MASTER
AMERICAN
HISTORY

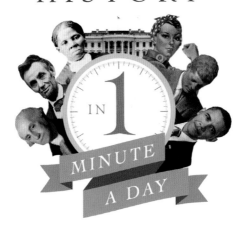

IN 1 MINUTE A DAY

FAMILIUS

FAMILIUS

Published by Familius LLC, www.familius.com

Familius books are available at special discounts for bulk purchases, whether for sales promotions or for family or corporate use. For more information, contact Familius Sales at 559-876-2170 or email orders@familius.com.

Library of Congress Cataloging-in-Publication Data
2018963781

Print ISBN 9781641701235
Ebook ISBN 9781641701723

Printed in China

Edited by Joseph Webb and Alison Strobel
Cover design by David Miles
Book design by David Miles and Derek George

Images sourced from WikiCommons, Library of Congress, or licensed from Shutterstock.

10 9 8 7 6 5 4 3 2 1

First Edition

MASTER
AMERICAN
HISTORY

IN **1** MINUTE A DAY

DAN ROBERTS

Professor of Liberal Arts and History
Chair, Department of Liberal Arts
School of Professional and Continuing Studies
University of Richmond
Executive Producer and Host, *A Moment in Time*

For Daniel McDonald Roberts.
He conveyed to me both his name and
a passion for the historical quest.

CONTENTS

ACKNOWLEDGMENTS

From the beginning, the radio program *A Moment in Time* has been a collaborative effort. In a classic student-professor joint research endeavor, many of the episodes have borne the imprint of my students' enthusiastic exploration of the topic. Too numerous to acknowledge individually, these students are the heroes in the development of the radio program and, by extension, this book. Often their contribution is recognized in transcripts at www.amomentintime.com.

Over the years, others have lent this project their energies and intellects and made the program more than it could ever have been were it solely an individual enterprise. Many of the programs and these chapters have benefitted from the careful writing and research of Ann Houmans Johnson. Since she first began her time with the venture, Nancy Waldo has provided administrative guidance and support to those involved. She has helped with the book and is still helping with the program and website. For that, she has earned the author's ongoing gratitude. Jackson Pieters devoted his summer to this and other projects and helped secure many of the images that will grace the pages of this volume.

The home base of *A Moment in Time* is WCVE-FM, Richmond. I am most grateful to General Manager and Vice President Bill Miller and his staff for taking a chance on a fledgling historian with an idea and little experience. Their unflagging enthusiasm for this mission was an inspiration to me and kept us going for now more than two-and-a-half decades. I am particularly grateful to my longtime producer, Steve Clark, who, over the course of almost twenty years taught me everything I know about broadcasting and helped shape me as a presenter of complex subjects, guiding both the style and content of the radio program.

I am grateful for the work of Rob Richards, who serves as current production manager of *A Moment in Time* and for all the station managers and program directors at the scores of stations nationwide that provide the means by which many of these stories have been told. I am also appreciative of the listeners who have provided praise and the occasional helpful critique, which keep my interest keen and my mind focused on the purpose of the venture.

The support and encouragement of my colleagues at the University of Richmond has enabled me to pursue the path of a public historian. I appreciate the backing of teaching colleagues from the Department of History, but especially John Gordon, Hugh West, and Debbie Govoruhk. At the School of Professional and Continuing Studies, I am most grateful for the backing of my faculty and staff colleagues, but especially the ongoing uplift provided by Dean Jamelle Wilson and former Dean James Narduzzi. I will always treasure the home I found at the university. The school's design to reach out to the community dovetailed perfectly with my scholarly pursuits in the field of public history.

I am most grateful to the visionaries at Familius who helped conceive this book and bring the dream into reality, primarily David Miles and Brooke Jorden, who supervised construction of the project. I have particularly enjoyed the collaboration with my editor, Joseph Webb. His careful attention to detail and ideas for improvements that often grew out of our conversations have made this book so much better. He was meticulous in insuring accuracy of narrative in addition to proper presentation and documentation.

This volume was conceived and executed in the year following the author's diagnosis with throat cancer. Fundamental to his recovery and ability to power through to its completion was the treatment and buttressing of the staff and physicians at Hunter Holmes McGuire VA Medical Center.

The author is also deeply indebted to the leaders and members of River Road Presbyterian Church and Providence Presbyterian

Church who he was privileged for a time to serve as pastor for their regular and intense spiritual support.

Finally, no author can successfully work without the support of his family. My sister Fran and her husband, Marty; my sister Julia and her husband, Ned; and all their wonderful children have provided welcomed encouragement during the assembly of these stories. I am most appreciative of the keen interest my children have shown in my work. Many thanks and much love go to Heather Elizabeth Roberts Gill, her history-loving husband, Gerald, and their newborn daughter, Gerika; Kathleen Roberts and my dear granddaughter Ava; and Daniel Roberts III and his amazing wife, Carolyn. In addition, I am most grateful for the inspiration and dream-sharing of my friend and husband, Mario Mejia Roberts.

INTRODUCTION

The late Daniel Boorstin, who was a very good historian and Librarian of Congress, said that trying to plan for the future without a sense of the past is like trying to plant cut flowers. We are trying to raise a lot of cut flowers these days. Public policy, journalism, foreign adventures, and many other parts of modern life are crafted with little understanding of the warnings or opportunities arising from what has come before.

Prior to the nineteenth century, much of written history was hagiography—the glorification of some leader, dynasty, or national or ethnic group. Often it involved the casual repetition of unexamined legends and stories passed between generations, with little concern for accuracy of fact or interpretation. By the turn of the twentieth century, however, historians were insisting on a more exact, even scientific, search for data, and on a more dispassionate analysis. The best historical work today involves the meticulous examination of primary documents, periodic reexamination of long-held conclusions, and rigorous debate about interpretation. Like all university-based historians, along with teaching and institutional service, I have been engaged in similar scholarly pursuits—specifically, examining the nexus of religion and politics in seventeenth-century Puritan London.

I am also a public historian; that discipline takes historical inquiry to another important level, making academic history accessible to a wider audience. Many people hunger to understand the historical context of events and personalities that affect our world today but are so caught up in immediate pressures of life that they have little time for serious inquiry. Public historians help craft a conduit through which important insights are made informative and arresting to such people.

One such conduit has been *A Moment in Time*, a brief historical examination of events and personalities from the past, heard on many domestic public-radio stations and Armed Services Radio around the world. This book and *A Moment in Time* come from the same animating impulse.

My associates and I have learned several things as we have produced the radio program:

- People learn differently now. They get their information in thirty-second bursts, tweets, and other forms of social media and are uncomfortable with long scholarship. The short-form delivery of high-quality information can help people improve their overall knowledge base.
- To make an impact on a mass audience, historians have to go where the people are, not wait for the people to come to them. Public historians create accurate and compelling historical vehicles for radio, television and the internet—interactive and multimedia tools to aid parents, schools, teachers, and students as they expand their historical perspective.
- People of all ages, particularly baby boomers and their children, respond to compelling and effective ways of teaching history.
- One of the most effective ways of teaching history, or for that matter science, literature, and the arts, is to convey it as a story. Recapturing the narrative tradition is an integral part of the work of public history.

Herein, I present three hundred stories that follow the American journey from the age of discovery to the recent era of social and political upheaval. Naturally, none of them tells the complete story. Readers should consider each a historical snapshot, an abbreviated conversation starter, hopefully whetting the appetite for more.

Most of these vignettes originated as radio programs, but each radio script was crafted from a much lengthier and more complex transcript that can be found at www.amomentintime.com. All visitors may access the website, but subscribers receive a daily email journey into history, crafted from the daily programs heard on *A Moment in Time*.

After each title in this book is a date associated with the events described in the vignette. After that is a reference (e.g., 03-007) that ties the story to a transcript at www.amomentintime.com, where the reader can examine a discussion of the topic in greater detail. Some vignettes have more than one reference.

Each story has a corresponding entry in the Bibliographic Appendix with a list of resources. These lists are not exhaustive but will help readers begin a voyage of discovering more about the topic.

Those of us at Familius wish you "fair winds and following seas" as you begin your journey into the exciting and challenging American experience.

COLUMBUS DID NOT DISCOVER AMERICA, 1492

Columbus Day is the annual celebration in the United States of that fateful dawn in October 1492 when Italian explorer Christopher Columbus, in service to the Spanish crown, made landfall in the Bahamas. Columbus, however, was late in the European discovery of the Western Hemisphere.

The second group to settle parts of America was Norsemen from Scandinavia. In several attempts around the year 1000 CE, the Vikings tried to settle the flat, wooded country they called Vineland, but the Norse were not colonizers. They lacked capital and infrastructure for permanent settlements, and soon cold, wolves, and hostile natives caused them to abandon their attempts after about a dozen years.

The real Eurasian discoverers of America were Stone Age hunter-gatherers sometime between 60,000 and 15,000 BCE, who crossed what was then the narrow treeless Bering Land Bridge between present-day Russia and Alaska. It took probably another one thousand years for these explorers and their descendants to work their way south and east to become the original inhabitants or discoverers of North and South America. (19-011, 19-012)

| 1400 | 1450 | 1500 | 1550 | 1600 | 1650 | 1700 |

Era of Exploration and Discovery

TRANSATLANTIC COD BRIDGE, 1492

I n the decades before Columbus's voyage in 1492, Basque fisher-men, from the northern part of Spain, may have beaten him to the New World. Author Mark Kurlansky presents strong evidence that the Genoese sailor was perhaps a "Christopher-come-lately."

Near the Pyrenees Mountains between Spain and France lies Basque Country, inhabited by a hearty people, jealous of their independence. In the Middle Ages, Basque fishermen supplied Catholics with salted cod for holy days. What was their special source of cod? When Germans monopolized Icelandic cod and cut off English supplies in 1475, Basque fishermen quickly stepped in with a steady supply of superb-quality dried and salted cod.

Evidence is strong that the tight-lipped Basques had discovered the desolate shores of Newfoundland, Nova Scotia, and perhaps even New England and the Grand Banks offshore, teeming with cod. The Basques never challenged Columbus's claims. Perhaps they knew how to keep a trade secret. (12-012)

JOHN CABOT, 1497

Soon after Columbus's first voyage, another Italian sailed the Atlantic in search of Asia. Born in Italy about the same time as Columbus, John Cabot was a wealthy importer of Asian spices by the 1490s. With Columbus's success, he began to look for a northern route through America to the Far East. Cabot approached King Henry VII of England for financing. Henry had earlier rebuffed Columbus and was eager to catch this opportunity. Cabot set sail from Bristol on May 20, 1497.

A month later he sighted the rugged coast of northern Newfoundland not far from where, 500 years previously, Scandinavian explorer Leif Eriksson had planted a colony. Cabot claimed the land for King Henry, which began the basis for England's settlement of North America. Cabot returned to England, and in 1498 five ships left England for Newfoundland. Only one returned. Cabot and the rest of the expedition disappeared without a trace.

(02-138, 02-139)

| 1400 | 1450 | 1500 | 1550 | 1600 | 1650 | 1700 |

ANTONIO PIGAFETTA AND
THE MISSING DAY, 1522

After three years, on September 7, 1522, *Victoria* returned to Spain from the first round-the-world voyage. It was the last remaining ship of Ferdinand Magellan's tiny armada. Crewman Antonio Pigafetta had sailed west with the captain general through the tip of South America, endured the terrible three-month Pacific crossing, and witnessed Magellan's death in the Philippines. All during the trip, Pigafetta had kept a daily journal. He was now puzzled. His journal marked the day as September 6, a day off.

Most people at the time believed the Bible taught that the earth was the center of the universe and the sun, moon, and stars revolved around it. Polish mathematician Copernicus believed the earth revolved around the sun and was slowly turning eastward, one trip around per day. By sailing westward, Magellan and Pigafetta ate up a day. The missing day confirmed Copernicus in the struggle between religion and science. (03-057, 03-058)

DON LUÍS'S REVENGE, 1570

E ven from Columbus's time, Spain had its eye on North America. In 1561, a Spanish expedition arrived in the Chesapeake Bay and took away with them Paquiquino, son of a local native chieftain. In the decade he remained with Spaniards, he was converted to Christianity and became fluent in Spanish. He became the ward of the governor of Mexico and took the official's name.

In September 1570, Jesuit priests on a mission to convert Native Americans landed not far from the future site of the Jamestown settlement. They were guided by Paquiquino, now newly renamed Don Luís. Soon, the boy was reunited with his family, and he reverted to his native roots with all its intense hostility to European "invaders." He broke with the Jesuits. Later in the winter, the starving priests reached out to the American Indians. During negotiations, Don Luís led a raiding party that killed all the priests. With the collapse of this colony, Spain never again attempted to settle Chesapeake Bay. (12-004)

LOST COLONY I, 1585

Twice in the 1580s, the English tried to establish a colony at Roanoke Island on the coast of Carolina. Twice they failed. After the initial voyages of John Cabot in the 1490s, interest in America waned. Late in the reign of Elizabeth I, tensions with Spain made a North American military outpost desirable if not a necessity. Leading this effort was Sir Walter Raleigh, the handsome son of a prominent family. He had distinguished himself fighting in France and Ireland and was one of the Queen's favorites. In 1585, he sent a 108-man expedition to plant the flag on tiny Roanoke Island off the coast of present day North Carolina. Unfortunately, Roanoke had barren soil and poor water supply, and it was located in the dangerous waters of Cape Hatteras.

On this first attempt, the settlers arrived at mid-summer and were saved from starvation by the Roanoke clan, part of the Native American Algonquian confederation. (04-014, 04-015, 04-016)

LOST COLONY II, 1587

In 1587, England made a second attempt to create a military outpost on the outer banks of today's North Carolina. John White led this endeavor; to create a permanent settlement, he brought families with him, including several pregnant women. White's own granddaughter, Virginia Dare, was the first English child born in the new world.

Of the Native American confederation in the area, only the Croatoan tribe remained on good terms with the English. So White became convinced that only a substantial resupply could insure the colony's survival. Later in 1587, he returned to England to organize aid for Roanoke. He was delayed during his trip back to America by an attack of the Spanish Armada (1588) and did not arrive back in Roanoke Island until August 1590. He found the settlement deserted. Only the cryptic word *Croatoan* carved in a tree offered a clue as to the fate of the Lost Colony. (04-016, 04-015, 04-016)

BRITAIN AND VIRGINIA, 1607

Since the Middle Ages, England's wealth came from wool. Each year, tons of raw wool were harvested from sheep on English hillsides and shipped to the European continent, where the material was fashioned into cloth. By 1600, however, the wool trade had been disrupted by religious and economic fighting in Europe. There was a glut of wool in France and Holland, which before had bought England's raw wool. English King James I, who derived much of his income from export taxes, began to look elsewhere for funds to make up for the shortfall in tax on English wool. His openness to colonizing North America was fueled by fears of Spanish encroachment on English claims in the region and the age-old hope that gold and silver, similar to that found by the Spanish in Mexico and Peru, might be secured by the English colonists because there never seemed to be enough money in circulation to pay for all the goods the English wanted to buy.

There never seemed to be enough money to pay for all the goods Englishmen wanted to buy. With a growing population, jails filled to overcapacity, and increasing unemployment, the government began to look for places to put people. And religious dissenters feeling oppressed by the Church of England wanted a place to practice their faith freely. These and other reasons created the desire to plant colonies in North America. (11-070, 11-071, 11-072)

FOUNDING JAMESTOWN, 1607

With failure of the Roanoke Colony, by 1606, England was even more determined to increase its grip on North America. England called the colony Virginia in honor of the King James I cousin and predecessor the Virgin Queen, Elizabeth I. Three ships set sail in December, and after a four-month voyage, the colonists arrived at the mouth of the Chesapeake Bay. They then traveled sixty miles westward and on May 14, 1607, made their settlement Jamestown on a small peninsula on the James River, naming both for England's reigning king.

Paying for this expedition was the Virginia Company of London, a group of wealthy Englishmen who were convinced that gold, silver, and other riches were there for the taking. They also sought a northwest passage to the riches of the Far East. The company promoted Virginia as a base for English occupation as well as the opportunity for the conversion to Christianity of native peoples. (07-066, 07-067)

| 1400 | 1450 | 1500 | 1550 | 1600 | 1650 | 1700 |

POCAHONTAS, 1610

F̲ew figures have captured the American imagination as has the Powhatan Indian woman, Matoaka, or as she is popularly known, Pocahontas. From the moment that, as a thirteen-year-old, she intervened and, by his testimony, saved the life of Captain John Smith, Pocahontas was a Jamestown fixture. Baptized as Rebecca, she was married in 1614 to John Rolfe, an early developer of Virginia's tobacco industry. She helped bring a measure of peace to the region.

In 1614, John and Rebecca went to England to recruit new settlers for the colony. Soon this gracious and charming young Indian woman had transfixed London society. She attended the theater, gala balls, and many dinners given in her honor; was entertained by the Bishop of London; and received at the court of King James I. The Rolfes conveyed such a positive impression that the English shifted in a more conciliatory direction in its dealings with Native Americans. (03-059, 03-060)

JOHN SMITH, 1610

Perhaps no early leader was more instrumental in saving and bringing prosperity to the Jamestown colony than mercenary, adventurer, explorer, and mapmaker Captain John Smith. The early years were marked by disease, hunger, attacks from Native Americans, and serious divisions within the leadership. By 1608, Smith was the president of the colony.

First, he got the local Powhatan tribes to trade for food the colony desperately needed. Then, he tightened the defenses of the colony and forced colonists to work if they wanted to eat. His leadership style aroused resentment in the colony, and by the summer of 1609 rumors of an assassination plot were rampant in Jamestown. At about that time, he was terribly burned in a gunpowder accident and had to return to England for medical care. Smith never returned to the Chesapeake area. Although he could inspire people, he also infuriated them. Nevertheless, under his leadership the colony survived, and his maps of the Chesapeake Bay proved an excellent resource for the colony in the decades ahead. (12-053, 12-054)

| 1400 | 1450 | 1500 | 1550 | 1600 | 1650 | 1700 |

BARON DE LA WARE, 1610

In the English settlement of North America, settlers and investors were hopeful of rich harvests, gold and silver, and friendly natives eager for trade. The largest investor in Virginia was Thomas West, the twelfth Baron De La Ware, a distant cousin of Queen Elizabeth I, and a member of the Queen's Council.

In 1609, word came of the worsening situation in Virginia. West was appointed governor and set off for the Chesapeake to rescue his investment. He arrived just as the colonists, who numbered sixty, down from a high of five hundred, were in the process of abandoning the colony. The baron reinvigorated colonial morale and built forts on the river for protection. After some time, West's health deteriorated, and he went back to England to recover. He died in mid-Atlantic on his return to Jamestown. Later, the colony of Delaware was named in honor of the man who saved Virginia.

(11-073)

JOHN ROLFE, 1615

Often overlooked because of Pocahontas, his more famous
wife, planter John Rolfe discovered the key to Jamestown's
economic survival. Rolfe and others knew that if Virginia was to
truly prosper it had to find a cash crop. Sometime around 1612,
he began experimenting with *Nicotiana tabacum*, a sweet strain of
tobacco imported from the Caribbean. In early summer 1613, he
sent a small shipment of this aromatic weed back to England. It
instantly caught on and eventually proved Virginia's salvation.

Two years after their marriage, tragedy struck the couple. At
the end of a triumphant recruitment tour of England, Pocahontas
died, probably of respiratory complications due to the cooler and
more moist climate in England. Upon his return, Rolfe received
a number of rich land grants. During the Powhatan uprising in
1622, his holdings at Bermuda Hundred were destroyed. He may
have died during the attack, but whatever his end, John Rolfe
played a leading role in the commercial, social, and diplomatic
life of first-decade Jamestown. (12-055, 12-056)

| 1400 | 1450 | 1500 | 1550 | 1600 | 1650 | 1700 |

SLAVES COME TO VIRGINIA, 1619

In the early 1600s, Robert Rich, Earl of Warwick, wanted to trade in the Caribbean, but this conflicted with the pro-Spanish policies of his monarch, King James I. Blocked from legitimate trade, Rich proposed a privateer campaign in the Caribbean—quietly attacking Spanish shipping for profit under the secret commission of the King. The monarch of course would get a cut from the take. James approved.

In 1619, Rich's ship, *Treasurer*, captured a Spanish vessel with a cargo that included forty African slaves. The ship then headed north to Virginia to sell the slaves. Virginia Governor Yeardley felt this might anger the Spanish and threaten the supposedly neutral port of Jamestown. *Treasurer*'s captain quickly crossed to Bermuda and deposited half the slaves on a plantation owned by Robert Rich. *Treasurer* then returned, and its captain began negotiations with Yeardley. They divided the Africans, sending most to outlying plantations far from prying Spanish eyes. African Americans as slaves had come to Virginia. (05-112)

MAYFLOWER COMPACT, 1620

One of the icons of democracy is the Mayflower Compact, the Pilgrim's commitment to justice and equality. It was signed on the *Mayflower* when it landed on Cape Cod in 1620. The Pilgrims, a tiny radical outgrowth of the English Puritan movement, had first tried to settle in Holland but found few chances there to make a living. They returned to England and then set sail for New England.

The crisis for the Pilgrims in Massachusetts came as non-Pilgrims began to move into the colony. Quakers arrived and started to press for rights of citizenship and worship. To maintain control, the Pilgrims dictated that voters had to own property. As much as one-third of the male population lost the right to vote. Civilian control collapsed and brought on the dissolution of the colony in the 1690s. Democracy had collided with the need to maintain ideological religious control of the colony. (10-040, 10-041, 10-042)

| 1400 | 1450 | 1500 | 1550 | 1600 | 1650 | 1700 |

TOBACCO, 1620

By 1615, Jamestown was almost defunct. Since 1607, the Virginia Company had invested $11 million (in today's currency) in what was shaping up to be an organizational and institutional disaster. Two things helped turn the situation around.

First, the company gave up control of the colony's property. Many of the settlers were either gentlemen seeking adventure and quick riches or poor people swept up off the streets of London or other English cities and forced onto company ships. Hard work was not something with which either groups were familiar. But once they owned their property, attitudes began to change and the settlers began to work—hard.

Second, the colony found a cash crop, *Nicotiana tabacum*, or sweet tobacco, from the Caribbean. Three years after John Rolfe sold his first shipment home in 1613, Virginia sent 20,000 pounds to feed the mother country's growing addiction. Along with immense prosperity, the golden weed would also bring much sorrow: soil depletion, slavery, monocrop farming, and, of course, serious health problems. But Virginia had found its salvation; it never looked back. (10-009, 10-010)

VIRGINIA COMPANY'S DEMISE, 1624

After nearly two decades of heroic effort, in 1624 the Virginia Company finally surrendered. It was brushed aside by a royal government hungry for tobacco profits. Thousands of settlers the company had sent to Virginia had died of disease, starvation, or conflict with Native Americans. Not until mid-century did the annual death rate drop below 25 percent and natural growth take over. By 1616, it had spent over £50,000, a huge sum for those days, equivalent to about $11 million in today's currency. And then in 1622, Opechancanough, the Algonquian chief, attacked the colony.

When word reached England that the Native Americans had killed a third of the colony's European population, the royal government threw in the towel. Frustrated by the company's failures and hungry for increased tobacco revenues, the crown terminated the company charter and made Virginia the first royal colony of England's new empire. (12-018)

ANNE HUTCHINSON, 1640

In the 1630s, Anne Hutchinson and her family immigrated to New England to escape religious persecution. An intelligent and independent thinker, Anne began to hold a weekly discussion group in her home, where she criticized the colony's religious and political leaders for narrow views on morality and religion.

The colony saw Hutchinson as a threat and passed a law banning women from organizing, leading, or even attending such meetings without their husbands. When Anne refused to stop, Governor John Winthrop put her on trial. She sealed her fate with an emotional outburst, claiming God spoke to her directly and some ministers in Boston did not teach the truth. She was found guilty and then later, in a church trial, was excommunicated and banished.

The Hutchinson group settled in what became Rhode Island. Then, fearing annexation by Massachusetts, the family fled to present-day Long Island where in 1643 they were killed in an American Indian uprising. (07-024, 07-025)

ROGER WILLIAMS AND RHODE ISLAND, 1645

English Puritan preacher Roger Williams immigrated to Massachusetts in 1631. Almost immediately, he began to clash with local leaders. Williams opposed government involvement in church affairs. Furthermore, he argued that the colony should not take land belonging to Native Americans unless they were paid.

Williams was banished from the colony in 1635, escaped south during the bitter winter, and settled in the region of Narragansett Bay near present-day Newport. He became friendly with the local American Indians and purchased from them land at the head of the bay, where he built the town of Providence. Rhode Island represented a unique stage in American constitutional evolution. It adopted the principles of complete religious freedom, toleration, and separation of church and state.

Williams, a prolific writer, spent the rest of his life writing and speaking his mind on religious freedom and became an outspoken advocate of fair treatment for Native Americans. (07-104, 07-105)

1400   1450   1500   1550   1600   1650   1700

ALGONQUIAN ANNIHILATION, 1645

Any fair and balanced study of Virginia cannot but provoke admiration. A primitive democracy was established. Tobacco cultivation laid the foundation for a rich commercial culture. Yet, Virginia's hard-won success had a dark side. Tobacco fortunes were built on the backs of black slaves, and the mass migration of whites slowly brought the Native American confederacy to the brink of extinction. In 1607, 24,000 Algonquians lived in the Chesapeake Basin. By 1669, through disease, forced starvation, ethnic cleansing, and direct military action, that number had been reduced to about 2,000. It seemed Native Americans had stepped onto the slippery slope to annihilation. If they resisted, as they did, sometimes violently, they died. If they gave in and accommodated the whites, they died.

The tide of European population never seemed to ebb. By the end of the century, the few Algonquians left alive were herded onto tiny reservations and ruthlessly compelled to stay there. (12-026, 12-027)

| 1700 | 1750 | 1800 | 1850 | 1900 | 1950 | PRESENT |

CAROLINA COLONY, 1670

In 1660, English King Charles II returned to the throne two decades after his father was executed by Parliament. Three years after that, Charles paid back eight supporters who helped him regain the English throne with an enormous land grant named Carolina, in honor of his father. The eight nobles were called Lords Proprietor (ruling landlords), and the vast territory contained the present-day states of North and South Carolina.

In 1670, 130 people from England and Barbados settled at the magnificent port of Charles Town, and by the early 1700s, Carolina supported about 8,000 persons, more than half of whom were slaves imported to work the huge rice and indigo plantations that dotted the lowlands.

By 1719, settlers had come to believe they were not being protected from piracy and American Indian uprisings. These mounting frustrations led to a bloodless overthrow of the Proprietary government. Ten years later, the Carolinas became royal colonies. (08-101, 08-102)

BACON'S REBELLION, 1676

In spring 1676, Bacon's Rebellion ripped Virginia apart. The causes? Decades of dissatisfaction with Virginia Governor Berkeley, falling tobacco prices, rising costs, class tensions, and even bad weather contributed to the discontent. But in later years, the governor made friends with some American Indian tribes, hoping they would act as a buffer between the colony and hostile clans. Many settlers considered the only good American Indian to be a dead one. The disgruntled found a champion in wealthy planter and recent immigrant Nathaniel Bacon.

When Bacon attacked the Native Americans, Berkeley declared him a rebel and had him arrested. Bacon escaped, and the rebellion was on. Eventually Berkeley prevailed when Bacon died of dysentery in October. The governor then pounced on Bacon's followers with such ferocity London removed him from office.

Some scholars have seen in Bacon's Rebellion a whiff of revolution that would sweep America a century later, but most have concluded it was mostly due to local conditions and the titanic clash of two great aristocratic egos. (13-015, 13-016, 13-017)

WILLIAM PENN'S HOLY EXPERIMENT, 1680

The Society of Friends, known derisively in England as Quakers, despaired of the dry, tedious orthodoxy animating regular Christian services. The Quakers were noted for incendiary preaching, boisterous worship in small groups, which earned them vicious persecution by church authorities. The persecution not only vastly increased the sect's numbers but also pushed them to seek a place of refuge in America.

Their leader was William Penn. He had abandoned his fun-loving ways as a young man and embraced Quakerism. Penn's father, Admiral William Penn Sr., had helped restore King Charles II to the throne in 1660 and had extended the new king a large loan for royal expenses. At the death his father, William proposed that the King exchange the debt for a very large land grant on the western side of the Delaware River—in the king's words, "Penn's Woods" or Pennsylvania. There, Penn and his followers in 1682 established a refuge for religious refugees. (08-040, 08-041)

WITCHCRAFT IN
MASSACHUSETTS I, 1692

In spring 1692, Massachusetts Governor William Phipps heard rumors asserting that there were witches in Salem. Samuel Parris was the minister in the village; his children were in the charge of Tituba, a Caribbean Indian Parris had brought to the colony. During that spring, Parris's daughter and niece began displaying symptoms similar to epilepsy. It was discovered that they had been pouring egg whites into a glass of water, which they pretended was a fortune-teller's crystal ball.

What began as girl play soon took a darker turn when several other girls in the community came down with like symptoms. Salem citizens panicked, and soon Tituba and two older women, Sarah Good and Sarah Osbourne, were accused of practicing witchcraft.

The governor appointed a special court, and by the time he called a halt to the proceedings in September, the court had convicted twenty-seven people, most from Salem. Nineteen had been hanged, and a hundred were awaiting trial. (01-042, 01-043, 01-044)

WITCHCRAFT IN
MASSACHUSETTS II, 1692

The village of Salem was part of present-day Danvers, Massa-chusetts. In spring 1692, Salem witnessed an outbreak of witchcraft. In the seventeenth century, the power of witchcraft was real, not because it actually worked but because people believed that it worked. Witchcraft works on the mind. This outbreak of practice and persecution was due to a deep-seated fear of witchcraft in the population as a whole, not, as it has been alleged, the work of preachers whipping the community into a frenzy. Eventually, the colony's leaders, led by prominent clergymen, intervened with Governor Phipps. In September, he brought the trials and executions to an end.

It is difficult to know how many were actually practicing witchcraft in that dreadful spring and summer, but the greatest victim of all was Salem, which lost control of itself, hounded some of its finest citizens to false confessions, and put nineteen of them to their deaths. (01-042, 01-043, 01-044)

1400	1450	1500	1550	1600	1650	1700

JOHN LAW AND THE
MISSISSIPPI BUBBLE, 1715

In 1717, Scotsman John Law, in service to the king of France, established la Banque Générale and issued paper money backed by government gold and silver. With this paper, people conducted business, and the government paid off its enormous debts. But Law became much too ambitious. He created the Western Company to develop land along the Mississippi River in French-controlled Louisiana, at the time no more than a semi-tropical swamp. He then merged this company with his bank. The wild increase in share prices for this royal bank became the Mississippi Bubble. And of course, eventually, the bubble burst and stock prices collapsed.

Law had created much of what constitutes the modern banking system, but because he was not cautious, it would be decades before people trusted national banks, a century before stocks were considered a safe investment, and nearly 200 years before people would put their trust in paper money. (03-093, 03-094, 03-095, 03-096, 03-097)

JAMES OGLETHORPE AND THE FOUNDING OF GEORGIA, 1732

Like his father and brother before him, beginning in 1722, James Edward Oglethorpe served in Parliament. In that capacity he chaired a committee investigating debtor's prisons. He was appalled. Should a debtor survive the corruption, disease, and brutality of a prison term, the rest of his life was washed up.

At the same time, there was much fear about the threat posed by hostile Native American clans and the Spanish against the rich colony of Carolina. Oglethorpe began to argue for another colony that would protect Carolina and give released debtors and Protestant dissenters a place in which they might start a new life. In 1732, Oglethorpe and a group of trustees were issued a charter for the establishment of a new colony, named Georgia for King George II. The following year, he led a group to settle Yamacraw Bluff, which eventually became the city of Savannah. (09-037, 09-038)

| 1400 | 1450 | 1500 | 1550 | 1600 | 1650 | 1700 |

TRIAL OF JOHN
PETER ZENGER, 1735

In 1731, William Cosby became royal governor of New York. He quickly established a reputation as arrogant, greedy, and corrupt. His popularity plummeted in part due to bitter criticism by the *New York Weekly Journal* and its publisher, John Peter Zenger. Cosby brought Zenger to trial for seditious libel in 1735. The judge was an appointee and vigorous supporter of the governor. When Zenger's lawyers demanded his recusal, the judge disbarred them. Their replacement, John Chambers, was also pro-Cosby but got several jury members removed since they were in the employ of the governor and likely to be biased. Zenger's real defense, however, was conducted by an imported Philadelphia lawyer, Andrew Hamilton.

Hamilton attacked the current libel-law theory designed to protect the government. The judge ruled that libel, true or not, was still wrong. Following Hamilton's idea that "truth is not defamatory," the jury acquitted Zenger. This confirmed America's radical and newly developing common-law vision that rulers should fear the people, not the other way around. (08-022)

1700	1750	1800	1850	1900	1950	PRESENT

GREAT AWAKENING, 1740

During the 1740s, a religious revival, the Great Awakening, transformed American Protestantism and in part paved the way for the American Revolution. The movement received a boost from the roving preaching of Anglican evangelist George Whitefield and Jonathan Edwards, pastor of the Northampton, Massachusetts, Congregational Church. Edward's Enfield, Connecticut, sermon of July 1741, "Sinners in the Hands of an Angry God," is considered typical of such preaching. While harsh to modern ears, it is a reasoned analysis of the sinner's predicament from the viewpoint of an evangelical Calvinist.

The Great Awakening caused not only splits in several Protestant denominations but also spectacular church growth. Furthermore, it created bitterness toward established religion such as Anglicanism. In the next generation, those touched by the Awakening, particularly Baptists and Presbyterians, provided support for the growing independence movement and produced many of the troops who fought in the colonial militias and the Continental Army during the Revolution. (07-049, 07-050)

| 1400 | 1450 | 1500 | 1550 | 1600 | 1650 | 1700 |

GILBERT TENNENT, 1743

Gilbert Tennent was one of the leaders of the Great Awakening, the eighteenth-century revival in American Protestantism. He taught that the proper Christian life consisted of three steps: conviction of sin; a personal, emotional, even born-again encounter with the living God; and a life of personal piety. As a traveling preacher, he thundered against ministers whose spiritual intensity did not measure up to his ideal. His most famous sermon is "The Danger of an Unconverted Ministry" (1740).

In 1743, Tennent moved to a large Philadelphia church. There he shifted in emphasis from simple conversion to pastoral care and doctrinal purity. He also began to recoil from the extremes of the spiritual enthusiasts of the Great Awakening and pressed for harmony and reunion within the church. Tennent became a strong supporter of the College of New Jersey (later to become Princeton University). Prior to his death in 1764, he saw a partial healing of old church wounds he himself had helped create.

(11-074, 11-075, 11-076)

SCOTTISH SETTLEMENT IN NORTH CAROLINA, 1745

In the 1740s, thousands left the rugged mountains and wind-swept islands of the Scottish Highlands and laid course for Carolina's Cape Fear Valley. Despite their love of land and kin and clan, their way of life was changing. The demand for beef in the urban lowlands and England was met with huge and highly profitable cattle drives, which concentrated wealth in the hands of an upper class elite. The elite raised land rent and made life miserable for their tenants known as *fir-bhaile*, or in English, "tacksmen."

These middle-class farmers and cattlemen recognized the squeeze they were in, and rather than pay many simply departed. Beginning in 1739 with the establishment of the Argyle Colony near present Fayetteville, North Carolina, Highland Scots made their home in a foreign land. They had concluded, in the words of a Gaelic song of the time, "better to leave willingly than to descend like slaves." (03-039)

1400   1450   1500   1550   1600   1650   1700

FLORA MACDONALD, 1747

In 1745, the Scottish Highlands rose against the English in support of Charles Edward Stuart, but in April 1746, the English destroyed Charles's Highlander army at the Battle of Culloden near Inverness. With the help of Flora MacDonald, Charles escaped to Europe. MacDonald's prospects in Britain seemed dim and, with her family, she joined a colony of Highland Scots in southeast North Carolina. When the Revolution came, because of the oath they had sworn to England after Colloden, the Scots had to fight as Tories.

The Loyalist cause in the region collapsed on February 27, 1776, at the Battle of Moore's Creek Bridge. MacDonald's husband was captured and their estates confiscated, and she was forced to return to Scotland. MacDonald died in 1790 and in death continued her lifelong devotion to the ancient regime. She was shrouded in a sheet used by Charles Edward Stuart during his escape. (01-087)

WHITEFIELD AND FRANKLIN: THE PROFITS OF RELIGION, 1750

During the Great Awakening, an American religious revival in the 1740s, two men formed a strange alliance. George Whitefield needed publicity for his revival efforts. Benjamin Franklin was out for profits.

Franklin, a deist, was skeptical of religion, which he felt, at its best, promoted hard work and civic morality. Whitefield was an itinerant evangelist who preached the "new birth" in Jesus Christ to vast crowds. At first reluctant, Whitefield soon embraced the concept of advertising to promote his books and increase his crowds. To Franklin, Whitefield was a powerful salesman, holding out the possibility of powerful profits.

Franklin's *Pennsylvania Gazette* poured out glowing stories about the evangelist's tours. This helped stimulate sales of Whitefield's journals, books, sermons, and pamphlets, which by agreement Franklin was publishing at an ever-increasing rate. Basically, the two used each other: Franklin made money; Whitefield made converts. (03-028, 03-029)

GEORGE WASHINGTON ON THE FRONTIER, 1754

Growing competition for control of the American heartland brought Virginia and therefore Britain into conflict with France. Young George Washington recommended that Virginia secure control of the place where the Allegheny and Monongahela Rivers converge to form the Ohio River (also known as the Forks). By building a fort there at the site of modern-day Pittsburgh, Washington believed this would make it impossible for the French to stem the flood of British settlers set to move west.

The French, however, beat the Virginians to the punch: they had already established Fort Duquesne at the Forks and ambushed Washington's Virginians when they arrived. His unit suffered heavy casualties. Washington was forced to retreat.

This incident ignited the Seven Years' War, known in American history as the French and Indian War. At its conclusion, France lost most of its overseas possessions, including Canada and India; Britain laid the foundation for its worldwide empire; and the world heard for the first time, but certainly not the last, the name of George Washington. (12-072, 12-073)

1700	1750	1800	1850	1900	1950	PRESENT

Era of Revolution: Colonial

PATRICK HENRY AND THE
PARSON'S CAUSE, 1763

In early Virginia, clergy were paid in tobacco. If there was a drought, the preachers benefitted greatly because the price of their guaranteed tobacco portion went up. In 1758, the General Assembly fixed clerical salaries at two cents per pound. On appeal, the king decided for the clergy.

In December 1763, clergy sued for back pay in Parson Maury's case. The defense lawyer was young, inexperienced Patrick Henry, but he carried the day when he shifted from advocate to actor. "Was not the king a tyrant for invalidating a law so crucial to his people's welfare?" Amidst shouts of "treason," Henry turned his venom on the clergy. "Instead of feeding the hungry . . . these rapacious harpies . . . [would] snatch from the honest parishioner his last hoe-cake, from the widow her last milk-cow."

The jury decided in favor of the parsons but awarded them in payment only a single penny. A triumphant Henry was borne from the Hanover Courthouse on the shoulders of the crowd. (13-022)

1400   1450   1500   1550   1600   1650   1700

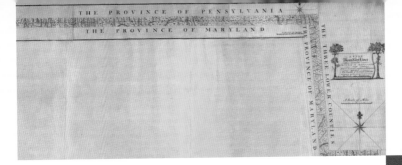

THE MASON–DIXON LINE, 1768

The last part of Maryland to be developed was northeast of present-day Baltimore. The heavy soil in this region was hospitable to the cultivation of wheat and corn, which could be shipped to the hungry West Indies. As more settlers flocked into this area, tensions grew between Maryland and Pennsylvania. Years of court battles were punctuated by violent raids and reprisals between partisans of the two colonies.

Finally, London stepped in and appointed a Boundary Commission, which in 1763 hired two surveyors, Charles Mason and Jeremiah Dixon, to survey the dividing line. In 1769 after six years, the border between Pennsylvania and Maryland was fixed: a near straight line east to west, just north of the thirty-ninth parallel. Milestones marked the 244-mile barrier, each with a P on the north and M on the south. This boundary became the traditional border between North and South, between slave and free states—the Mason–Dixon Line. (01-187)

| 1700 | 1750 | 1800 | 1850 | 1900 | 1950 | PRESENT |

Era of Revolution: Colonial

MONTICELLO, 1770

Perhaps no private residence in America reflects the tastes and disposition of its builder as does Monticello, the home of Thomas Jefferson.

The term *Renaissance man* seems created to anticipate Thomas Jefferson—lawyer, farmer, writer, philosopher, inventor, musician, politician, and father of the University of Virginia. Jefferson seemed to embody the Renaissance scholar's ideal of virtue as the governing principle of life.

By 1768, Jefferson was busy preparing his little mountain, part of his inheritance, for a home. He admired the classical style of sixteenth-century Italian builder Andrea Palladio and the octagonal designs of British architect Robert Morris. He spent the next half century building, altering, putting up, and pulling down until he realized his vision. It was only barely finished four years before his death because Jefferson's mind never left for long the path of creation. (04-021)

1400   1450   1500   1550   1600   1650   1700

BOSTON MASSACRE I, 1770

As late as 1770, most Americans considered themselves loyal subjects of the king. In just six short years, a Continental Congress had declared independence. What led to this transformation?

Strapped to pay for its victory in the Seven Years' War (aka the French and Indian War), in 1763 Britain began to tax Americans, many of whom considered this illegal "taxation without representation." Soon, Boston became the cockpit of opposition. In 1768, London sent troops to keep order, but people were always picking fights with the hapless troopers.

Monday night, March 5, 1770, was cold and clear. At the Customs House on King Street, Private Hugh White stood guard. A silly argument with a teenager ended when White struck the boy with the butt of his musket. A crowd gathered and began threatening White. At the barracks, a warning bell began to ring. Soon, accidentally, church bells picked up the call. Since bells at night often warned of fire, the unwary citizens of Boston began to spill out of their homes to fight the nonexistent fire. (03-064, 03-065, 03-066, 03-067)

BOSTON MASSACRE II, 1770

On March 5, 1770, Captain Thomas Preston led a group of British soldiers to rescue Private Hugh White, who was besieged by a mob at the Boston Customs House. But soon the troopers were surrounded and being pelted with rocks and snowballs—bells ringing, noise deafening. Then fatefully, Preston ordered his men to load. Private Hugh Montgomery was knocked down. In his rage he came up yelling, "Damn you, fire." Without aiming, in panic, he pulled the trigger. At that precise moment, someone struck Captain Preston just as he was saying, "Do not fire." His men only heard the word *fire*. In minutes, several citizens lay dead or dying.

The Boston Massacre was an accident—tragic for those who died, but basically a nonevent. Blown-up by patriot propagandists, the so-called massacre entered the realm of mythology. For years, parades were held on March 5 to whip people into a patriotic frenzy in support of the Revolution. (03-064, 03-065, 03-066, 03-067)

CRISPUS ATTUCKS, 1770

On March 5, 1770, in Boston, British soldiers led by Captain Preston fired into an unruly crowd of protesters. One of the first to fall was Crispus Attucks.

Attucks was, at forty-seven, a six-foot drifter, a powerful mulatto, a light-skinned black man. He had escaped slavery by going to sea. On the day of the so-called Boston Massacre, Attucks was at the head of the crowd.

At Preston's trial, a witness testified that a stout mulatto had weighed in and struck one of the soldiers. The soldier turned and fired, several others followed suit, and soon five men lay dead or wounded. Attucks was among the first to fall. Later, John Adams said few battles "were more important . . . than the battle of King Street on the 5th of March, 1770." Given America's original sin of slavery, it is ironic that the first to fall at that most singular event was a man of color, Crispus Attucks. (05-105)

1700   1750   1800   1850   1900   1950   PRESENT

Era of Revolution: Colonial

BOSTON TEA PARTY, 1773

In 1773, the Parliament passed the Tea Act. First, it gave a monopoly on tea shipped to America to the financially strapped British East India Company. Second, it permitted the company to ship tea directly from China to the colonies. By the time tea reached America, company tea was so cheap that it threatened the fortunes of American importers who had been selling smuggled Dutch tea at a premium to colonists resentful of the tea tax. Finally, Parliament left the tea tax in place as a reminder of its power to tax Americans.

On December 17, 1773, approximately sixty men dressed in Indian garb boarded three vessels anchored in Boston Harbor. They tossed 340 chests of prime Cantonese East India tea into the bay. They were led by a shadowy group of radical leaders such as Samuel Adams, most probably in alliance with an equally shadowy group of wealthy tea smugglers whose business was about to evaporate. (06-017, 06-018, 06-019)

FIRST CONTINENTAL
CONGRESS, 1774

Parliament was so enraged by the Boston Tea Party that it passed what Americans called the harsh, arbitrary Intolerable Acts. The Port of Boston was closed, Massachusetts' legislative powers were restricted, and colonials were required to house royal troops in their homes. Intercolonial Committees of Correspondence began making plans for a continental gathering of colonial representatives to discuss a response.

The First Continental Congress met in September 1774 with Peyton Randolph of Virginia as president. Its work was not a move toward independence but rather to craft a petition of complaint and to encourage repeal of the Intolerable Acts. If Britain did not respond favorably, Congress endorsed a general boycott of British goods. King George III said, "The die is now cast. The colonies must either submit or triumph." Parliament and the king had confirmed the law of unintended consequences. In their attempt to suppress colonial rights, they sparked a revolution. (08-042, 08-043)

| 1700 | 1750 | 1800 | 1850 | 1900 | 1950 | PRESENT |

Era of Revolution: Colonial

PATRICK HENRY'S
PERSONAL TRAUMA, 1775

At the time Patrick Henry gave his famous "liberty or death" speech at Richmond's St. John's Church in March 1775, few people knew his wife was at home suffering a severe mental illness. Her dementia was so acute that she had to be restrained to stop her from harming herself. Each day, Henry went down through the trapdoor in the hall near the house entrance to feed her.

Those who look at the past must avoid too much speculation about how personal trauma affects political actions. But it is useful to consider how Henry's quiet struggle to comfort a suffering loved one might have given intensity to his political rhetoric.

"Shall we try argument? Sir, we have been trying that for the last ten years. . . . We have petitioned, remonstrated, prostrated ourselves before the throne . . . and we have been spurned, with contempt. . . . Is life so dear or peace so sweet as to be purchased at the price of chains and slavery?"

Patrick Henry lived another quarter-century. Mrs. Henry was dead within a year. (01-010)

| 1400 | 1450 | 1500 | 1550 | 1600 | 1650 | 1700 |

DANIEL BOONE IN
BOONESBOROUGH, 1775

Founded in 1775, the settlement of Boonesborough, Kentucky, became a target for Native American tribes angry at white intrusion into their territory. During an expedition to gather salt for the besieged outpost, Daniel Boone was captured by a Shawnee raiding party. Hearing of a coming campaign against the central Kentucky settlements, Boone escaped and made his way back to warn the pioneers.

He organized the defense of Boonesborough, and in late summer 1778, a strong party of Shawnee arrived before the gates of the village. On September 9, the sides held a major parley. At first it seemed a solution was at hand, but a misunderstanding led to a breakdown in communications. Gunshots rang out all over the meadow.

The siege continued for eight days, during which time the Shawnee regularly attempted to gain the fort but sustained heavy losses from fort snipers. On September 18, they pulled out. A few days later, reinforcements arrived from Virginia. (01-171, 01-072, 01-073)

1700	1750	1800	1850	1900	1950	PRESENT

Era of Revolution: Colonial

PAUL REVERE'S RIDE, 1775

The political atmosphere of Massachusetts in spring 1775 was toxic. In April, Governor Gage heard there was a Patriot munitions store in Concord and dispatched several hundred British troops to capture it. American activists Paul Revere and William Dawes were sent to warn of the enemy approach. Their efforts were not so much to protect the arms, which had been spirited away two days prior, but to warn John Hancock and Samuel Adams, who were hiding in Lexington. Along the way, Revere was arrested by British soldiers. In response to a gun placed to his head, Revere revealed all, but he got away and helped the two leaders escape. He never made it to Concord and so was

| 1400 | 1450 | 1500 | 1550 | 1600 | 1650 | 1700 |

not present for the clashes on April 18, 1775, at Lexington and Concord, nor did he witness the gauntlet the British soldiers had to negotiate to escape back to Boston. But his escapades that night inspired some of the most heroic, if inaccurate, verse in American literature:

> So through the night rode Paul Revere;
> And so through the night went his cry of alarm
> To every Middlesex village and farm,—
> A cry of defiance and not of fear,
> A voice in the darkness, a knock at the door
> And a word that shall echo forevermore!
> For, borne on the night-wind of the Past,
> Through all our history, to the last,
> In the hour of darkness and peril and need,
> The people will waken and listen to hear
> The hurrying hoof-beats of that steed,
> And the midnight message of Paul Revere.

HENRY WADSWORTH LONGFELLOW (1860)

(02-155, 02-156)

VIRGINIA DECLARATION OF RELIGIOUS FREEDOM, 1775

A serious question facing early America was state support for religion. In Virginia, the Anglican Church was the state church. Citizens were taxed to pay the church's cost of doing business. By 1776, however, an alliance formed that would bring this to an end. Enlightened thinkers such as Thomas Jefferson and James Madison took common cause with evangelical Christians to end tax support for churches. The result was the Virginia Statute for Religious Freedom, written by Jefferson in 1777 but passed only after ten years of bitter dispute. He wrote, "It is . . . tyrannical to compel a man to support opinions he disbelieves, but even forcing him to support this or that teacher of his own religious persuasion is wrong."

The statute shaped the First Amendment, which in turn allowed religion to expand. Religious historian Philip Schaff put it well: "The United States is the most religious country in the world . . . just because religion is there most free." (01-063)

| 1400 | 1450 | 1500 | 1550 | 1600 | 1650 | 1700 |

LEE-DEANE CONFLICT, 1776

Connecticut native Silas Deane had been in Paris during the early months of 1776, sent by Congress to open trade, buy munitions for the Army on credit, and work for French recognition of American independence. He was very successful in large part because the government of Louis XVI was looking for a path of revenge against Britain for France's losses in the Seven Years' War, which ended in 1763. Even before the crucial Battle of Saratoga, New York, in 1777 demonstrated that the Americans might just succeed in the Revolution, a supposedly neutral France secretly sent supplies to help.

Despite his success, Deane's reputation suffered because of personal and professional animosity between him and another member of the Congressional delegation, Arthur Lee of the prominent Virginia family. Under Lee's influence, Congress inappropriately recalled Deane in an early example of political and regional divisions. Here Congress began airing its dirty linen. It has not stopped since. (09-032, 09-033)

1700   1750   1800   1850   1900   1950   PRESENT

Era of Revolution: Colonial

BENJAMIN FRANKLIN I, 1776

In a life distinguished by business success (by the 1740s he was financially secure), intellectual curiosity, and innovation, Ben Franklin embarked on a course of extraordinary public service. His reputation as a reformer, in which he advocated action by the colonies as a group, carried him after 1764 to London as agent for several of the colonies. There, he vigorously articulated the colonial position in the press and before Parliament and the government.

After eighteen years in London as agent arguing the colonies' case in the press and before Parliament and government, Ben Franklin returned home convinced the only course for America was independence. He arrived in Philadelphia on May 5, 1776, and was immediately appointed to the Pennsylvania delegation. For the next two months, he helped John Adams and others marshal the case for independence in the Congress. Once the Declaration he had helped craft was signed and the course set, he began perhaps his greatest service to the infant republic. (11-054, 11-062, 11-063, 11-064)

| 1400 | 1450 | 1500 | 1550 | 1600 | 1650 | 1700 |

BENJAMIN FRANKLIN II, 1776

I n late 1776, Benjamin Franklin, accompanied by two grandsons on the small, swift warship *Reprisal*, was sent as the United States' first ambassador to France. His skillful diplomacy secured that nation's support and therefore the success of the American Revolution.

The breakthrough came in fall 1777 with the crushing defeat of British General John Burgoyne's army at the Battle of Saratoga. The American revolt was not going quietly into the night. In February 1778, France and the United States signed a Treaty of Alliance. French loans, troops, and naval forces were soon in the service of George Washington. Franklin remained in France for negotiations until 1785. His counsel at the Constitutional Convention in 1787 led to the great compromise, which provided for a House of Representatives proportioned by population and a Senate with equal representation from each state. Franklin died, honored and admired at age eighty-four, in 1790. (11-054, 11-062, 11-063, 11-064)

BATTLE OF SARATOGA, 1777

In late summer 1777, British forces, led by General John Burgoyne, marched south from Quebec. His objective was to seize control of the Hudson Valley and cut off New England from the South.

Unable to secure supplies from the countryside, he had to haul his provisions, arms, and ammunition with him. This gave the Americans time to lay a trap for him north of Albany. On September 19, he faced 6,000 Americans under General Horatio Gates. The clash was indecisive, but the British casualty rate was twice as high as that of the rebels. On October 7, Burgoyne was defeated by forces led by Benedict Arnold. Days later at Schuylerville, he was surrounded by 17,000 Patriots and forced to surrender.

Saratoga is considered a decisive American victory and the turning point of the Revolution. Its diplomatic consequences were even greater. This triumph convinced the French to recognize the fledgling American republic and aid in the cause of independence.

(08-089, 08-090)

1400   1450   1500   1550   1600   1650   1700

MOLLY CORBIN—
REVOLUTIONARY SOLDIER, 1777

During the eighteenth century, most armies allowed women to accompany units on campaign. They cleaned and cooked and performed other dubious social duties associated with men alone far from home. Molly Corbin's husband, a matross (a gunner's assistant), fought together with Molly in the Battle of Fort Washington, near present-day 183rd street in New York City in November 1776.

Her husband was killed, and she took over, fighting as hard as any man. The British overran the position, and she was terribly wounded. Her arm was nearly shot off, and her breasts were lacerated. For most of the rest of her life "Captain" Molly was an invalid, drawing a small government pension. With her nasty temper and sharp tongue, she made life miserable for her caregivers. After her death in 1800, memory of her heroism in war helped rehabilitate her reputation. She is buried in the post cemetery at West Point. (01-0184)

| 1700 | 1750 | 1800 | 1850 | 1900 | 1950 | PRESENT |

Era of Revolution: Military

BENEDICT ARNOLD, 1780

In fall 1777, Connecticut native Benedict Arnold was a bitter man. He was recuperating from a leg injury received at the Battle of Saratoga where his leadership in this decisive American victory had been critical. Unfortunately, his commander Horatio Gates and the Continental Congress were tardy in according him proper recognition. Arnold, however, had the confidence of General Washington, who made him commandant of Philadelphia. There, he met and married Tory socialite Peggy Shippen. Arnold's resentment at the slights he had received from Congress and his fellow officers, his perception that the Revolutionary effort was flagging, and the toxic pro-English influence of his wife had probably pushed him toward betrayal.

He first told the British of a proposed American invasion of Canada, and when he received word that Washington was giving him the command of the highly strategic stronghold of West Point on the Hudson River, Arnold began a secret correspondence with the British Commander Henry Clinton. The plan was to surrender the Point to the British in exchange for payment and a commission. At the last minute, the plot was exposed, and Arnold barely escaped to a British vessel. (09-035, 09-036)

In the last years of the Revolution, New York–based British General Henry Clinton had an extensive spy network in the Hudson Valley, probing for American weaknesses and stirring up trouble among quiet British supporters in the region. Clinton's intelligence chief was Major John André, an officer of Huguenot descent who was ambitious, cultured, elegant, and artistic.

In spring 1779, André received word from American General Benedict Arnold that he wished to defect to the British and surrender the strategic outpost of West Point. For months the two negotiated. They met on the moonless night of September 21, 1780, to finalize the deal. The meeting went longer than expected, so André could not return home by ship; he had to travel overland to British lines. Near Tarrytown, New York, he was detained by American pickets who discovered notes from Arnold to General Clinton in his boot. Ironically, the notes, confirming Arnold's treachery, were unnecessary because the British had the information already. André was arrested and eventually hanged as a spy. Arnold escaped. In 1801, he died in England, ignored and nearly penniless; his name became an epithet for treason in the nation he originally served but then betrayed. (03-020, 03-021, 03-022)

FRANCIS MARION—
THE SWAMP FOX I, 1780

By 1780, Revolutionary fighting had shifted south. After taking Charleston, the British began a series of raids into the interior, climaxing in a great victory at Camden in August 1780. Complete conquest seemed imminent, but the British had two problems.

Politically, they failed to exploit the fact that half the colonials did not support the Revolution and might have responded to negotiation and compromise. Instead, they treated Americans as undisciplined children needing to be whipped into order.

This arrogance led to their second error, this one military. Americans were often outnumbered, ill-clothed, deficient in supplies, and poorly led, but they were not stupid. Patriots were not going to stand up in pitched battle against the finest European troops money could buy. When odds were against them, Americans melted away and returned to fight again. After Camden, the cause was pursued by partisan militia groups. The most successful individual partisan was Francis Marion. (05-015, 05-016, 05-017)

1400   1450   1500   1550   1600   1650   1700

FRANCIS MARION—
THE SWAMP FOX II, 1780

After the British victory at Camden in August 1780, the Revolution in the South was kept alive by partisan guerrilla groups such as Francis Marion's. His band was racially mixed and lived in the swamps of the Pee Dee River on Snow's Island near present-day Florence, South Carolina. The partisans in Marion's group sniped at the Redcoats, attacked baggage trains, and harassed patrols.

Marion was a natural leader, inspiring near fanatical loyalty in his troops. He never risked the lives of his men unnecessarily and understood he was fighting a civil war. Many of his opponents were his neighbors, so winning their hearts was as important as winning battles.

At first shocked at Marion's success, the British finally sent Lieutenant Colonel Banastre "Butcher" Tarleton after Marion, but despite tactics of destruction, he could not find him. After seven days of wandering around in the muck, Tarleton arrived empty-handed at Ox Swamp. Tradition records that he said, "Come, my boys, let's go back. . . . As for this damned old fox, the devil himself could not catch him." (05-015, 05-016, 05-017)

JAMES CALDWELL—
SOLDIER'S PARSON, 1780

Much of the Revolution's leadership came from clergymen. Rev. James Caldwell was chaplain of the Third New Jersey Regiment. His devotion to the Patriot cause cost him his home and church at Elizabethtown, burned by a Tory raiding party. On June 7, 1780, Mrs. Caldwell was killed by a British soldier.

The British raided northeastern New Jersey, falsely believing it might be won back to the royalist cause. Two weeks after his wife's death, Pastor Caldwell was among the defenders at Springfield. When paper wadding used to load weapons ran low, he rode to the village church, gathered hymnbooks, and distributed them to his soldiers. Invoking the memory of the great hymn writer, he shouted, "Now, boys . . . let them have Watts." Soon the British withdrew from the area. Whether the sacrifice of the Springfield hymnbooks helped is a matter of speculation, but for James Caldwell, the sound of his men's guns was music to his ears. (01-030)

1400   1450   1500   1550   1600   1650   1700

BATTLE OF KING'S MOUNTAIN I, 1780

S eeking to mine a rich vein of loyalist sentiment and exploit bitter partisan conflict already ripping the Southern heartland, beginning in 1779, the British Army shifted its strategic focus to the Carolinas. First Savannah, then Charleston fell. Southern commander General Charles Cornwallis began to move northwest from Charleston in summer 1780. He divided his Army into three groups. The right was led by Lieutenant Colonel Banastre Tarleton, already infamous for his brutality following the Battle of Waxhaws on May 29, which earned him the sobriquet *Butcher Tarleton.*

Cornwallis defeated a Continental army under Horatio Gates at Camden in August. Complete victory in the South seemed inevitable. His left flank was led by Major Patrick Ferguson, whose reputation for brutality was only slightly less than Tarleton's. In September 1780, camped near Charlotte, he threatened Patriot groups with severe consequences if they continued their resistance. It was as if he stuck his arm in a hornet's nest. (07-002, 07-003, 07-004)

BATTLE OF KING'S
MOUNTAIN II, 1780

After several victories, British General Charles Cornwallis seemed poised to shut down Patriot hopes in the Carolinas by late summer 1780. Covering his left flank in a three-pronged assault into the southern heartland was a force of Loyalist militiamen under Major Patrick Ferguson. The major made a serious error when he threatened Patriot groups in the alpine valleys east of the Appalachians. Among them were the backwater men, hard-working, tough, hearty, and deeply religious Scot-Irish immigrants who had settled those valleys to protect their families, secure their independence, and practice their fierce Presbyterian faith. His threat sealed his fate.

Seeing trouble ahead, Ferguson retreated to the slopes of King's Mountain, a rocky spur of the Blue Ridge not far from Charlotte. There on October 7, he was attacked from two directions by partisans whose approach was masked by heavy rainfall. It was over in seventy-five minutes. Ferguson was shot repeatedly, and his force surrendered. Writing later, theater commander Sir Henry Clinton said, "The instant I heard of Major Ferguson's defeat I foresaw the consequences. . . . [It was] the first link in a chain of evils that . . . ended in the total loss of America." (07-002, 07-003, 07-004)

| 1400 | 1450 | 1500 | 1550 | 1600 | 1650 | 1700 |

ELIZABETH ZANE, 1782

Ebenezer Zane established Fort Henry on the site that became Wheeling, West Virginia, in 1769. Several years later, Zane's sister, Elizabeth, returned to the area after her schooling in Philadelphia.

In fall 1782, Captain Andrew Brandt, with 40 British Rangers and 250 American Indians, laid siege to Fort Henry. After six hours of battle, the fort was low on gunpowder, and many defenders were wounded. Powder was stored in the basement of Zane's house, sixty yards outside the fort. Elizabeth convinced the commander to let her go get it.

She grabbed a cask of powder and ran back though gunfire, making it unscathed. Shortly thereafter, the siege was lifted. Though many historians question the accuracy of this story, even as legend it is a useful reminder of the sacrifices women made to help conquer the American frontier. Betty Zane's great-grand nephew, novelist Zane Grey, based his first novel, *Betty Zane* (1903), on his ancestor's life and heroism. (03-030)

| 1700 | 1750 | 1800 | 1850 | 1900 | 1950 | PRESENT |

Era of Revolution: Military

AMERICANS AND TAXES, 1782

Americans have a love/hate relationship with taxes. British taxes sparked the Revolution—"no taxation without representation." From ancient times, taxes were paid in goods and services, labor, and military service, but by the 1800s, governments began to tax things that could be measured: land, property, and income. In the United States, the constitution prohibited any direct tax, but during the Civil War emergency, Congress authorized an income tax to help finance the war. It was reduced after the war and repealed in 1872.

An income tax, however, appealed to advocates for the poor. They wanted a heavier burden put on the wealthy—a form of wealth redistribution, considered fairer than tariffs or excise taxes, which hurt middle income and poor people. Reviving the income tax failed in 1894. The Supreme Court ruled it unconstitutional. An alternative was to amend the Constitution. In 1913, the Sixteenth Amendment made the income tax a permanent part of American life. (07-052)

1400   1450   1500   1550   1600   1650   1700

YORKTOWN AND THE
TREATY OF PARIS, 1783

Until the twenty-first century, the American Revolution was the longest war in the history of the United States. From the first shot on the Lexington green in 1775 until the signing of the Treaty of Paris in 1783, Britain clung with desperate intensity to the colonies of North America. The beginning of the end took place in Virginia with the surrender of the southern commander, Lord Cornwallis, at the Battle of Yorktown, on October 19, 1781.

Cornwallis and his troops were completely trapped on the Yorktown peninsula. By late September, a joint American–French infantry taskforce, led by Generals George Washington and Jean-Baptiste Donatien de Vimeur, comte de Rochambeau and backed by a large French naval squadron in the Chesapeake led by François Joseph Paul de Grasse, locked up the besieged Brits. Their fate was sealed when the French fleet defeated attempts by the British Navy to rescue or resupply the Yorktown garrison. When Cornwallis recognized his hopeless situation, he sought terms of surrender from Washington and Rochambeau. Feigning illness, the British commander did not attend the surrender, sending his second in command to proffer his sword. Legend has it that when the British marched off the field their band played "The World Turned Upside Down." Though unconfirmed, the story nevertheless reflects the view of the British government toward the situation.

The United States achieved its independence from Great Britain with the Treaty of Paris, signed on September 3, 1783. It brought the Revolutionary War to an end and set the boundaries of British and American holdings on the continent.

| 1700 | 1750 | 1800 | 1850 | 1900 | 1950 | PRESENT |

Era of Revolution: Military

SHAYS' REBELLION I, 1787

Coastal merchants in New England, by the mid-1780s in debt and squeezed out of rich markets in the West Indies by Britain, called in many loans to frontier farmers. When they could not pay up, the merchants foreclosed. Opponents called themselves Regulators, although the movement became known as Shays' Rebellion, named for Daniel Shays, a former Continental Army officer and farmer from Pelham, already arrested twice for petty debt.

Frustrated in their attempts to get legislative relief, the Regulators turned to violence. Judges would convene a court session intending to foreclose on a farm, only for a large crowd to materialize and prevent the court from even meeting. Governor Bowdoin of Massachusetts assembled an army from the coastal counties, and in February 1787 at Petersham, 4,000 militia dispersed a crowd of Regulators half its size. The action ended the insurrection, but unwittingly Mr. Shays helped bring on a different kind of Revolution—a constitutional one. (01-193, 01-194, 01-195)

SHAYS' REBELLION II, 1787

The Articles of Confederation was a weak and ineffective compact. Federal taxes could not be compelled. The Confederation could not settle disputes between states by force. Leaders such as Alexander Hamilton understood the need for a more powerful central government. In August 1786, a convention met in Annapolis, Maryland, to study the issue but broke-up in failure. Only five states sent representatives. The Annapolis Convention, though, recommended a follow-up meeting in spring 1787.

Then word spread of rural insurrections, the most serious of which was Shays' Rebellion in western Massachusetts. Again Congress proved itself impotent to put down anarchy. State leaders, many of whom had resisted the idea of a stronger central government, began to clamor for one. George Washington believed the Shays' Rebellion so shocked local leaders that states sent delegates to Philadelphia ready to make serious changes. He did not create the new federal government, but Shays surely helped create the setting out of which it emerged. (01-193, 01-194, 01-195)

JAMES MADISON AND THE
CONSTITUTION I, 1787

The sense of euphoria that followed independence was short-lived. The problem was the national charter, the Articles of Confederation. It was so weak and ineffectual that by 1786 the Continental Congress was reduced to being a feeble debating society, so impotent that many state representatives simply did not attend. Into this chaos stepped James Madison of Virginia.

Madison attended the Annapolis Convention in September 1786, called to examine constitutional revision. Only five states bothered to send representatives, but the Convention called for a new Convention in Philadelphia in May 1787. On the way home, he dropped by Mount Vernon and convinced George Washington to lead the Virginia delegation and support reform. The Virginians were united in Philadelphia and presented Madison's ideas, known as the Virginia Plan.

The horse-trading went on all summer. The final document bore the marks of Madison's Plan, though he had been forced to make concessions. It was a brilliant exercise in Enlightenment jurisprudence. (09-011, 09-012, 09-013, 09-014)

1400   1450   1500   1550   1600   1650   1700

JAMES MADISON AND THE
CONSTITUTION II, 1787

When the Constitutional Convention met in Philadelphia in May 1787, its debates focused on the Virginia Plan, a structure devised by James Madison. It called for a two-branch legislature based on population, a strong executive elected by Congress, and a national judiciary. When complete, the new national charter insured that no part of the government was too powerful and envisioned equity between federal and state governments.

Having led in the crafting the Constitution, Madison joined in marketing efforts to win support for this fundamental change. John Jay, Alexander Hamilton, and Madison wrote eighty-five essays under the name Publius, entitled *The Federalist*. The collective effort, an intellectual triumph, was widely distributed and won broad support for ratification.

Madison then promised to work for a Bill of Rights to quiet the fears of those, including his friend and soul mate Thomas Jefferson, who were concerned that the Constitution failed to address the question of individual rights. (09-011, 09-012, 09-013, 09-014)

COMPROMISE OF SHAME, 1787

Roger Sherman's compromise at the Constitutional Convention in 1787 yielded a two-house Congress, one based on population, the other with equal representation between the states. Then the Convention deadlocked over how to count black slaves in determining the number of representatives in the House. Southerners wanted all slaves counted. Northern states wanted them counted not at all.

A few delegates were utterly opposed to slavery and later the convention took steps to end the slave trade, but for the most part, these men were not struggling with the morality of slavery. They were designing a constitution to protect property, and slaves were property. Their solution was that each slave would be counted as three-fifths of a person. It was the Three-Fifths Compromise, a compromise of shame.

It is unfortunate that the Constitution should be blighted with so repulsive an arrangement. Yet, without this compromise the constitution would likely have been aborted. For many, slavery appeared to be on the wane. That is, until Eli Whitney's cotton gin gave the South an enormously profitable cash crop needing slaves to cultivate it. Slavery's end would require the bloody Civil War, but the delegates were not future-tellers. Thus, in the steamy Philadelphia summer of 1787, for national unity, the Constitutional Convention adopted the compromise of shame. (01-009)

WHISKEY REBELLION, 1794

I n winter 1794, President George Washington sent an army into western Pennsylvania to put down a rebellion among farmers opposed to a federal tax on whiskey. Passed to pay revolutionary war debts, this tax was deeply resented by farmers in the west. Instead of storing their grain, they distilled it and used it for medicine and as well as a form of money. When a citizen militia led by backcountry lawyer David Bradford threatened violence and perhaps secession, Washington declared them traitors and sent an army to put down the rebellion. High tension filled the area around Pittsburgh as the army under Revolutionary War hero General "Light-Horse Harry" Lee moved slowly westward.

When Lee arrived, he required all citizens to sign a new oath of allegiance. Bradford escaped down the Ohio to Spanish territory. The United States would face many challenges in the decades ahead, but it had proven it had the power and the will to tax.

(02-157, 02-158, 02-159, 02-160)

1700	1750	1800	1850	1900	1950	PRESENT

Era of Revolution: Constitutional

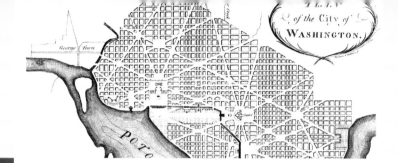

PIERRE L'ENFANT–
DC ARCHITECT, 1795

When the deal was cut to place the new federal city in the South, George Washington chose as architect Pierre L'Enfant, known for design originality combined with a prickly personality. His plan called for avenues 160 feet broad and a huge mall extending west from the base of Jenkin's Hill, the future location of the Capitol building. He selected dominating sites, a Capitol on the promontory, the president's house on flat low ground, and–his unique contribution to urban planning–radial avenues that, theoretically at least, made travel within the city more efficient.

Because of his personality, however, L'Enfant came into conflict with the people who were actually living there. He once ordered a home torn down because it lay seven feet within the survey lines of New Jersey Avenue. As a result, he lasted only one year as architect of the federal city, but the basic outlines of his plan remain to this day. (01-125)

XYZ AFFAIR I, 1796

In 1789, France was rocked with a bloody revolution and in the 1790s went to war with Britain. Both countries wanted US help, but Presidents Washington and Adams were determined to remain neutral. France seemed to have the best case. The French had virtually saved the American Revolution. They reasoned it was time to return the favor.

Complicating matters, both the French and British were attacking American ships caught trading with the other side. In 1794, Washington sent Supreme Court Chief Justice John Jay of New York to London to negotiate a settlement with the British. The resulting Jay's Treaty partly smoothed over relations with the British, but this angered the French, who accused the United States of breaking the Treaty of 1778.

The people of the United States were divided. Thomas Jefferson and his political allies were pro-French, though they were offended by many of the excesses of the revolution in Paris. Many of the president's supporters were pro-British. (03-099, 03-100, 03-101, 03-102, 03-103)

XYZ AFFAIR II, 1796

War with France was looming in the 1790s when President John Adams sent a delegation to calm the French. French Foreign Minister Charles Maurice de Talleyrand desired an apology for allegedly disparaging remarks about France by Adams and a $250,000 bribe for Talleyrand, and an enormous loan that everyone agreed would never be repaid.

One of the delegation's commissioners, future Supreme Court Justice John Marshall, rejected the French demands in a dispatch published in American newspapers. To protect the identity of Talleyrand's emissaries, several of whom were friends of America, he called them "Mr. W, Mr. X, Mr. Y, and Mr. Z." The so-called XYZ Affair turned fellow commissioner Charles Cotesworth Pinckney's witty rejoinder into one of America's earliest political slogans: "Millions for defense, but not one cent for tribute."

President Adams, aware of US military weakness, refused to allow public irritation at France draw America into war. The French and the United States finally settled their dispute at the Convention of 1800. (03-099, 03-100, 03-101, 03-102, 03-103)

| 1400 | 1450 | 1500 | 1550 | 1600 | 1650 | 1700 |

At the Second Session,

Begun and held at the city of *Philadelphia*, in the state of PENNSYLVANIA, on *Monday*, the thirteenth of *November*, one thousand seven hundred and ninety-seven.

An **ACT** *concerning aliens.*

BE it enacted by the Senate and House of Representatives of the United States of America, in Congress assembled,

ALIEN AND SEDITION ACTS, 1796

71

In 1798, anger against France provoked widespread war talk. The people were aroused. The Federalist Party in Congress, alarmed at the growth of the followers of Thomas Jefferson, passed the Alien and the Sedition Acts. The first more than doubled the time immigrants needed to achieve citizenship and allowed the president to deport foreigners he considered dangerous. The Sedition Act levied penalties for those convicted of criticizing the United States, the Congress, or the president.

The targets were obvious. French and Irish immigrants almost all supported the Democratic-Republicans. Nearly all prosecuted under the Sedition Act were Republican newspaper editors or activists. It was a repressive violation of the First Amendment's protection of free speech. Reaction was swift. The Virginia and Kentucky legislatures denounced the Acts as unconstitutional. In 1800, the dispute with France was resolved, war fever subsided, and rationality returned. The public turned against this perceived constitutional coup in the Democratic-Republican electoral tidal wave in 1800. And the Federalist Party began its long slide to political oblivion. (09-063, 09-064, 09-065)

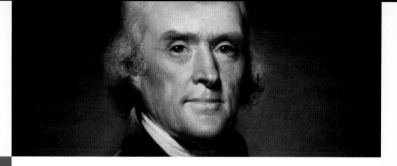

REVOLUTION OF 1800 I

In 1800, Thomas Jefferson defeated incumbent President John Adams in a closely fought election that brought what some have called the third American Revolution. The first was military and began in 1776, the second was constitutional, and this third was political, firmly establishing political parties in American life.

Adams was swept into office in 1796 with the support of the Federalists. He was not a naturally popular person and took positions that made matters worse. Adams kept the nation out of a declared war with competing European powers, particularly France, but did so in such a way as to offend the national honor. During the run-up to the election, the electorate was incensed that Adams seemed to cozy up to France when it made extravagant demands to secure US trade cooperation (see chapters on the XYZ Affair) and then engaged in the Quasi-War, a low-grade naval war against US interests.

In 1798, during a dinner honoring John Marshall, Representative Robert Goodloe Harper of South Carolina offered a toast of US defiance, rephrasing Charles Cotesworth Pinckney's response to the French. Harper's "Millions for defense, but not one cent for tribute," was on the lips and minds of many voters.

The Quasi-War with France kept the pot boiling, and in summer 1798, with prowar sentiment at a fever pitch, Adams reluctantly signed into law the Alien and Sedition Acts, a big mistake. (09-049, 09-050, 09-051)

The Democratic-Republican Party, the political ancestor of today's Democratic Party, was a coalition of southern planters and northern workingmen, organized by Aaron Burr and was quietly led by Vice President Thomas Jefferson. Republican political propaganda, very similar to modern negative television attack ads, falsely accused Adams of wanting to be king and for undermining freedom of the press. The Federalists went down to a crushing defeat. After a long battle in the House of Representatives, the states elected Jefferson as president over Burr.

Disillusioned, Adams did not even attend Jefferson's inauguration, but he had a bit of revenge. In the closing days of his administration, the lame-duck Federalist Congress vastly expanded the number of federal judges—called "midnight judges." One of those so chosen was Supreme Court Chief Justice John Marshall, whose longevity and intellectual horsepower helped firmly establish the federal government as preeminent in national affairs and the Judicial Branch as an equal partner in the federal constitutional order. (09-049, 09-050, 09-051)

LOUISIANA PURCHASE, 1803

The Louisiana Purchase secured for the United States over 800,000 square miles of French territory. For $15 million or four cents an acre, land from the mouth of the Mississippi to the Northwest Pacific Coast ensured that the United States would have almost limitless territory in which to expand. It would also become the dominant power on the continent.

For all the potential of this extraordinary purchase, President Thomas Jefferson believed it violated his republican principles that asserted the federal government could do nothing unless the Constitution specifically permitted it. If such an enormous purchase could be justified as part of the president's natural treaty-making responsibilities, he feared the Constitution could be stretched out of shape by any creative president. Despite his conviction that the purchase was an unconstitutional expansion of federal authority, he was also a clever politician. The purchase was powerful and popular politics. Therefore, he swallowed his convictions and bought the territory. (05-036)

| 1400 | 1450 | 1500 | 1550 | 1600 | 1650 | 1700 |

HAMILTON AND BURR–
DEADLY RIVALRY I, 1804

One of the earliest political rivalries in US history was that between Alexander Hamilton and Aaron Burr. It was personal, intellectual, political, social, and, at the end, quite deadly.

They first met as young officers in the Continental Army. Burr was a line officer, and Hamilton was on the staff of General Washington. Burr, the son and grandson of presidents of Princeton, was brash and brilliant and nursed a smoldering ambition for greatness. Hamilton soon detected a rival for Washington's attention and for future leadership. Hamilton harbored much social insecurity because of his dubious upbringing in the West Indies. Burr's rumored affinity for sexual liaisons, which irritated the general, gave Hamilton the perfect opportunity to impugn Burr's character with tantalizing gossip about his rival's exploits. Tragically, both decided to settle in New York—a boiling cauldron of competitive politics. Into the city stepped two of the most ambitious men ever to struggle for power in American history.

(01-021, 01-022, 01-023)

HAMILTON AND BURR—
DEADLY RIVALRY II, 1804

In the 1700s, two groups dominated New York politics. One was Episcopalian and only very late in the Revolution began to shift away from its loyalty to Great Britain. It was led by the Dutch, aristocratic Schuyler family. Alexander Hamilton married into the faction and quickly came to dominate it.

Another alliance was middle class and Presbyterian; it was headed by the Livingston family. A third coalition was emerging in upstate and western New York, led by Revolutionary War Governor George Clinton and his nephew DeWitt Clinton. Aaron Burr quickly perceived the importance of political parties in recruiting talent and organizing elections. Using his connections with Tammany Hall, a working-class political club, Burr brought together middle-class voters and the Livingston and Clinton groups. In the US Senate election of 1791, Burr defeated Hamilton's father-in-law, General Phillip Schuyler. From that point on, the Hamilton and Burr were implacable enemies. (01-021, 01-022, 01-023)

HAMILTON AND BURR—
DEADLY RIVALRY III, 1804

Alexander Hamilton was the nation's first Secretary of the Treasury. Aaron Burr, his great rival, sat in the Senate in a seat he won from Hamilton's father-in-law. Soon the character of Hamilton and Burr became obvious. Hamilton put the needs of the nation above his own ambitions. Burr was an unscrupulous politician who would do anything to attain power.

In the presidential election of 1800, Jefferson and Burr were tied with seventy-three votes each in the Electoral College. The election then shifted to the Federalist-controlled House of Representatives, where each state had a single vote. The Federalists would elect the president. Burr quietly signaled that he would shift parties. Horrified, Hamilton helped secure Federalist votes for Jefferson, thus ensuring his election.

Bad blood between Burr and Jefferson dictated that Burr was not included as vice president when Jefferson ran for reelection. Instead, he went home to New York to run for governor. Hamilton used his political clout to help defeat Burr in his gubernatorial run. Finally, Burr had had enough. He challenged Hamilton to a duel and on the morning of July 11, 1804, killed him. Hamilton shot in the air. Burr, whom no one ever accused of generosity, took careful aim and removed for good the barrier to his ambitions. (01-021, 01-022, 01-023)

| 1700 | 1750 | 1800 | 1850 | 1900 | 1950 | PRESENT |

Era of Nationalism

THE CHINCHA (GUANO) ISLANDS : MIDDLE ISLAND, AS SEEN FROM NORTH ISLAND.

GUANO, 1804

Guano is bird excrement. Among the most potent natural fertilizers, it contains up to 16 percent nitrogen, 12 percent phosphorus, and 3 percent potassium. In 1804, geographer Alexander von Humboldt returned to Germany and brought a sample of guano, taken from islands off the coast of Peru. Since many European and Eastern US farms were depleted, guano possibly could revive them.

Peru, the source of the richest deposits, jealously guarded its islands and charged premium prices to extract the guano, which, after thousands of years of bird visits, was in places 150 feet deep. The US then joined the worldwide guano rush, intensive expeditions to find undiscovered islands loaded with the stuff. In 1879, Peru and Bolivia fought the Guano War or War of the Pacific in part to secure the mineral-rich guano islands off the coast of South America.

By 1900, synthesized fertilizers had become universally accessible. Guano, however, has recently come back into fashion with growth of organic farming. (11-026)

LEWIS AND CLARK
EXPEDITION, 1805

"Great joy in camp. . . . We are view of the ocian. . . . This great Pacific . . . which we have been so long anxious to See," wrote William Clark inaccurately in his journal on November 5, 1805. He was actually viewing the huge estuary of the Columbia River, whose salty and brackish waters stretched twenty miles inland in present-day Washington State.

The journey of Clark and his partner Meriwether Lewis, President Jefferson's secretary, was an assertion of control over the enormous Louisiana Purchase. Lewis journeyed down the Ohio. After a winter layover near St. Louis, on May 14, 1804, the party began its trip overland to the Pacific.

On the afternoon of November 15, the party moved from its base camp four miles around Point Ellice to a sandy beach about a half mile southeast of Chinook Point, and there for the first time they could see the Pacific Ocean. Lewis and Clark had reached their goal. (01-207)

| 1700 | 1750 | 1800 | 1850 | 1900 | 1950 | PRESENT |

Era of Nationalism

ROBERT FULTON'S FOLLY, 1807

Although often incorrectly credited with the invention of the steamboat, Robert Fulton cobbled together the invention's components—engine, boiler, and paddle wheel—to produce the first commercially successful steamboat. He did so under contract to wealthy New York businessman Robert Livingston.

Fulton's steamboat, *Clermont*, derided as "Fulton's Folly" during construction, was a flat-bottomed vessel, 150 feet long and 16 feet wide, with 15-foot paddlewheels installed midway along the sides.

In early August 1807, heading north to Albany against the current, the steamboat appeared to observers like "a sawmill mounted on a raft and set on fire." After an overnight stop at Livingston's estate near Clermont, the village for which the craft was named, the party was off. Normally, a fast-sailing schooner took four days to reach Albany, but after only thirty-two hours of sailing, at 4.7 miles per hour, *Clermont* arrived in Albany to a cheering crowd led by the governor of New York. Fulton's Folly had produced a revolution in transport. (09-046, 09-047)

NEW JERSEY AND THE
WOMEN'S VOTE, 1807

New Jersey crafted its first state constitution in 1776. The only voting requirement was that a person be worth £50 or more. Among others, women and free blacks were eligible. The numbers were not large, since few women owned property independently of their husbands. A few prosperous single women and widows qualified.

In 1790, New Jersey revised the election laws of several counties and specifically extended the franchise to voters referred to as "he or she." This was later extended to the rest of the state. In 1807, however, Newark and Elizabeth were fighting over which would become the county seat. Newark won, and women voted in large numbers, perhaps a few more than once. Recoiling from this demonstration of female voting power and from the untidy voter fraud, the New Jersey political class revised the election rules to exclude women. They would have to wait until 1920, when the Nineteenth Amendment gave women the right to vote. (02-179)

END OF SLAVE TRADE, 1808

As delegates gathered in Philadelphia in summer 1787 to craft a new constitution, they confronted the problem of slavery. Surprisingly, even many southerners were aware that the institution had harmful effects on the character of slave and slaveholder, violated the principles on which the new republic was founded, and was becoming economically unprofitable. George Mason of Virginia spoke for slave skeptics when he called the slave trade "a moral corruption" and said that "every slave-holder was born a petty tyrant."

The convention compromised, and while it gave Congress the right to terminate slave importation in 1808, that did little to impede the institution. Southerners found that they could breed slaves like cattle more profitably than importing them. The number of slaves grew enormously as the cotton plantations in Alabama, Mississippi, and the rest of the Deep South, now mechanized with Eli Whitney's cotton gin, demanded and got their steady supply of human chattel. (11-046, 11-047)

TIPPECANOE AND
TECUMSEH TOO I, 1811

The treatment by whites of African slaves and Native Americans represents a moral stain on American history—the nation's original sin. In the early 1800s, the vision of Shawnee Chief Tecumseh and his brother The Prophet was perhaps the supreme challenge to white supremacy in the early years of the republic. Their program was spiritual as well as practical and was at fundamental odds with way whites organized their lives. Steeped in the Judeo-Christian tradition of private property, white Americans looked upon land as something owned by an individual. Indians saw land much the same as they saw air. It was a commodity owned and used by all.

The Prophet preached American Indian renewal, and in Native American villages throughout the Ohio Valley hundreds of warriors turned their backs on loose living and American whiskey and returned to traditional American Indian ideas of communal living and tribal solidarity. His brother had a different and potentially powerful approach. (01-079, 01-180, 01-081)

TIPPECANOE AND
TECUMSEH TOO II, 1811

In the early 1800s in the American Northwest, Tecumseh and his brother The Prophet offered a program of spiritual renewal and practical political and military unity as a means of resisting white expansion. Tecumseh was a shrewd and charismatic leader. He began a series of recruiting trips—north to Canada, south to Florida—urging other clans to adopt a form of intratribal solidary. He said resistance to whites was only possible if the tribes were united.

The great enemy of American Indians in the old American Northwest was territorial Governor General William Henry Harrison. Seeing the brothers as a powerful threat, he began a preemptive campaign against them in 1811. During one of Tecumseh's frequent absences, he brought an army up the Tippecanoe River in Northern Indiana and attacked and defeated The Prophet's poorly led forces at the Battle of Tippecanoe in November 1811. The Prophet survived, but with a diminished reputation. Unfortunately, he had promised victory over whites would be attended by American Indian renewal. Tecumseh returned to see the collapse of his vision among the scattered corpses on the battlefield. He continued to resist the onslaught of white civilization, allying himself with the British in the War of 1812. He was killed by forces led by Harrison at the Battle of the Thames in Ontario, Canada, on October 5, 1813. William Henry Harrison was elected president in 1840 using the slogan and song "Tippecanoe and Tyler Too." (01-079, 01-180, 01-081)

1400   1450   1500   1550   1600   1650   1700

WAR OF 1812 I

Three decades after winning its independence from Great Britain, the United States found itself at war with its former adversary. The United States was caught between Britain and France in the Napoleonic Wars, and neither of the rivals wanted America to trade with the other. Both attempted to block US ships from the other's ports. Britain also had the offensive habit of stopping American ships and impressing or kidnapping US sailors to crew English ships. On the western frontier, the British enlarged their forces by using their Native American allies in raids on US settlements in the Northwest. Indians were convinced that the only way to stop American aggression was to side with the British.

Both sides were divided on whether to go to war. Britain was distracted by its struggle with Napoleon. The US Congress was seriously divided between the war hawks (prowar western and southern Republicans) and sea traders in New England who would rather be trading than fighting. President Madison signed the declaration of war on June 18, 1812.

1700   1750   1800   1850   1900   1950   PRESENT

Era of Nationalism

WAR OF 1812 II

Neither Britain nor the United States was prepared for war in 1812. The Brits were distracted by their fight against Napoleon. At first, the United States was plagued by serious military incompetence. The war was fought in three arenas: Canada, the Atlantic, and the Southwest.

American strategy focused on taking Canada or what Thomas Jefferson called "the final expulsion of England from the American continent." Every encounter with the British on this front failed with the exception of Oliver Hazard Perry's great naval victory on Lake Erie and the defeat and death of Britain's Native American ally, Tecumseh.

American ships such as *Constitution* scored impressive victories in single-ship actions on the Atlantic in the early months of the war, but the British Navy soon blockaded the whole coast, bottling up the heavy frigates and crushing US overseas trade. In 1814, British forces sailed into the Chesapeake Bay and burned parts of Washington, DC, but failed to take Baltimore. Francis Scott Key memorialized that failure in his poem that, set to music, became "The Star Spangled Banner."

In the Southwest, Andrew Jackson secured his reputation by crushing the Creek Confederation. Then, before word arrived of the war's end by the Treaty of Ghent (1814), Jackson blocked the British invasion of Louisiana with his victory at the Battle of New Orleans. Both sides were tired of war and were willing to settle for a military stalemate. Most historians agree that the United States had successfully defended its honor and that Britain was willing to return to the prewar status quo.

| 1400 | 1450 | 1500 | 1550 | 1600 | 1650 | 1700 |

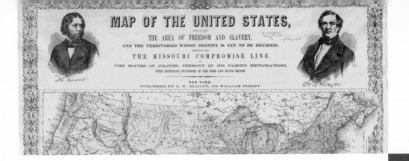

MISSOURI COMPROMISE, 1820

By 1820, the debate over slavery had focused on whether slavery could be banned in territories applying for statehood. Southerners insisted on no restrictions. Northerners wanted no spread of slavery.

If Missouri, which leaned toward slavery, became a state, it would upset the balance in the US Senate. In 1820, Henry Clay of Kentucky, the Great Compromiser, suggested that both Missouri and Maine become states at the same time. Maine, free, was admitted as the 23rd state; Missouri, slave, was admitted as the 24th state.

In the future, slavery was to be banned in states north of a line drawn along the southern boundary of Missouri out to the west coast. Most people north and south were relieved by the compromise, but Thomas Jefferson called it "a fire bell in the night, awakened and filled me with terror." The compromise only delayed the inevitable. Slavery would last until it was torn from the national fabric by a bloody civil war. (08-068, 08-069)

MONROE DOCTRINE, 1823

By the 1820s, with all the brashness and optimism of a youthful republic, the United States was increasingly committed to manifest destiny. Americans believed they had a God-given right to stretch their land claims from Atlantic to Pacific. When Russia began to expand south from Russian America (the future Alaska) into California, in 1823 President James Monroe issued the so-called Monroe Doctrine. The United States would consider land claims or military or political interference in North and South America by European powers to be acts hostile to the interests of the United States.

Remarkably, thanks to Britain's quiet support, America's extravagant claim of continental independence worked. Not until the 1860s, with the United States distracted by the Civil War, did Europeans attempt further interference in the Western Hemisphere. The attempt by Spain, France, and England to install Austrian Archduke Maximillian as Emperor of Mexico ended in 1866 with his execution by Mexican revolutionaries. US power and proximity largely kept the Americas free of outside meddling.
(06-040, 06-041)

| 1400 | 1450 | 1500 | 1550 | 1600 | 1650 | 1700 |

THE STRANGE DEATH OF
JEFFERSON AND ADAMS, 1826

In 1826, the United States was enjoying an exuberant adolescence: its borders stretched ever westward, its ambitions were ravenous, its future was seamless—without limit to prosperity and peace.

High on his small Virginia mountain, Thomas Jefferson, had grown increasingly feeble. On July 2, he began his last sleep. Sometime in the day, Jefferson inquired, "Is this the 4th?" Hearing a yes, he lay back. This gentle and yet false reply surely brought him comfort.

In Massachusetts, John Adams's health had also declined. On the morning of the 4th, his attendant asked him, "Do you know, sir, what day it is?" His reply: "Oh yes, it is the glorious 4th of July. God bless it; God bless you all." Sometime that afternoon he uttered his last intelligible words: "Thomas Jefferson survives." The moment he said this was near Jefferson's last, and by sunset the two men, so honored by their fellow citizens, so important in the birth of freedom, and, in the end, so close as friends, were dead. It was July 4, 1826, fifty years to the day since together they signed the Declaration of Independence. (01-051)

AMERICA'S FIRST RAILROAD, 1830

In 1828, Horatio Allen, an American engineer, visited England to study railroads and was so impressed that he bought four locomotives. He first used them in South Carolina, which was to have the honor of hosting America's first commercial railroad. It ran due west from Charleston to the river port of Hamburg on the Savannah River. Goods could be transshipped from Hamburg to Charleston, thus avoiding the rival port of Savannah. Eventually, it was 130 miles long and was briefly the world's longest railroad.

Allen also built America's first locomotive, *The Best Friend of Charleston*. In June 1831, the engine's boiler exploded, killing the fireman and blowing iron around the landscape like an exploding artillery shell. Rebuilt and aptly renamed *Phoenix*, for years it remained in active service. At the end of 1830, there were twenty-three miles of working track in the United States, most of them across the low country of South Carolina. (01-080)

HAYNE–WEBSTER DEBATE, 1830

It started as a debate on tariffs. In January 1830, Senator Robert Hayne of South Carolina attacked what southerners called the "Tariff of Abominations." This tariff (1828) raised taxes on imports to help native industries, mostly in New England. Overseas retaliatory tariffs hurt southern exports of cotton and rice. Southerners had an alliance with western states to maintain cheap federal land to increase western settlement. Hayne advocated low tariffs and cheap land, but soon the debate turned to nullification, the idea that a state could cancel any federal law it did not like.

He was opposed by Senator Daniel Webster of Massachusetts. Webster insisted that if nullification prevailed then the Union was bound with a "rope of sand"—the most full-throated Union defense prior to Abraham Lincoln. Staring down Vice President John C. Calhoun, the author of nullification who was presiding over the debate, he declared, "Liberty *and* union, now and forever, one and inseparable." (04-001, 04-002, 04-003)

| 1700 | 1750 | 1800 | 1850 | 1900 | 1950 | PRESENT |

Era of Nationalism

NAT TURNER SLAVE
REBELLION I, 1831

Nat Turner was a gifted and powerful slave preacher. His owners from the early days encouraged him to read those portions of the Bible that tell slaves to live lives of dutiful and submissive obedience. Yet, he also read subversive portions of the scriptures that gave him hope that one day he might achieve freedom. By the mid-1820s, Nat Turner was attracting large groups of slaves to his preaching services on Sundays near Cross Keys in Southampton County, Virginia.

He was otherwise a hard worker during the week—sober, smart, honest, and respectful—but Nat Turner raged inside. He may have had prodigious preaching ability, but he was still a cotton-patch Negro, slaving behind a mule. By 1831, Nat was assembling a group of trusted comrades, all disaffected slaves, warning them to prepare and recruit others for an uprising to destroy their oppressors and free their people. (11-006, 11-007, 11-008)

NAT TURNER SLAVE
REBELLION II, 1831

In mid-August 1831, an atmospheric phenomenon caused the sun to dim and change colors. Nat Turner, the powerful slave preacher in South Side, Virginia, saw this as a divine signal to lead a rebellion. On August 21 and for part of the two following days, Nat and his lieutenants, joined by a number of slaves, killed at least fifty-seven whites—men women, and children—beginning with Nat's owners. White reaction was swift and brutal. Dozens of blacks, many having nothing to do with the insurrection, were killed. Turner escaped and was not captured until October 30. He spoke extensively of his motives in interviews prior to his execution less than two weeks later.

Among whites, Turner's Rebellion aggravated already intense fear of the huge number of slaves in their midst, whose anger at the South's peculiar institution smoldered just beneath the surface and, if appropriately organized and inspired, might sweep them all away. (11-006, 11-007, 11-008)

1700	1750	1800	1850	1900	1950	PRESENT

Era of Nationalism

CYRUS MCCORMICK–INVENTOR AND SALESMAN, 1831

In the early 1800s, harvesting wheat was labor-intensive and expensive. The first commercially practical reaper was invented in Rockbridge County, Virginia, in 1831 by Cyrus Hall McCormick. It consisted of a vibrating cutting blade, a reel to bring the stalks within reach and a platform to receive the falling grain. This basic design has changed but little in the years since.

In 1844, McCormick concluded that the Midwest was ripe for harvest. Three years later, he sold 800 machines. When denied a renewal of his original patent, McCormick decided he could only make his fortune if he could improve the machine and beat the competition in sales. McCormick's strategy was to buy the rights to improvements from other inventors and quickly get them onto the machines and out to the customers. He was an extraordinary salesman, and by 1856 he was selling 4,000 machines a year. When he died in 1884, the McCormick reaper dominated the market. (01-188)

JACKSON AND THE
SECOND US BANK, 1832

I n 1832, President Andrew Jackson vetoed the renewal of the Bank of the United States. The bank was popular with many businessmen, North and South, but to Jackson and his supporters it violated states' rights. Also, the bank issued bank notes or paper, not "real money" like gold and silver. Most of all, to them the bank concentrated too much power in the hands of rich, aristocratic, big-city easterners.

Prodded by Jackson enemies Henry Clay and Daniel Webster, the bank applied for an early recharter, confident they could override Jackson's expected veto. The president's allies orchestrated a campaign accusing the bank of economic abuse and corruption. In July, Jackson vetoed the recharter, successfully fended off the override, and made it an issue in the 1832 campaign. Jackson's overwhelming 1832 victory sealed the bank's fate. America's experiment with a central bank was not revived until the Federal Reserve was established in 1913. (06-070, 06-071, 06-072)

COMPROMISE OF 1833

A ngered over protective tariffs benefiting northern industry but hurting farmers in the South, southerners, led by Vice President John C. Calhoun, advocated nullification. States could nullify, or declare inoperative, federal laws they considered unconstitutional. Opposing this defiance was President Andrew Jackson, himself a southerner and also unsympathetic to high tariffs, but determined to enforce federal law.

In late 1832, a convention in South Carolina declared the recently passed high tariff bill, the so-called Tariff of Abominations, to be null and unenforceable in the state. In January 1833, Jackson declared that nullification violated the Constitution and that "disunion by armed force" was "treason." He reinforced federal forces, and South Carolina called up the militia.

Led by Senator Henry Clay of Kentucky, Congress developed a compromise. The tariff was reduced over a ten-year period, thus reducing its protective nature. Calhoun successfully orchestrated a moderate response from South Carolina. Both sides had stepped back from the brink, but the South had learned that mere threats could get results. (02-191, 02-192, 02-193, 01-194)

1400   1450   1500   1550   1600   1650   1700

ALEXIS DE TOCQUEVILLE, 1835

After touring America for nine months in the early 1830s, aristocratic Frenchman Alexis de Tocqueville wrote *Democracy in America* (1835). The book was based on Tocqueville's interviews, observations, and personal thoughts after touring seventeen of twenty-four states. He was brutally honest, acknowledging both the good and bad parts of American democracy.

He praised America for self-government and the deep involvement of its citizens in the local affairs. Tocqueville warned, however, that rule by an unrestrained majority could threaten individual liberty and freedom. For example, he pointed to the malignant power of white male supremacy in the treatment of black slaves, Native Americans, and women. He correctly predicted that continued slavery would lead to a civil war, concluding, "I confess that in America I saw more than America; I sought the image of democracy itself, with its inclinations, its character, its prejudices, and its passions, in order to learn what we have to fear or hope from its progress." (06-064, 06-065)

SARAH ALDEN BRADFORD RIPLEY, 1836

A descendant of one of New England's earliest and most prominent families, Sarah Bradford Ripley became one of America's most influential intellects. Her marriage to Samuel Ripley, a Unitarian minister and uncle to Ralph Waldo Emerson, coupled with her classical education—rare for a woman in those days—placed her squarely in the path of the heady literary and philosophical ferment sweeping across America.

To supplement their meager income, the Ripleys opened a school to prepare boys for admission to Harvard. Her infectious intellect inspired in her students a love of learning. She was mentor to Henry David Thoreau, Nathaniel Hawthorne, Margaret Fuller, William Ellery Channing, and of course, Emerson. It was said that Sarah could shell peas and rock a cradle with her foot while tutoring a student in Greek. As guide to many in the so-called transcendentalist movement, Sarah struggled for years to reconcile religion and science. Eventually resolving the two, she described herself as a deist. Though she considered Jesus an outstanding human being, Ripley reserved judgment on his divine nature. (07-072, 07-073)

1400   1450   1500   1550   1600   1650   1700

TRAIL OF TEARS, 1838

The removal of the Cherokees, the infamous Trail of Tears, is one of the saddest episodes in American history. The Cherokee tribe had established schools and written laws, and some Cherokees even built plantation homes, bought slaves, and became Christians. Despite this accommodation, the invention of the cotton gin generated a lust for Cherokee land to grow cotton, and the discovery of gold in the north Georgia Mountains brought a flood of whites, all this bolstered by the idea of white superiority.

After 1828, President Andrew Jackson actively sought the removal of the Cherokee to Oklahoma. Sensing victory, Georgia abolished Cherokee government and divided up Cherokee land. The Supreme Court declared for the Cherokee, but Georgia ignored the Supreme Court, and Jackson refused to enforce the law.

By 1838, only 2,000 out of 16,000 Cherokee had moved west, and the government sent in militia to root the rest out. They were rounded up at bayonet point, with very little time to gather their possessions. In June, they were sent on their way. They endured extreme weather, disease, and poor food in the march to the Oklahoma. On the way, as many as 8,000 people died. (01-065, 01-086)

AMISTAD, 1839

After overwhelming their captors off the coast of Cuba in summer 1839, slaves on *Amistad* sailed their ship north to New England. They were arrested and held for trial. Abolitionists adopted them as a cause, supplied their legal counsel, and began teaching them English. The Spanish government wanted them returned to Cuba for trial and presumably execution. In the meantime, the prisoners, led by their powerful leader Joseph Cinqué, had become a national sensation, provoking an outpouring both of sympathy and disdain.

At a preliminary hearing, the parameters of the case emerged. Were these free men or property liable for return to their owners? After riveting testimony before a packed New Haven courtroom, the judge ruled for the prisoners. The US Supreme Court also decided for the "Amistad's." A charity appeal secured their passage home and on November 27, 1841, they sailed from New York for Sierra Leone. The *Amistad* story became a tribute to the unquenchable human yearning for liberty. (06-033, 06-034, 06-035)

JOHN C. CALHOUN, 1840

When he first came to Congress from South Carolina in 1812, with Henry Clay of Kentucky, Calhoun was a nationalist arguing for the War of 1812 and the American system—federal support for a national road system, a national bank, and a protective tariff. Calhoun's perspective changed when cotton transformed the southern landscape and additional tariffs threatened his region's prosperity. He developed the idea of nullification—states ignoring federal laws they did not like. This crisis (1833) was eased with one of Clay's compromises, but that just papered over sectional differences.

By 1832, his relationship with President Andrew Jackson was malicious, and Calhoun resigned as vice president. He returned to the Senate and spent the balance of his life a staunch opponent of protective tariffs and supporter of slavery and states' rights. He died in 1850, eleven years before his beloved state led the way in breaking the Union he so endangered by his advocacy of the southern cause. (08-038, 08-039)

THE BOWERY, 1840

When the Dutch settled Manhattan in the 1600s, the land that runs diagonally from present day Chatham Square to 4th Avenue and 8th Street was farmland, or *bouwerij*, the old Dutch word for "farm." By 1807 it was named the Bowery.

Nineteenth-century New York was a bustling metropolis, eventually topping 3 million in population. In the Bowery, waves of immigrants settled and then quickly moved on. Its tenements were multistoried, of cheap construction, and poorly lit and rarely had clean drinking water or adequate sanitary facilities.

While the area had a retail base—Lord & Taylor, E. Ridley and Sons, and A&P all originated there—the Bowery's main business was entertainment. From mid-century, it was the city's theater district, though its houses were mostly saloons with a stage, beer gardens, dime museums, and concert halls with female attendants of questionable morals. By the 1880s, the once-vibrant Bowery had become a slum and would remain as such until modern urban renewal transformed the area. (08-044)

1400   1450   1500   1550   1600   1650   1700

SAM HOUSTON, 1840

Virginia-born Sam Houston (1793–1863) developed an early love for Native American life, spending several years with the Cherokee when he was adopted by an esteemed chieftain and received his American Indian name, The Raven. This connection did not prevent him from admirable service with Andrew Jackson in the American Indian wars. Jackson became something of a mentor to the young Houston. When he found himself caught up in the rivalry between Jackson and his enemies, he moved to Nashville, read for the bar, served in the US House and as Tennessee governor.

His marriage to Eliza Allen in 1829, daughter of a politically prominent family, ended under bitter and mysterious circumstances, and he moved west, eventually becoming involved in Texas politics. With his old friend Jackson, he worked for the eventual annexation of the territory, and in March 1836 Texas declared independence. Led by Houston, Texans defeated the Mexicans at San Jacinto, forcing President Santa Anna to give Texas independence. He served as president of Texas for two terms, and through his work Texas joined the United States in 1845.

As events tumbled toward Civil War in the late 1850s, Houston was once again elected governor, but when he refused to take a loyalty oath to the Confederacy, he was deposed in 1861. The Raven returned to Huntsville, where he enjoyed a restful retirement with his wife, Margaret, and their eight children. (10-032, 10-033, 10-048)

TEXAS INVADES NEW MEXICO, 1841

Texas achieved independence from Mexico in 1836, but establishing a successful nation proved to be difficult. Some like President Sam Houston wished to swiftly join the United States. Others wanted Texas to go it alone. Washington showed itself to be a reluctant suitor. President Martin Van Buren did not want another slave state in the Union, and by treaty with Mexico the United States had abandoned claims to territory west of the border between Texas and Louisiana.

With hopes for annexation fading, those who advocated an independent Texas rose to power. Houston's successor, Mirabeau Lamar, wanted to grab Mexican lands east of the Rio Grande River in what is now New Mexico.

When the Texas Congress refused money for this scheme, he sent the troops anyway. On June 21, 1841, a ragtag collection of soldiers, merchants, and adventurers left to claim Santa Fe for Texas. They ran out of food within six weeks, and when they arrived, the locals remained loyal to Mexico. The invading troops were captured without a shot. Sam Houston returned to the presidency in late 1841, interest in annexation revived, and Texas, its plans for a western empire in shambles, joined the United States in 1845. (02-066)

1400   1450   1500   1550   1600   1650   1700

CHARLES DICKENS
AND AMERICA, 1842

On his tour of America in 1842, British author and social critic Charles Dickens created a firestorm by criticizing American publishers, which in the absence of an international copyright law simply stole his books.

Americans loved Charles Dickens, whose stories, they correctly concluded, were in part autobiographical. But they didn't like to pay for them. Dickens would serialize his novels in London newspapers. American publishers would copy the texts, and release them, much to the delight of American readers who got Dickens on the cheap. When he bitterly complained, the press was especially harsh. It stood to lose much if required to pay for reprints.

When he returned to England he published a "travel book," *American Notes*. Arguably one of Dickens' dullest books, it berated American prison conditions, slavery, noisy and filthy steamboats, and tobacco-spitting, second-rate politicians. Americans, their vanity wounded, gave back in equal vitriol. The argument between Dickens and America continued until after the Civil War, when a contrite author and a US society, somewhat humbled by the pain of conflict and a recognition that he had been right in many ways, embraced each other in a triumphant tour. The United States, however, did not sign onto an international copyright agreement until 1892. (07-074, 07-075)

1700   1750   1800   1850   1900   1950   PRESENT

Era of Nationalism

SOMERS MUTINY, 1842

To make the choice of young officers less political and their training more efficient, in 1842 the US Navy commissioned a training brig, a fast, sleek two-masted ship, USS *Somers*. On the return passage of its first training cruise to West Africa, it endured the most notorious mutiny in US naval history. The main agitator was nineteen-year-old Philip Spencer, son of the Secretary of War. He had built a reputation for insubordination and troublemaking in college and on two ships prior to his service on Somers. Spencer recruited two other members of the crew, Cromwell and Small, and allegedly several of the "ratings" (trainees) by plying them with cigars and liquor. His plan was to seize the ship, kill the officers and uncooperative crew, and turn *Somers* into a pirate ship operating out of Cuba.

When Captain Alexander Slidell Mackenzie received word of the planned mutiny, he arrested Spencer, then Cromwell and Small, chained them on deck and then watched as tension escalated on board. Mackenzie's officers investigated and recommended execution. Mackenzie agreed. The three were hanged and buried at sea.

A subsequent court-martial vindicated Mackenzie, but he was forced to endure a highly critical national debate. The result was the establishment in 1845 of the US Naval Academy in Annapolis to standardize the training of naval officers. (02-203, 02-204, 02-205)

1400   1450   1500   1550   1600   1650   1700

SENATOR BENTON'S
CONSPIRACY, 1844

Thomas Hart Benton, senator from Missouri in the 1830s, wished to push the United States to the Pacific. There were problems: Native Americans didn't wish to be pushed aside, Mexico controlled vast sections of the area into which white Americans wished to expand, and the British shared occupancy of the Oregon territory with the United States. The biggest problem, however, was American apathy. The risks associated with settling the West appeared too great.

To counteract this pessimism, Benton sponsored an expedition led by his son-in-law, John Charles Fremont, to cross the continent, establish its opportunities, and report back.

During 1842 to 1844, Fremont, Kit Carson, and the rest traveled 5,000 miles in the mountains and prairies of the West. Fremont sent reports back to his wife, Jesse, who retold them in vivid detail for newspapers and books. The influence of her reports, combined with land gains after the Mexican War, unleashed a flood of Americans heading west to seek a better life. Senator Benton's conspiracy had paid off. (01-108)

FIFTY-FOUR FORTY
OR FIGHT, 1844

With the Louisiana Purchase in 1803, the United States acquired a vast amount of territory, which brought it into conflict with Great Britain. By 1840, many new settlers had settled along the rivers emptying into Puget Sound in present-day Washington State. The prospect of a transcontinental railroad made the ports of the area vital to the future prosperity of the nation that successfully claimed them.

Negotiations with Great Britain dragged on until 1844. Democratic Candidate James Knox Polk of Tennessee ran on a platform that pledged to demand territory up to the 54th parallel (and 40 degrees), which led to the slogan "Fifty-Four Forty or Fight." Polk believed in manifest destiny, the idea that the United States should stretch from Atlantic to Pacific. In addition, Polk's commitment to annex Texas won over the voters. He beat Henry Clay of Kentucky. Talks were reopened. Polk's hostile rhetoric in public combined with a flexibility in negotiation brought a fair settlement with the border at the 49th parallel, thus smoothing relations between Britain and the United States. (02-010)

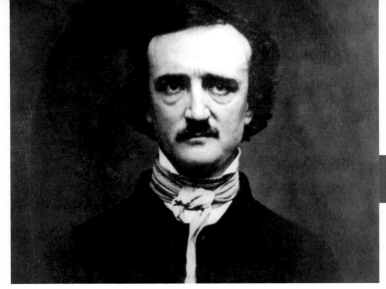

EDGAR ALLAN POE, 1845

After a classical education in Europe, stumbling attempts at Virginia and West Point led to grief. Edgar Allan Poe (1809–1849) descended into gambling and especially drink, the scourges of Poe's life. Despite his inner struggles and unrealized potential, Poe's intellectual radiance and unique ability to describe the fears and desires of the human condition could not but break through.

Living the life of the gypsy author, he wandered the East Coast seeking patrons and work, all the while churning out a prodigious and increasingly popular collection of detective stories, poems, narratives, stories of supernatural horror, and dark journeys of inner terror that, all too often, seemed autobiographical.

After a life of brilliant dissipation Poe, whose lyrical musings delved deep into the shadowy precincts of the soul, died on October 7, 1849, in a Baltimore death shrouded in mystery. No better example of his deep emotional struggle can be found than these closing lines from his most famous poem, "The Raven":

> *"Be that word our sign of parting, bird or fiend!" I shrieked, upstarting—*
> *"Get thee back into the tempest and the Night's Plutonian shore!*
> *Leave no black plume as a token of that lie thy soul hath spoken!*
> *Leave my loneliness unbroken!—quit the bust above my door!*
> *Take thy beak from out my heart, and take thy form from off my door!"*
> *Quoth the Raven "Nevermore."*
>
> *And the Raven, never flitting, still is sitting, still is sitting*
> *On the pallid bust of Pallas just above my chamber door;*
> *And his eyes have all the seeming of a demon's that is dreaming,*
> *And the lamp-light o'er him streaming throws his shadow on the floor;*
> *And my soul from out that shadow that lies floating on the floor*
> *Shall be lifted—nevermore!*

(05-067)

JAMES KNOX POLK AND
"HAIL TO THE CHIEF," 1845

The stirring, heroic song "Hail to the Chief" was ritualized by First Lady Sarah Childress Polk to encourage respect for her husband President James Knox Polk. He was short, sported a bad haircut, and wore cheap oversized suits. People ignored him when he came into the room. Despite this, during his presidency the United States extended its boundaries to the Pacific Coast, annexed Texas, and won the Mexican War.

Sarah Polk decreed that whenever he entered the room, the Marine Band should play "Hail to the Chief." It is taken from Sir Walter Scott's epic poem *Lady of the Lake*, which describes the fickle nature of public opinion and the fall of a Scottish chieftain betrayed and executed by his archrival.

Perhaps each president, prior to first being welcomed by "Hail to the Chief," should read all of Sir Walter Scott's *Lady of the Lake*, a story of the rise and triumph of heroes and their swift and painful fall. (09-045, 09-048)

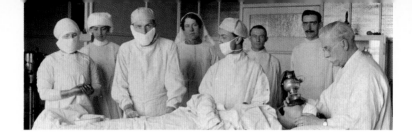

MIRACLE OF ANESTHESIA, 1846

In 1772, Joseph Priestly, the English clergyman and chemist who would later describe the gas now termed oxygen, isolated one of the oxides of nitrogen, a colorless gas with a sweet odor and strange narcotic effect. He called it nitrous oxide. Later another English chemist, Sir Humphrey Davy, inhaled nitrous oxide and described its effects: first laughter, then euphoria, and then, after prolonged use, relatively harmless and short-term unconsciousness. He suggested its usefulness for surgery, but few took him seriously. Nitrous oxide was something of a novelty in the early 1800s. It was the subject of public lectures and the source of entertainment among well-to-do socialites who would bring a bag of the stuff to enliven their private parties.

In 1842, Crawford Long, a physician in Jefferson, Georgia, who had provided another form of laughing gas, diethyl or sulfuric ether, to several parties for his friends, successfully tried it during minor surgery on some of his patients. In 1845, a Connecticut dentist, Horace Wells, tried nitrous oxide while one of his own teeth was painlessly removed. He failed in an attempt during a demonstrated tooth extraction at Massachusetts General Hospital, but the following year his friend and future rival for the honor of discovery, William Morton, returned to Masschusetts General and successfully used ether to induce controlled unconsciousness on two patients. Oliver Wendell Holmes Sr., father of the famous jurist and an eminent surgeon, suggested the name "anesthesia," and from that point the science of surgery began to make even greater contributions to the progress of medicine. (03-153, 03-154)

LINCOLN'S QUEST
FOR CONGRESS, 1846

Moving through various occupations, Abraham Lincoln (1809–1865) developed a style of sociable behavior that would eventually take him to the White House and immortality. He served four terms in the Illinois legislature, read for the law exam, settled finally in Springfield, and, in 1842, married Mary Todd, who animated his political ambitions.

Lincoln's successful law practice took him throughout the central Illinois circuit where he tried cases in civil law and some criminal trials. There he cemented a growing reputation for fairness and down-to-earth humor, which helped carry him into a single term in the US House of Representatives in 1846.

In Washington, Lincoln was not supportive of the Mexican War, considering it imperialistic and to have been provoked by President James Knox Polk. His opposition to slavery began to take concrete shape while in Congress. His antiwar stance was unpopular, and he left politics for a time and threw himself back into a law practice that became one of the largest in the state. (12-024, 12-025)

DONNER PARTY TRAGEDY, 1846

Seeking a better life, in the mid-1800s thousands crossed the deserts and mountains, heading west. In 1846, eighty-nine emigrants led by George Donner following bad directions, got lost, and wasted three precious weeks slogging through the Wasatch Mountains east of the Great Salt Lake in Utah. They had to make it over the crest of the Sierra Nevada Mountains by mid-September, or they might be blocked by snow in the high mountain passes. The Donner Party lost its battle with time.

They arrived at the base of Truckee Pass near Lake Tahoe on November 1, but when they attempted to scale the 1,200-foot crossing they were forced back to Truckee Lake by a terrific blizzard. They built shelters, but snow overwhelmed them. The food ran out, and then as the deaths multiplied they were forced to cook and eat the bodies of the dead to survive.

In December, a small number of the marooned party left, and, after enduring great hardship while crossing the mountains, got to California and brought a rescue party back to the Truckee camp. On April 22, 1847, the last survivor of the eighty-nine who started out arrived in California. Their ordeal is a testimony to the dangers facing those who immigrated west and the courage required to make that journey. (01-160, 01-161, 01-162)

1400   1450   1500   1550   1600   1650   1700

Since its founding by Joseph Smith Jr., the Church of Jesus Christ of Latter-day Saints, the largest group among those better known as Mormons, had attracted hostility and intolerance in a supposedly tolerant nation. So the Mormons moved constantly, eventually settling in Illinois. When Smith was murdered by a mob in June 1844, the demoralized community chose Brigham Young as leader. His superb organizational instincts restored confidence in the church and prepared them to seek a new and more permanent home where they could consolidate their spectacular growth without persecution.

Young's advance party left in February 1846, and soon more than 10,000 of the faithful were in wagons following along. Their destination was Utah's Great Salt Lake basin. The advance party arrived on July 21, 1847, and began to plant crops and prepare for the arrival of the rest. The migration was one the best organized in American history. Within three months, the valley was home to thousands, ready for commerce and government. (01-134, 01-140)

SENECA FALLS CONVENTION, 1848

Elizabeth Cady Stanton and Lucretia Mott met in 1840 at the World Anti-Slavery Convention in London. They had been involved in the abolitionist movement in the United States but in London found they shared another common concern: the rights of women. By early 1847, they were ready to act. A mutual friend, Jane Hunt of Seneca Falls—a small village just west of Syracuse, New York—brought together an informal group that planned a convention in Seneca Falls the following year.

Prior to the convention, the group met and drafted a Declaration of Sentiments. Following the Declaration of Independence, group members substituted "all men" in the phrases that contained "King George." Mirroring Mr. Jefferson's sentiments, they identified lack of voting rights, the right to equal wages, and equal custody of children, property, and inheritance. The convention opened on July 19, 1848. Most of the Declaration passed. It was the beginning of the long struggle for women's suffrage, culminating in 1920 in the Nineteenth Amendment to the Constitution.

(05-018)

| 1400 | 1450 | 1500 | 1550 | 1600 | 1650 | 1700 |

HENRY BARBER, Commander, AT PIER 13 EAST RIVER.

CALIFORNIA DOCKS IN
SAN FRANCISCO, 1849

In early 1848, builder James W. Marshall discovered gold on the
property of John Sutter near Sacramento, California. From all
over the world, the gold-frenzied converged on California. Some
scaled the treacherous Sierra Nevada Mountains. Some sailed for
six months around the Horn of South America. Others went to
Panama, crossed the Isthmus, and tried to catch a mail packet to
San Francisco.

On January 17, 1849, a light, sleek, fast new steam packet ship,
the *California*, arrived in Panama City for its first trip. During the
next week, by a combination of lottery, bribery, trickery, and ticket
scalping, 365 were let on board, some having paid as much as
$1,000 for the trip.

It took four weeks, and on February 28, 1849, *California* sailed
through the Golden Gate to the cheers of thousands standing on
hilltops and wharves. Within minutes of dropping anchor, it was
deserted. Gold fever! In time, the *California* trickle became a flood.

(01-105)

SECOND GREAT AWAKENING, 1850

In the decades following independence, politics, economics, culture, and religion were transformed by a new spirit of freedom, resistance to authority and orthodoxy, and a fascination with novelty and experimentation.

On the southern frontier, Methodists, Baptists, Disciples, Christians, and other evangelical Protestant sects surged in numbers. Through the ministry of often poorly educated but enthusiastic itinerant preachers, and emotionally charged revivals, these new denominations serviced the emotional, spiritual, and social needs of thousands of believers. In the Midwest, Presbyterian Charles Grandison Finney demonstrated how to use emotion to excite and convert thousands to Christianity.

Traditional denominations, such as Congregationalists and the Presbyterians led by Yale President Timothy Dwight and his students, Lyman Beecher and Nathaniel Taylor, prospered by moving away from the rigid Calvinist emphasis on predestination and original sin and toward a more inclusive theology based on personal faith, social improvement, and free will.

Volunteer organizations, such as the American Bible Society, the American Sunday School Union, and later the YMCA and the Salvation Army, provided cross-denominational means of outreach and social service. The result of the Second Great Awakening was that by 1850, pan-Protestant evangelicalism was the dominant religious force in America. (12-048, 12-049)

ABRAHAM LINCOLN'S ADVICE TO YOUNG LAWYERS, 1850

Abraham Lincoln was gifted and successful attorney. He had good instincts about people and liked them; they liked him back. Tall, gangly, and awkward in his appearance, he knew he was no beauty, but he also knew he shared that defect with the vast majority of jurors and, later, voters. He was shrewd; he could see to the heart of a case and usually won it.

Notes have survived, written in his clear hand, of a law lecture probably given in summer 1850 to what seems to be a group of young law students. His advice was at once practical and idealistic:

- Be diligent—leave nothing for tomorrow that can be done today.
- Cultivate extemporaneous speaking. People won't bring a lawyer business if he can't make a speech. On the other hand, a glib tongue cannot substitute for hard work nor relieve a lawyer from the drudgery of the law.
- Discourage litigation and persuade clients to compromise.
- Above all, cultivate a reputation for honesty. If a lawyer can't be an honest one, he should choose some other occupation.

(05-078, 05-079)

HERMAN MELVILLE, 1851

Born in to an old and prominent New England family—one of his grandfathers had taken part in the Boston Tea Party—Herman Melville was shocked by the bankruptcy and death of his father. He went to sea for several years, including time on a Pacific whaling vessel. He returned in 1844 with a memory well stocked with fascinating stories. Some of them he turned into the novel *Typee*, a semiautobiographical description of his life among cannibalistic natives on a South Pacific island. The novel was an instant success, and Melville became an overnight celebrity.

In 1851, he began *Moby-Dick*. This novel, with its unrelenting journey into the depths of human darkness, received unenthusiastic reviews, and only in the 1920s—a more cynical and jaded era—did it reemerge, considered then as a masterpiece. After *Moby-Dick*, Melville endured periodic bouts of depression and long creative dry spells. Despite this, he produced four additional novels (including *Billy Budd*, based on the mutiny on USS *Somers*), along with short stories and poetry. Melville died in 1891. (03-006)

| 1400 | 1450 | 1500 | 1550 | 1600 | 1650 | 1700 |

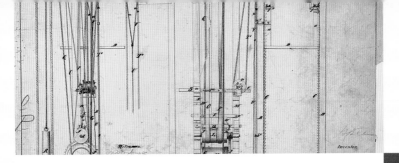

ELISHA GRAVES OTIS AND
THE ELEVATOR, 1853

A case can be made that little known Elisha Otis, a Yonkers, New York, machinist, gave birth to the modern urban landscape. In the early 1850s, he created a braking device that made elevators safe.

From the dawn of civilization, humans have been drawn to cities. The resulting overpopulation created conditions of poverty and squalor—too many people, too little space. The solution was to build up, but until the advent high-grade steel and reinforced concrete, buildings were structurally limited in height. Otis solved the problem of too little space; his elevators made possible the efficient movement of people and goods between the floors of increasingly tall buildings.

He demonstrated his invention at the New York World's Fair in 1853, and from that point, he and his sons, who took over the company upon his death in 1861, sold elevators into an exploding market. For them, the sky was the limit—well, almost. (09-061)

WINDMILLS, 1854

Evoking visions of charming Dutch country scenes, the tilting object of slightly confused Spanish knights, and fights between green power and wealthy islanders, one of things that modernized rural America was the windmill. In 1854, Daniel Halladay, a New England inventor, applied for a patent for a self-regulating windmill that automatically closed its blades in high wind to avoid damage.

Much of the continent west of the Mississippi lacks reliable sources of surface water. Ranchers and farmers were forced to draw underground water. From the middle of the nineteenth century, increasingly efficient windmills helped transform rural areas by automating the pumping process, spinning up water for thirsty livestock and crops.

By the 1930s, electricity had come to rural America, and windmills, for a time, went out of fashion. In recent decades, however, they have enjoyed something of a renaissance, partly out of environmental concerns but also because modern, efficient windmills can provide cost-effective power in remote locations.

(11-038)

| 1400 | 1450 | 1500 | 1550 | 1600 | 1650 | 1700 |

KNOW-NOTHING PARTY I, 1854

The United States is nation of immigrants. Crowding out Native Americans, more strangers arrived each decade in search of a new life. Soon established, they looked at the next batch of immigrants with fear and loathing. Between 1845 and 1854, nearly 3 million immigrants, split almost evenly between Germans and Irish, poured into northern ports. They spoke little English, were considered by natives to be dirty and disease-ridden, and worst of all were Roman Catholic.

By 1853, organized to galvanize this growing nativist sentiment, the Order of United Americans established lodges all over the country. They were secret, and only native-born Protestants needed apply. An old legend is that inquiries were met with the words "I know nothing."

In the off-year elections of 1854, with little organization and few national leaders, the Know-Nothings elected over one hundred congressmen, eight governors, and countless local officials. Their legislative program, born as it was of bigotry and prejudice, proved to be surprisingly progressive. (03-141, 03-142)

KNOW-NOTHING PARTY II, 1854

The Know-Nothings advanced a program that was remarkably progressive for a movement steeped in bigotry against immigrants. Except in the Deep South, the Know-Nothings opposed slavery. In Massachusetts, the Know-Nothing General Court desegregated public schools, passed laws forbidding imprisonment for debt, and allowed married women to bring legal suit in court, make wills, and work without the consent of their husbands.

The Know-Nothing movement almost immediately began to die. It had been a coalition of wildly varied interests united only by a temporary upsurge of immigration. In 1856, the party's candidate, former President Millard Fillmore, only carried one state. The wave of new immigrants had begun to recede, and Americans had moved on to more pressing concerns. War over slavery and state sovereignty loomed just over the horizon, and a new, vigorous political movement, the Republicans, had risen out of the Midwest to take the place of the dying Whig Party. The spectacular career of the Know-Nothing Party was over, but similar and periodic explosions of anti-immigrant fervor have been an ironic but regular feature of the political life of this nation of immigrants.

(03-141, 03-142)

HARRIET TUBMAN, 1855

Born in the early 1820s of slave parent, Harriet Tubman as a girl was intelligent and determined. Her willfulness often got her in trouble, so she endured especially intense abuse from her owners. In 1824, she rode the Underground Railroad (a secret system that helped slaves escape to freedom) and then began returning the favor. From 1850 to 1860, she made nineteen trips into the South and brought 300 slaves out. With large rewards posted for her capture, Tubman was smart and cunning and was never apprehended. Among African Americans, she was known as "Moses" after the leader who brought the Jews out of slavery.

During the Civil War, she worked in service jobs in the Union Army but also served as a scout and spy. An activist until her death in 1913, she was a strong supporter of the suffrage movement for women's rights. She was buried with full military honors. Tubman's epigraph ends with "She Overcame Every Obstacle." (07-090, 07-091, 07-092)

1700   1750   1800   1850   1900   1950   PRESENT

BLEEDING KANSAS, 1857

In an effort to damp down sectional animosity, Congress in 1854 passed the Kansas–Nebraska Act. As part of that act, the majority of those living in a territory could vote to be slave or free. In the first three years of settlement, a large number of proslavery settlers moved from proslavery Missouri to develop the rich river valley bottomlands of the Kansas territory. By 1855, they controlled the territorial legislature and voted Kansas a slave state.

Alarmed, northern abolitionists recruited freedom-loving settlers to move to Kansas. The pace was slow at first, but more and more free-soil settlers began to arrive. Both sides engaged in violent tactics, as one bloody act followed another, but in the end Kansas's status was resolved by sheer numbers. By 1858, antislavery settlers outnumbered their opponents, and by extension the territorial legislature was more antislavery. Kansas adopted an anti-slavery state constitution, and submitted it to Congress.

That year, in a speech Abraham Lincoln quoted the Bible: "A House divided against itself cannot stand." He was largely referring to bleeding Kansas. In 1861, a bloodied and exhausted Kansas was admitted to the Union as a free state. (01-174, 01-175)

| 1400 | 1450 | 1500 | 1550 | 1600 | 1650 | 1700 |

JOHN BROWN, 1857

In 1855, restless drifter-turned-abolitionist-zealot John Brown took five of his sons to Bloody Kansas. After proslavery ruffians raided the small town of Lawrence in May 1856, Brown led a revenge strike along Pottawatomie Creek. The Brown party brutally murdered five proslavery settlers.

Later at an 1858 abolitionist meeting in Canada, he announced his intent to forcefully free the slaves by leading an "army of emancipation" through the South. On October 16, 1859, Brown and twenty men struck the federal arsenal at Harpers Ferry, Virginia. Within a day, a small force of US marines commanded by Colonel Robert E. Lee forced his surrender. Seventeen people on both sides were killed, including two of Brown's sons.

Brown was charged, tried, and found guilty of murder, slave insurrection, and treason. He was hanged. He left an eerie yet predictive note with his jailer: "I, John Brown, am now quite certain that the crime [slavery] of this guilty land will never be purged away but with blood." (08-122, 08-123)

DRED SCOTT DECISION, 1857

Dred Scott, slave of army surgeon John Emerson, served his owner on military postings in free states and slave states. When Emerson died in 1843, Scott sued in Missouri to secure freedom for himself and his family. Until then, Missouri courts had ruled that slaves living for a time on free soil automatically became free. The Missouri Supreme Court rejected this precedent and ruled that since Missouri was a slave state, Scott must continue as a slave. Scott then sued in federal court and on March 6, 1857, Supreme Court Chief Justice Roger Taney decreed that slaves were property and that Congress could not restrict lawfully maintained property.

Scott almost immediately obtained his freedom, but the Supreme Court had given the South a great, if temporary, victory. This case ignited a firestorm of denunciation in the North. The increased tension further doomed the efforts of those seeking a resolution short of secession and civil war. (01-176)

1400   1450   1500   1550   1600   1650   1700

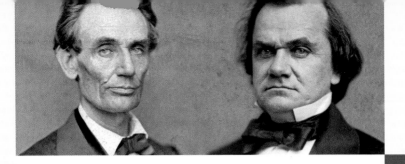

LINCOLN-DOUGLAS DEBATES, 1858

These seven encounters are justly famous. In the 1858 Illinois US Senate election, Republican Abraham Lincoln challenged Democratic incumbent Senator Stephen A. Douglas. The subject was the future of slavery.

Douglas shamelessly exploited the prejudice of whites. To great applause, he asserted that Lincoln's insistence that blacks had a claim to the "created equality" of the founders was a "monstrous heresy." Lincoln reminded his opponent that the founders believed slavery was morally wicked, in violation of the spirit of freedom, and destined to become extinct. Lincoln's problem was that, like many pre–Civil War northerners, he vigorously opposed slavery but was unsure how he felt about full political and social equality for the black people.

The Senate seat went to Douglas, but history has given the debate victory to Lincoln. He had gone toe-to-toe with the most powerful Democrat in national life, outlined the core beliefs of his party, and won a prominent place in national affairs. This last was vital, as he sought the presidency two years later. (17-032, 17-033, 17-034)

HARRIET BEECHER STOWE, 1859

One of those most offended by the Fugitive Slave Law (1850) was Harriet Beecher Stowe. The mother of seven, she was the wife of a Bowdoin College professor. She took her offense to paper, specifically a novel composed at her kitchen table and serialized in the weekly abolitionist newspaper *National Era*. Despite her lack of firsthand experience with slavery, her rich narrative and vivid descriptions were convincing. Periodically, a new chapter would describe the lives, challenges, sufferings, and pleasures of a cast of characters whose names were soon world famous: Little Eva, Sambo, Quimbo, the tragic Lucy, cruel master Simon Legree, and, of course, Uncle Tom.

Uncle Tom's Cabin sold 3 million copies before 1860. It confirmed the worst fears of the abolitionists, offended many white southerners, and inflamed opinion on all sides of the slavery question. When Abraham Lincoln first met Mrs. Stowe in 1862, he is said to have greeted her, "So you're the little lady who made this big war!" (04-062)

1400   1450   1500   1550   1600   1650   1700

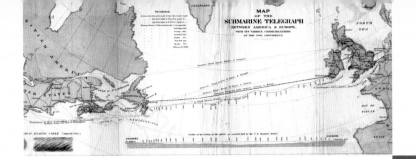

TRANSATLANTIC CABLE, 1858

The problem was primitive cable construction, transmission equipment, and laying apparatus. After the brief exchange between Queen Victoria and US President James Buchanan in 1858, massive celebrations on both sides of the Atlantic heralded a new day in communications. The new day lasted only 271 messages; then, the 1858 transatlantic submarine cable sputtered out. Nevertheless, cable advocates, including engineer Fleeming Jenkin and New York businessman Cyrus Field, went back to work. An analysis by the Atlantic Telegraph Company and the British Board of Trade produced a plan that led to success.

By 1865, after significant improvements in cable design and the purchase of the giant failed passenger liner *Great Eastern*, the only ship that could carry enough cable for the entire crossing, they began the second attempt. Two days out of Newfoundland, however, the cable snapped. A year later, *Great Eastern* was back with a second cable, which went the distance. The company found the old one and spliced it; in the summer of 1866, it delivered two cables into transatlantic telegraph service. (09-006)

CHARLES NALLE AND THE FUGITIVE SLAVE LAW, 1859

Worried about escaping slaves, southerners demanded and Congress passed the Fugitive Slave Law (FSL), in 1850. If an escaped slave was caught in a free state, federal law required his return to his owner.

In 1858, Virginia-born Charles Nalle escaped, was reunited with his family, and moved to Troy, New York, where he hired out as a coachman. He could not read or write, and the person who had helped him betrayed him to his former owner in Virginia, who happened to be Nalle's half-brother.

On April 27, 1859, Nalle was arrested and was immediately taken before a commissioner. When he was moved to face a judge, a crowd, 1,000 strong, led by activist Harriet Tubman, attacked the police, separated Nalle and eventually spirited him away to Canada. Nalle's experience confirmed that northerners hated the FSL and refused to enforce it. As a result, the law returned few slaves to the South and stirred up the already tense political situation. (05-111)

1400   1450   1500   1550   1600   1650   1700

PONY EXPRESS, 1860

I n the late 1850s, overland mail was carried from Little Rock through Texas to San Diego and then to San Francisco. It took twenty-five days. Midwest-based entrepreneur William H. Russell wanted the contract to deliver mail to California, but Russell wanted to take it straight across from Missouri to Denver and then on to the Pacific.

To prove this central route he and his partners developed the Pony Express as an elaborate marketing scheme. It was a highly organized relay of riders—190 stations, 500 horses, and 80 riders— who would move at top speed from one station to the next and cut the time for a letter to ten days.

The first rider left St. Joseph, Missouri, on April 3, 1860. The transcontinental telegraph was completed in late October 1861, and the last run of the then-obsolete Pony Express was just over a month later. The irony was that Russell and his collaborators failed to get the overland mail contract and went bankrupt. Nevertheless, despite its expiration, the system was an organizational marvel. (01-163)

FREDERICK DOUGLASS AND THE BATTLE FOR FREEDOM, 1860

"All the other speakers seemed tame after Frederick Douglass. He stood there like an African Prince, majestic in his wrath." The witness was future women's rights champion Elizabeth Cady Stanton. She knew her activists.

He escaped from slavery as a teenager and spoke of slavery's horrors to northern church audiences. He thundered, "Other abolitionists can tell you something about slavery; they cannot refer you a back covered with scars." After a triumphant European tour, he returned to the United States and began his own newspaper, *North Star*. Douglass hated slavery but advocated emancipation within the political system.

During the Civil War, he pressed for equal treatment of black soldiers and for President Lincoln to free those still held as slaves. After the war, he fought on for black rights. Douglass died in 1895 in the Jim Crow era when laws in the South were restricting African American rights and in the North enthusiasm to protect those rights was ebbing. (02-078, 02-079)

SHOWDOWN IN
CHARLESTON I, 1860

In spring 1860, the Democratic National Convention met in Charleston, South Carolina. It failed to achieve unity, compromise, or peace. The Charleston convention was a snapshot of the republic itself: Politics was becoming arthritic. Compromise, the lubricant of democracy, was in decline as if sand had been thrown into the machinery of American civilization. The reason was slavery.

The front-runner for the presidential nomination was Stephen A. Douglas of Illinois. He had a majority of the delegates, but the nomination required a supermajority—two-thirds of the vote—and many were ready to deny him his dream. President Buchanan loathed Douglas particularly due to the admission of Kansas as a state.

Proslavery politician and orator William Lowndes Yancey of Alabama was one of the secessionist fire-eaters and had long plotted the destruction of the United States. He desired to break the Democratic Party. The resulting Republican victory would stampede the cotton states out of the Union. He attacked Douglas using the idea of a slave code. (01-079, 01-080, 01-081, 01-082)

SHOWDOWN IN
CHARLESTON II, 1860

When the Democrats met to pick a presidential candidate in spring 1860 in the beautiful port city of Charleston, South Carolina, John Brown's raid on Harpers Ferry hovered over the gathering like some evil specter. Panicked southern delegates demanded that the party nominee advocate a slave code. Under this, all the power of the US government would be marshaled to protect their slave property, and western territories could not reject slavery prior to becoming states.

The slave code would be ruinous to any candidate running in the North, and both the front-runner Stephen Douglas and the Convention rejected it. On principle, the party committed suicide. Six Deep South delegations left and set up a rival convention across town. In despair, the Democrats adjourned, reassembled in Baltimore, and gave Douglas its then-worthless nomination. In November, there were four candidates for president. As a result, Abraham Lincoln was elected a minority president, the South seceded, and the dogs of war were loosed on the nation. (01-079, 01-080, 01-081, 01-082)

| 1400 | 1450 | 1500 | 1550 | 1600 | 1650 | 1700 |

CIVIL WAR—STATES' RIGHTS
OR SLAVERY? I, 1860

From the standpoint of history, the American Civil War is most unique. A whole school of thought has twisted the story of the conflict, promoting a fraudulent interpretation of the heart of the republic's greatest crisis. This school, loosely identified as neo-Confederate, justifies the continued obsession with rebel flags, equestrian monuments, southern denialism, and thinly veiled racial animus by insisting that the American Civil War was fought to preserve states' rights. Nothing could be further from the truth. In fact, the Union was sundered specifically because the South realized that it had reached the limits of its ability to command the federal, legal, and social apparatus in support of its peculiar institution, chattel slavery.

In the Confederate Constitution, the various state constitutions, and those declarations justifying their secession, there was no mention of states' rights. In fact, it was the southern disdain of northern states exercising their states' rights to restrict slavery and its spread that compelled them into the Confederacy.

CIVIL WAR—STATES' RIGHTS
OR SLAVERY? II, 1860

In 1787, the South was able to insert into the Constitution a demand in Article IV that states had to restrain and return any escaping slave to his master. This committed the federal government and all the states, no matter what their desires or opinions concerning slavery, to the preservation of the southern slave interest and "billions of dollars of human property." This provision was enforced in the Fugitive Slave Act of 1793 and all its siblings up until the 1850s and reinforced by the infamous Three-Fifths Clause, which increased slave-state representation; the Missouri Compromise; and the Compromise of 1850. The last thing the South was interested in was states' rights. The South wanted federal power to restrict antislavery activity in the free states and prevent free states from using their growing power to impede the spread of slavery into the territories.

In the end, the South broke the Union because it was convinced that northern states were hostile toward its economic well-being. The southern agribusiness grandees were petrified that they would endure enormous losses if slavery were restrained or ended by federal edict. Mississippi was refreshingly candid when it declared its reason for seceding: greed. "Our position is thoroughly identified with the institution of slavery—the greatest material interest of the world." Far from championing the principal, southerners instead saw states' rights as a profound threat to the South's slave-based, moneymaking enterprise.

LINCOLN'S PRESIDENTIAL
WIT, 1860

Abraham Lincoln's use of humor was brilliant. He was not a handsome man and was often the butt of insulting remarks about his rough appearance. Many times, he used humor to diffuse the attacks of his enemies. After one of his periodic losses at the ballot box, Honest Abe said he felt like the man who had been tarred and feathered and run out of town on rail. When the man was asked how he was feeling, the victim said that if it weren't for the honor of the thing, he would just as soon have passed it up.

His relations with General George B. McClellan, commander of Union forces in Virginia, were notoriously frosty. Lincoln felt that McClellan was a martinet who would rather parade-march his troops than take Richmond. McClellan, whose approach to battle was a study in strategic inertia, felt that Lincoln was a crude politician who could be safely ignored. During one extended period of inaction, Lincoln sent a telegram to the general, "If General McClellan does not want to use the Army, I would like to borrow it for a time, provided I could see how it could be made to do something." (32-155)

THE PHASES OF THE AMERICAN CIVIL WAR I

During the American Civil War (1861–1865), major combat often shifted from one state or theater to another and came in fits and starts, with idle periods for refitting and rest. One way of looking at the war is to see it in phases, as described here and in the next few pages.

PHASE ONE: CONFEDERATE CONSOLIDATION– DECEMBER 1860–JULY 1861

From the secession of South Carolina through the southern victory at the First Battle of Bull Run, a new southern regional government and military enterprise were hammered together almost from scratch, an extraordinary accomplishment.

PHASE TWO: UNION ASCENDANCY– AUGUST 1861–MAY 1862

Most of the fighting shifted to the West as Union forces were nearly everywhere victorious. This effort culminated in the bloody fighting at Shiloh Church and saw the beginning fruits of the strategy to split the Confederacy along the Mississippi with the capture of New Orleans. (18-038, 18-039, 18-040, 18-041)

| 1400 | 1450 | 1500 | 1550 | 1600 | 1650 | 1700 |

THE PHASES OF THE
AMERICAN CIVIL WAR II

PHASE THREE: CONFEDERATE ASCENDANCY—
MAY 1862-JULY 3, 1863

Union morale collapsed as rebel forces were victorious from Jackson's valley campaign to the Seven Days, Second Bull Run, Fredericksburg, and Chancellorsville battles. Only the strategic Union victory and reversal of the Lee's first northern invasion at Antietam and the Emancipation Proclamation brightened northern prospects. Lee's victories tempted him north a second time toward the disaster of the third day at Gettysburg.

PHASE FOUR: UNION REASCENDANCY—
JULY 3, 1863-MAY 1864

The tide began to turn with unambiguous Union victories at Gettysburg and Vicksburg and with ever-larger Union land forces regaining momentum and eating away at Confederate territory.

In the East, Robert E. Lee faced a new determined opponent in Ulysses S. Grant, whom Lincoln chose because "he fights." Grant, determined to use his superior numbers and material resources, hammered away at Lee in the Overland Campaign, and though Lee was tactically successful in the Battle of the Wilderness, at Spotsylvania, and in the terrible fighting at Cold Harbor, Grant refused to let up, each time wheeling around Lee's right flank. Soon the southern miracle worker ran out of miracles. Lee was slammed back on the defenses of Richmond and forced to endure nearly a year of siege. (18-038, 18-039, 18-040, 18-041)

| 1700 | 1750 | 1800 | 1850 | 1900 | 1950 | PRESENT |

Era of Republican Crisis

THE PHASES OF THE AMERICAN CIVIL WAR III

PHASE FIVE: STALEMATE AND UNION CONSOLIDATION, MAY 1864–SPRING 1865

It was stalemate in Virginia but dynamic movement and significant Union victories in the Deep South at Atlanta and Nashville and during William Tecumseh Sherman's March to the Sea and into South Carolina.

PHASE SIX: CONFEDERATE COLLAPSE, APRIL 1865

By late winter 1865, the ever-shrinking Confederacy was facing collapse, ensured by the overwhelming number of Union land forces, the industrial and financial strength of the North, the almost perfect Union naval blockade, and the improving quality of Yankee generals.

The noose around Petersburg and Richmond was daily squeezing the life and hopes out of rebel leaders, civilians, and soldiers alike. Many of the latter began walking away. When twice in early April Union forces breached the Rebel siege lines, General Lee and President Davis recognized the inevitable. Escape seemed impossible, though Lee would try. But by April 9, he had no choice except to meet General Grant at Appomattox and surrender. (18-038, 18-039, 18-040, 18-041)

FORT SUMTER, 1861

On April 12, 1861, after months of threat and posturing, Civil War erupted between the formerly "united" States of America. Southern forces attacked Fort Sumter in Charleston harbor. South Carolina, the first state to secede, had seized all federal property in South Carolina except Fort Sumter. Major Robert Anderson, commander of the fort, refused to surrender. Early in the morning of April 12, Confederate commander General Pierre G. T. Beauregard sent an ultimatum: the fort would be attacked in one hour. Anderson still refused to surrender.

The stalemate ended at 4:30 a.m. when Confederate batteries around the harbor opened fire on the fort. In the fort were ten officers, sixty-eight soldiers, forty-three civilians, and eight musicians. Two federal relief vessels arrived, but Confederate fire drove them away. Finally, with little food and almost no ammunition left, Anderson was forced to surrender. The same tattered flag he carried away was raised over the fort on April 14, 1865, by Robert Anderson. (07-109, 07-110, 07-111)

| 1700 | 1750 | 1800 | 1850 | 1900 | 1950 | PRESENT |

Era of Republican Crisis

STRUGGLE FOR MISSOURI, 1861

In late spring 1861, Missouri's fate hung in the balance. Would the state secede or remain loyal to the Union? It was a slave state surrounded by free territory. The governor, legislature, and many prominent citizens wanted to take Missouri out of the Union. Opposing these forces were Congressman Frank Blair and Captain Nathanial Lyon, commander of the federal arsenal in St. Louis. Both sides wanted the arms in that arsenal, amounting to thousands of weapons and tons of ammunition.

On April 25, Blair and Lyon, under the cover of darkness, spirited most of the weapons across the river into Illinois. On the night of May 8, a shipment of cannon from Confederate forces in Louisiana was taken to a militia camp in Missouri filled with fighters loyal to Governor Jackson. Sensing the need to act, on May 10, 1861 Lyon, at the head of two regular companies and several thousand Union supporters, marched out to the militia camp and arrested the prosouthern soldiers. Missouri was saved for the Union. (03-188, 03-189)

| 1400 | 1450 | 1500 | 1550 | 1600 | 1650 | 1700 |

DUPONT'S SALTPETER MISSION, 1861

By summer 1861, federal leaders realized the war was not going to be short and they were running low on potassium nitrate (saltpeter), essential for making gunpowder. India, controlled by Great Britain, was the primary source of American saltpeter, and strong economic ties between Britain and the Confederacy threatened the flow of nitrates to the North. The Lincoln administration sent Lammot DuPont to London to buy up all the saltpeter he could find. Within ten days, armed with US gold, he had 2,000 tons of saltpeter on London wharves awaiting shipment, but the British embargoed it in retaliation for the Trent Affair.

In November 1861, the US Navy boarded the British mail ship *Trent* and detained two Confederate diplomats, James Mason and John Slidell. Britain demanded their release, and Lincoln reluctantly did release them, in part because the Union desperately needed DuPont's embargoed saltpeter. The DuPont family then became immensely wealthy by supplying the US military with munitions through World War II. (06-039)

WEST VIRGINIA SECEDES
FROM VIRGINIA, 1861

B y the onset of the Civil War, there was major tension between
the eastern region of Virginia and the counties on the
western side of the mountains. Political and economic power lay
in the East with slaveholders and their allies. By contrast, western
Virginia was filled with immigrants who worked small farms.
Slaves were rare.

On April 17, 1861, the Virginia Secession Convention voted to
leave the Union. Most of the west voted against secession. Within
weeks, pro-Union conventions met in Wheeling, and in October
thirty-nine counties voted for separate statehood.

According to the Constitution, a new state cannot be carved out
of an existing state without consent from the original state's legislature. To admit West Virginia implied that Confederate Virginia
was out of the Union, something President Abraham Lincoln was
loath to do, but such emphatic loyalty overcame hesitation. The
West Virginia Statehood Bill passed Congress and was signed into
law by President Lincoln on June 20, 1863. (09-141, 09-042)

1400   1450   1500   1550   1600   1650   1700

TRENT AFFAIR, 1861

In early November 1861, two Confederate emissaries, James Murray Mason of Virginia and John Slidell of Louisiana, en route to England, were arrested when the British mail packet *Trent* was seized by USS *San Jacinto*. The Confederates were imprisoned in Boston. The British government demanded their immediate release. The Brits were prepared to go to war because San Jacinto had violated international maritime law.

On Christmas Day, Lincoln summoned his cabinet, explained the situation, and capitulated. Lincoln said he could not countenance the folly of "having two wars on his hands at a time." The next day, he admitted the seizure was a violation of international law. Mason and Slidell were released, and they proceeded to their destinations. War with Britain was averted.

Mason and Slidell's diplomatic efforts in Europe were not successful. Neither France nor Great Britain ever recognized the Confederacy, but the Trent Affair revealed the diplomatic and military weakness of the federal government in the early years of the Civil War. (06-050, 06-051)

STEPHEN RAMSEUR
SEES THE DEATH OF THE
WOODEN NAVY, 1862

Stephen Ramseur was a twenty-four-year-old Confederate major of artillery who was in Norfolk, Virginia, in March 1862 when CSS *Virginia* and USS *Monitor* ushered in the iron navy. He wrote a letter to a kinsman describing the clash of the iron monsters.

Virginia was a masterpiece of improvisation. The Confederates took *Merrimack*, a scuttled Union steam frigate, sliced off the upper hull, replaced it with a constructed barn-shaped super-structure, and armored it with iron. The rechristened *Virginia* was a bit clumsy and required half an hour to turn around in the water, but on March 8, 1862, the ship cut up the Union blockade fleet. USS *Cumberland* was destroyed, USS *Congress* was in flames, *Minnesota* had run aground, and two other blockaders had fled to shallow water.

When *Virginia* came out the next morning to finish the job, out from behind *Minnesota* came a vessel Ramseur called "the famous

1400   1450   1500   1550   1600   1650   1700

Erricson iron battery," USS *Monitor*. Back and forth the two odd shapes passed on opposite courses, firing away, neither penetrating the armor of the other. At about noon, the *Monitor* withdrew after its captain was blinded by flying iron splinters. By the time it came back out, the *Virginia* had retreated to the Confederate shore.

The fight had been a tactical draw, but actually *Monitor* was the victor. The federal fleet continued its blockade. *Monitor* sank in a storm off Cape Hatteras on December 31, 1862. *Virginia* never fought again. When the Confederates abandoned Norfolk, it was abandoned and scuttled for the second time. (01-107)

NEBRASKA AND THE
HOMESTEAD ACT, 1862

In May 1862, President Lincoln signed the Homestead Act.
Anyone twenty-one years or older, a citizen or on the way to
becoming one, who had never borne arms against the United
States government, for $10, could receive 120 acres of unimproved
government land. After five years of living on and cultivating
it, the citizen could receive the land title free and clear. This act
and others allied to it formed the foundation for the explosive
settlement of Nebraska and other western states.

The first claimant under the Homestead Act was Daniel
Freeman. A Union soldier at home on furlough, he persuaded
the registrar of the Land Office in Brownville to open up shortly
after midnight on January 1, 1863, the date the law went into
effect. He claimed land along Cub Creek northwest of Beatrice,
near the Kansas border. Thanks to the Homestead Act, in the
years between 1862 and 1900, more than a million others joined
Freeman in making Nebraska home. (02-020)

| 1400 | 1450 | 1500 | 1550 | 1600 | 1650 | 1700 |

LINCOLN AND HIS ENEMIES I, 1862

When democracies are in peril, those in power become the focus of the peoples' discontent. By 1862, northerners blamed Abraham Lincoln for inflation, high taxes, inept generals, one battlefield loss after another, and a horrific body count. Lincoln faced a growing number of politicians seeking to be rid of him; they were as aggressive and hostile as any southerner.

On January 14, 1863, Clement Laird Vallandigham, a lame-duck congressman from Ohio, rose in Congress and urged immediate peace with the rebellious southern states. Stop the war, he said; quit insisting on the end of the slavery, and the South would come home. He was a peace Democrat, which was then called a "copperhead." His problem was that whatever their frustrations, many northerners, having surrendered their sons to the ocean of blood that was this war, thought copperheads were making light of their sacrifice. Northerners were slowly coming to the conclusion that for all their stated support for the Union the copperheads were really friends of Jefferson Davis. (02-093, 02-094, 02-095)

LINCOLN AND HIS
ENEMIES II, 1862

After 1860, congressional leadership was held by a faction soon to be known as "radical Republicans." Led by Senator Charles Sumner and Congressman Thaddeus Stevens, they desired immediate emancipation. Lincoln hesitated because such an act might anger the South and prevent reunion. To the radicals, this was moral timidity. They began to plot against him.

Ironically, by late 1862 the President had concluded that reunion was impossible as long as the South continued to win on the battlefield. If he did nothing, Europe might throw its power on the side of the South. His Emancipation Proclamation was on track for January 1, 1863, but the disastrous December defeat at Fredericksburg animated the radicals. They began to conspire with cabinet members, particularly Treasury Secretary Salmon P. Chase of Ohio. Aware of the plotting, Lincoln summoned a joint meeting of concerned senators and his cabinet. After a short speech on the need for harmony, he called for public support. Chase was caught in public and had to back the president. Checkmate. (02-093, 02-094, 02-095)

MORRILL ACT, 1862

Justin Smith Morrill was elected to Congress on an antislavery ticket in 1854. He shifted to the new Republican Party and served as House Speaker. He then became Finance Committee chair. There, he insured the Washington Monument completion, but he is best remembered for the Morrill Act (1862). It established a network of colleges funded by federal land grants to boost the teaching of agriculture, mechanical and industrial arts, and military science. Thirty thousand acres of land was set aside for each senator and congressman. Land would be sold and proceeds used for higher education.

Some schools used their grants wisely, Cornell, for instance, sold its million acres for over $5.50 per acre, a princely sum in that era. Others were not so fortunate. Morrill responded in 1890 with a second act that provided regular cash grants to land-grant colleges. For those states that continued segregation, the second act required that an equal amount be devoted to starting black colleges before the money would flow. (02-180)

LANE AND QUANTRILL, 1862

In the years before the Civil War, bleeding Kansas produced two disreputable guerrilla leaders, James Henry Lane and William Clarke Quantrill, who laid waste to the countryside, inflaming passions on both sides of the question of slavery.

Lane headed a guerrilla group in Kansas and became a US senator and supporter of Abraham Lincoln. During the war, he continued his guerilla activities as head of "Lane's Brigade," which conducted operations against Confederate forces in Western Missouri. Particularly vicious was his raid against Oceola, where his brigade burned and looted everything in its path. He died by his own hand in 1866.

Quantrill failed at most things he tried and by 1860 had joined a band of antislavery fellow drifters who claimed to support anti-slavery settlers for a fee but whose main occupation was petty theft and murder. His actual sentiments on slavery were only loosely moored; during the Civil War, Quantrill changed dramatically. He formed a guerrilla gang that raided towns and farms of Union sympathizers. His raid on Lawrence, Kansas, in summer 1863 was particularly egregious, killing over 150 men, including several young boys. Toward the end of the war, his gang broke up due to infighting. Quantrill was a killed in a May 1865 raid into Kentucky a month after Lee's surrender at Appomattox. (02-222, 02-223, 03-001)

1400   1450   1500   1550   1600   1650   1700

WHITE OFFICERS AND BLACK TROOPS, 1863

Up until the Civil War, blacks were not officially permitted to serve in the Army. With the Militia Act (1862) and the Emancipation Proclamation (1863), northern whites became more willing accept black troops—particularly as the need for manpower in the Union Army escalated after the heavy body count in 1862.

Initially, the federal government did not have a national plan for organizing colored troops. The Bureau of Colored Troops was established to streamline the process of activating black units. Only white men were permitted to command black troops. To prepare these officers, a school was established in Philadelphia. After an intensive thirty-day curriculum, applicants could present themselves for examination in Washington. More than 6,000 officers commanded 179,000 African American troops during the Civil War. At first, because of racial prejudice in the North and fears of southern retribution, black soldiers were not used in combat situations as extensively as their white counterparts. This changed as the war continued. (07-114, 07-115, 07-116)

1700	1750	1800	1850	1900	1950	PRESENT

Era of Republican Crisis

MASSACHUSETTS COLORED REGIMENT, 1863

The 54th Massachusetts Infantry was made up of black troops and white officers. Early in 1863, Governor John Andrew, an ardent abolitionist, organized the unit. He selected as leader Robert G. Shaw. He was a battle-tested, well-educated, young officer from a prominent Boston abolitionist family. Shaw quickly earned the respect of his unit, which included former slaves and free blacks. Shaw was sure that well-trained blacks could fight just as well as white troops. At Battery Wagner, they proved him right.

On July 18, 1863, the 54th attacked the fort, a strong Confederate position near Charleston, South Carolina. Unfortunately, Confederate cannons were well positioned to fire down into the charging soldiers. The black troops braved the fire, scaled the parapet, and held their ground for one hour. Eventually they were pushed back after brutal hand-to-hand combat. The unit lost half its troops including Shaw, who died in the initial charge. During the fight, Sergeant William H. Carney lofted the regimental flag. He was the first African American to win the Congressional Medal of Honor. (11-011, 11-012)

1400   1450   1500   1550   1600   1650   1700

Espionage, someone has said, is the "second oldest profession." Of the many roles women played during the American Civil War, the most dangerous, daring, and deadly was spying. Civil War women spies were amateurs often motivated by fervent regional patriotism.

Rose Greenhow was a Washington hostess who ran a Rebel spy ring in DC and used her political connections and perhaps the occasional romantic liaison to harvest a treasure trove of valuable military information. She helped the South win the first Battle of Manassas before being exiled south. Sent as a goodwill ambassador to Europe, she wrote a best-selling spy memoir. Legend has it that when her boat capsized off the North Carolina coast while on her way home she was dragged to her death by the gold sovereign book profits sewn into her dress.

Gender-bending Union spy Sarah Emma Edmonds used elaborate disguises in her work. Masquerading as a man, she enlisted and often used disguises to infiltrate Confederate lines. In 1863 behind Rebel lines in Vicksburg, she contracted malaria and deserted to seek treatment in Illinois. Once recovered, she spent the balance of the war as a nurse in Washington. (07-010, 07-011, 07-012, 07-012, 07-013)

CIVIL WAR WOMEN SPIES II

A staunch Confederate, young Belle Edmondson lived in Memphis after Union forces occupied the city in 1862. She slipped information and supplies to the Confederates. Belle hid letters, brass buttons, medicine and amputation tools, and money in her dresses and rather ample bosom. In July 1864, Belle was forced to flee south to Mississippi because the federals were on to her. After the war, Belle returned to Memphis and there befriended the Jefferson Davis family in the early 1870s. After announcing her engagement to a mysterious "Colonel H," she died in 1873 at the age of thirty-three. According to family tradition, Colonel "H" was a Yankee officer.

Elizabeth Van Lew was a closeted abolitionist and Union sympathizer living in wartime Richmond. She ran an elaborate spy operation, sending coded information through the lines to Union intelligence officers. One of her operatives was a very attentive servant in the White House of the Confederacy. Van Lew expended her inheritance financing the spy ring and died in 1900 penniless and a social outcast. Friends from Massachusetts sent a stone for her unmarked grave. Her epigraph reads as follows:

She risked everything that is dear to man—friends, fortune, comfort, life itself, all for one absorbing desire of her heart—that slavery might be abolished and the Union preserved.

(07-010, 07-011, 07-012, 07-012, 07-013)

| 1400 | 1450 | 1500 | 1550 | 1600 | 1650 | 1700 |

STONEWALL JACKSON—
VICTIM OF FRIENDLY FIRE

At Chancellorsville, Virginia, in May 1863, Robert E. Lee achieved perhaps his greatest military victory, but at a terrible price. Among the thirteen thousand Confederate casualties was his right arm, Thomas "Stonewall" Jackson. Friendly fire (or casualties inflicted by those on the same side) happens in most combat situations. Distinguishing between friend and foe in the heat of battle has always been difficult.

In spring 1863, ambitious Union General Joseph Hooker desired to remove Lee and take Richmond. He sent the main body of his army, 70,000 men, west up the Rappahannock, across the river, and then southeast to attack Lee's rear. Hooker established his headquarters in the dense woods of the Wilderness at Chancellorsville, a crossroads ten miles west of Fredericksburg.

Aware of Hooker's move, Lee divided his army, sending about 45,000 men to check Hooker. He then sent Stonewall with 26,000 Confederates on a two-and-half-mile march to hit Hooker's exposed, weak right flank. Caught by surprise, Hooker's army began to fall apart. After dark, Jackson went on a nighttime reconnaissance. When he and his aides returned, nervous Confederate pickets mistook them for federal cavalry and fired. Jackson was struck three times, and his left arm was later amputated. He contracted pneumonia and died on May 10. His absence at Gettysburg may have been decisive in the Rebel defeat there. (10-001, 10-002)

PICKETT'S CHARGE, 1863

Tempted into another invasion of the North by his stunning victory at Chancellorsville, Robert E. Lee and his Army of Northern Virginia moved into Pennsylvania, eventually converging on the small crossroads village of Gettysburg on July 1, 1863. There he was blocked by steadily increasing elements of the Union Army of the Potomac under newly appointed General George G. Meade.

Three days of intense fighting marked the high point of Confederate military ambitions in the Civil War. The first two days had indecisive results, with Rebel units battering away at a Union line that benefitted from steadily strengthening interior defensive positions. On the third day, Lee, acting on the skill and confidence that nearly always served him well, cast all of the South's hopes on a go-for-broke attack on the Union Center on Cemetery Ridge.

Around 3:00 p.m. on July 3, after perhaps the largest artillery bombardment of the war with over 150 Confederate cannon engaged, 12,500 southern soldiers under General George

Pickett moved off the ridgeline, crossed the Emmitsburg Road, and attacked the Union line. For a brief moment, the Union line wavered at the "Angle," in a stone fence on the Ridge, but reinforcements closed in and repulsed the Confederate advance. Half of Pickett's command did not return, chewed up by withering artillery and musket fire and bitter hand-to-hand combat.

Lee retreated into Virginia, never again to return to the strategic offensive. The war would last nearly two more terrible years, but from that point the military initiative would be clearly in the hands of the Union.

GETTYSBURG ADDRESS I, 1863

At Gettysburg, the casualties on both sides were enormous. Over the three-day period, in excess of 50,000 were killed, wounded, missing, or captured.

With contributions from eighteen Union states, seventeen acres were purchased near the center of the Union line for a "national cemetery." Dedication was set for November 19, 1863. The principal speaker was to be Edward Everett, orator, statesman, and president of Harvard College. President Lincoln would make a few remarks. After Everett's two-hour oration, Lincoln stood in his black frock coat and white gloves and delivered his 272-word, three-minute speech.

His simple yet eloquent words defining the purpose of the war were a moving tribute to the fallen. They are recognized by many as perhaps the most profound expression of freedom and the democratic spirit in the English language. The next day, Everett wrote Lincoln, "I should flatter myself that I came as near to the central idea of the occasion in two hours as you did in two minutes." (08-008, 08-009)

1400   1450   1500   1550   1600   1650   1700

*F*our score and seven years ago our fathers brought forth, on this
continent, a new nation, conceived in liberty, and dedicated to the
proposition that all men are created equal. Now we are engaged in a great
civil war, testing whether that nation, or any nation so conceived, and so
dedicated, can long endure. We are met on a great battle-field of that war.
We have come to dedicate a portion of that field, as a final resting-place
for those who here gave their lives, that that nation might live. It is
altogether fitting and proper that we should do this. But, in a larger sense,
we cannot dedicate, we cannot consecrate—we cannot hallow—this ground.
The brave men, living and dead, who struggled here, have consecrated it
far above our poor power to add or detract.

   The world will little note, nor long remember what we say here, but
it can never forget what they did here. It is for us the living, rather, to be
dedicated here to the unfinished work which they who fought here have
thus far so nobly advanced. It is rather for us to be here dedicated to the
great task remaining before us—that from these honored dead we take
increased devotion to that cause for which they here gave the last full
measure of devotion—that we here highly resolve that these dead shall not
have died in vain—that this nation, under God, shall have a new birth of
freedom, and that government of the people, by the people, for the people,
shall not perish from the earth.

ABRAHAM LINCOLN
GETTYSBURG, PENNSYLVANIA
NOVEMBER 19, 1863 (08-008, 08-009)

1700	1750	1800	1850	1900	1950	PRESENT

Era of Republican Crisis

CITY POINT EXPLOSION, 1864

In mid-1864, General Ulysses S. Grant established his head-quarters and supply depot in the village of City Point (now Hopewell) at the confluence of the Appomattox and James Rivers ten miles northeast of Petersburg, Virginia. From there, he conducted siege operations at Petersburg, which guarded the vital rail links between Confederate capitol Richmond and the rest of the beleaguered South.

Around noon on August 9, a huge explosion lit up and destroyed the *J. E. Kendrick*, a munitions barge anchored just below Grant's headquarters located on a bluff overlooking the harbor. Miraculously, Grant himself was unharmed, but 43 were killed and 126 injured, and damaged property was assessed in the millions. A board of inquiry ruled the explosion an accident, but it was actually sabotage.

That morning, John Maxwell, member of Confederate Secret Service, had walked down the dock with a "horological torpedo," a time bomb of his own design. He placed in onboard, and at 11:40 a.m. the *Kendrick* and everything in range were vaporized.

(05-093, 05-094)

MR. LINCOLN'S
CHRISTMAS GIFT, 1864

The Union occupation of Atlanta, Georgia, in early September 1864 was greeted in the North with elation and probably assured the reelection of President Lincoln. Nevertheless, defiant rebel armies were still in the field and especially around Richmond; stalemate was order of the day. William Tecumseh Sherman had a bold plan—to strike out with his army and through "utter destruction . . . make Georgia howl." With some reluctance, Lincoln permitted Sherman to cut a hole through the countryside, and on November 15, 1864, Sherman and his army of 62,000 disappeared into the hole.

They emerged a month later, having sliced a swath sometimes eighty miles wide across the southern heartland, collecting livestock and freeing countless slaves. Damage done to the Confederates? Sherman calculated it to be in excess of $100 million. His telegram to Lincoln created a sensation. "I beg to present to you as a Christmas gift the city of Savannah, with one hundred fifty heavy guns and plenty of ammunition, also about 25,000 bales of cotton." The President was glad of it. (01-118)

THE DOCTORS MAYO, 1864

William Worrall Mayo was born in 1819 in Manchester, England. While serving as a medical apprentice in Glasgow, he met a young postgraduate physician from Philadelphia who reinforced in Mayo the desire to seek a future in the United States. He immigrated and resumed his medical studies, settling in Rochester, Minnesota, in 1863. There he established an extensive surgical practice.

In the 1880s, first son Will and then Charles joined their father in what was becoming a medical practice famous throughout the state. In 1889, William and his sons established St. Mary's Hospital, and as the elder Mayo gradually retired the boys moved into important leadership roles. Will administered the hospital and specialized in surgery of the abdomen and kidney. Charles originated numerous surgical innovations and did pioneer work in orthopedic and cataract surgery. Charles's son by the same name joined the practice, and from this intergenerational partnership evolved the world-famous Mayo Clinic. (02-007)

| 1400 | 1450 | 1500 | 1550 | 1600 | 1650 | 1700 |

RAPHAEL SEMMES,
REBEL SAILOR, 1864

In 1861, Maryland-born Raphael Semmes, after a distinguished career in the US Navy, offered his services to the Confederacy. His most outstanding command was as captain of the 900-ton commerce raider CSS *Alabama*. The ship's most destructive voyage was a round-the-world cruise during which *Alabama* smashed sixty-two Union vessels. A Naval solicitor wrote eleven years later, "Never in naval history has there occurred so striking an example of the tremendous power of mischief exacted by a single cruiser as *Alabama* under Raphael Semmes."

On June 19, 1864, *Alabama* sailed out of Cherbourg, France, to engage USS *Kearsarge*. Unknown to Semmes, Captain Winslow of the Union ship had hung iron cable at mid-ships so *Alabama*'s shot just bounced off this ironclad in disguise. Thus protected from incoming fire, *Kearsarge* pummeled *Alabama* with relentless cannon shot. In just over an hour, Semmes' ship was dying. Rescued by an English yacht, he then commanded gunboats on the James River and later returned to Alabama after the fall of Richmond. The Confederate Navy's finest sailor ended his career as a practicing lawyer and newspaper editor. (01-084)

JOHN SINGLETON MOSBY, 1865

John Mosby, a country boy, graduated from Virginia and established a law practice in Bristol. He volunteered for service in the cavalry when war broke out. An excellent scout, he conducted reconnaissance patrols in Northern Virginia throughout the summer and fall of 1862.

Mosby began to engage in guerrilla operations behind Union lines. He was very good at what he did, piloting raids against supply lines, railroads, wagon trains, and isolated Union outposts. He was so good that Fauquier and Loudoun Counties were known as "Mosby's Confederacy." While keeping civilian casualties very low, he kept Union forces off balance until the end of the war.

After the surrender, he became friends with Ulysses S. Grant and supported his former antagonist for president. Mosby's neighbors shunned the former guerrilla fighter; one even took a shot at him one night at the Warrenton Depot. Grant, concerned for his friend's life, appointed him consul in Hong Kong. He served in other federal posts until his death in 1916. (08-026)

MATHEW BRADY, 1865

On the afternoon of his famous Cooper Union speech in early 1860, Abraham Lincoln dropped by the photography studio of Mathew Brady. There, using the efficient collodion wet-plate process, Brady fixed forever the rough but distinguished face of America's future leader. He put Lincoln's visage on cartes de visite, or calling-card-sized photos on cheap paper. Soon, the candidate's picture was in newspapers and magazines all over America. Lincoln said, "Brady and Cooper Union made me president."

With the coming of the conflict, Brady covered the war, employing teams of operatives to mark the passage of the fighting. They and their competitors captured over a million photos: leaders, the nameless, and many whose faces could little hide the emotional scars from the horrible event into which they had been swept. The Civil War project bankrupted Brady, and despite a Congressional pension he died alone and forgotten in 1896. His haunting images, however, will live on forever. (05-049, 05-050)

LINCOLN'S VISION: SECOND INAUGURAL ADDRESS I, 1865

In his Second Inaugural, Abraham Lincoln gently celebrated the emerging Union triumph and then pointed the way to national reconciliation. In the summer, he had been resolved to serving only a single term. The horrendous casualties of the Wilderness Campaign had sent northern public morale spiraling downward. The capture of Atlanta in September, however, restored national confidence in Lincoln's leadership.

As he stood to be sworn in, he spoke confidently of the brightening prospects of a reunited America. Frederick Douglass said that "the address sounded more like a sermon than a state paper." Lincoln's normal concision yielded a speech of 703 words in twenty-five exquisitely crafted sentences. He considered it his greatest speech.

Lincoln remembered the gloomy spirit under which the capitol labored four years before, with two circling antagonists, one of which would make war rather than let the nation survive and the other which would accept war rather than let it perish. The war was fought to resolve the issue of slavery, revealing his own struggle to see its purpose as bringing freedom to the African American as a divinely inspired mission. (13-072, 13-073)

1400   1450   1500   1550   1600   1650   1700

LINCOLN'S VISION: SECOND INAUGURAL ADDRESS II, 1865

Lincoln eschewed judgment against southerners, recognizing that they too had sought God's blessing on their own crusade. In the end, though, both prayed to the Almighty for success, and neither side had had their prayers fully answered. North and South had conspired over the decades through their complicity in slavery to bring this terrible scourge of war on the land. Author Ronald White says Lincoln is here speaking against any "God bless America" notion that does not recognize evil and hypocrisy in its own house.

His vision and path to understanding emerged in the final words. Though he would not preside over that reconciliation, his spirit insured that the Union, reforged in the bloody crucible of battle, would never again be threatened by sectional animosity:

With malice toward none; with charity for all; with firmness in the right, as God gives us to see the right, let us strive on to finish the work we are in; to bind up the nation's wounds; to care for him who shall have borne the battle, and for his widow, and his orphan—to do all which may achieve and cherish a just and a lasting peace among ourselves and with all nations.

(13-072, 13-073)

MAN PURSUED BY WAR, 1865

Wilmer McLean lived at Yorkshire, a 1,200-acre tract close by the small creek known as Bull Run just outside of the village of Manassas Junction, Virginia. In spring 1861, McLean realized that both sides wanted control of Manassas, as it was a vital rail link north, south, and west. Sometime before July 21, McLean moved his family out of Yorkshire; therefore, they were not present for the Battle of First Manassas, which took place in his front yard.

It was common in that time for many civilians caught in the line of fire to flee from the fighting. The McLeans settled in Appomattox Courthouse in south central Virginia. As a merchant, McLean prospered during the war, and their big home reflected that affluence. In April 1865, with Richmond abandoned and his escape blocked, Robert E. Lee had to surrender. He met General Ulysses S. Grant in the parlor of the McLean house in Appomattox. The man in whose front yard the war began now played reluctant host to the meeting at which it ended. (02-107, 02-108)

1400   1450   1500   1550   1600   1650   1700

THE HAUNTED
MAJOR RATHBONE, 1865

On the night of April 14, 1865, Major Henry Rathbone and
his friend Clara Harris were delighted to join President
and Mrs. Abraham Lincoln for the performance of *Our American
Cousin* at Ford's Theatre in Washington. At the point in the play
when the lines read, "Wal, I guess I know enough to turn you
inside out, you sockdologizing old mantrap," John Wilkes Booth
fired a bullet into the skull of the president. Rathbone went after
the now knife-wielding Booth. The assassin brought his arm up
and sliced the blade down into the major's arm, cutting it to the
bone from elbow to shoulder. Blood spurted in all directions.
Booth shoved him aside and jumped over the railing down to the
stage, yelling, "*Sic semper tyrannis* [thus always to tyrants]; the South
is avenged!"

In 1867, Clara Harris and Henry Rathbone married, but it was
clear Rathbone blamed himself for Lincoln's death. He began to
suffer delusions, physical ailments, and constant fears. On a trip
to Germany for treatment in the winter of 1883, on Christmas
Eve sometime before dawn, Rathbone entered the room and killed
Clara. He then took a knife and stabbed his own arm repeatedly
in the same spot Booth had cut him eighteen years before. After
Clara's burial, Henry Rathbone was committed to an insane
asylum where he remained in haunted isolation until his death
in 1911. (02-217, 02-218)

COLLINS'S OVERLAND
TELEGRAPH, 1866

L ooking back, Perry Collins's idea for a telegraph link westward through Alaska and across Siberia to Europe was exotic and complex, but it had unintended consequences.

Collins believed that a westward telegraph to connect the United States with European Russia would be far less complicated than laying an undersea cable. The project was adopted by Western Union, but the Civil War intervened. As the war was winding down, interest revived. Surveys across British Columbia and Alaska were completed, and construction of the line actually began.

At that point, on the other side of the continent, the steamer *Great Eastern* arrived in Newfoundland with a transatlantic telegraph cable. Soon two cables linked Europe and America under the Atlantic. This signaled the end of the Russian–American project, but the interest generated by Perry Collins's western telegraph project convinced the US government that it should buy Alaska. Negotiations led to the purchase of this vast new addition to the United States for about two cents an acre in March 1867.

(02-069)

GREAT EASTERN, 1866

I sambard Kingdom Brunel was one of the most successful engineers of the nineteenth century. He constructed the world's longest tunnel at the time, several unusual railroad bridges, and, finally, *Great Eastern*. Conceived as the first luxury liner, the ship was designed to carry 4,000 passengers in complete comfort, haul enough coal for a nonstop round-trip from England to Australia, and earn her investor's money back in a couple of years. No profit was made with *Great Eastern*.

The 12,000-ton iron-hulled vessel was powered by huge steam engines and driven by an underwater propeller, two massive side paddle wheels, and sails and spent most of her thirty years of life in the shop. The ship seemed to be cursed.

Great Eastern's great moment came in 1866 when, carrying an underwater telegraph cable, it helped connect Europe and North America electronically. After time as a floating amusement park in Liverpool, the ship was sold for scrap. It was a miserable end to Brunel's great dream. (02-049)

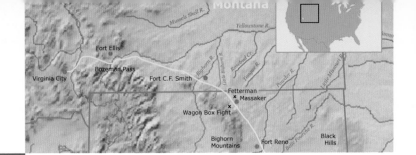

BOZEMAN TRAIL, 1866

The Oregon Trail and Overland Trail were the two premier trails immigrants took to the West Coast. Heavily traveled through the 1850s, the Oregon Trail went up the North Platte River through South Pass, the Snake River Valley, and the Blue Mountains and into the Willamette Valley. Yet, it was not easy, and word began to circulate of a new trail, a shortcut, with better water for stock and better grades that could cut nearly three months from the journey west. The problem was it was in Indian Territory. Repeated attacks on miners and wagon trains gave the Bozeman Trail its nickname, "Bloody Bozeman."

The number of travelers continued to swell, encouraged by the presence of three army forts built along the trail to protect them. Just before Christmas 1866, a huge war party led by the charismatic Chief Red Cloud wiped out an army detachment near Fort Phil Kearny near the start of the trail. For a time, the Bozeman Trail was abandoned. The American Indians had blocked the trail for a while, but the victory was short-lived. Red Cloud's words were prophetic: "Now we are melting like snow on the hillside, while you are growing like spring grass." (09-020)

LAURA INGALLS WILDER, 1867

Laura Wilder was born in Wisconsin in 1867, the second of four siblings. The Homestead Act of 1862 encouraged western migration by offering 160 acres of land to settlers who agreed to farm and reside on the land. Wilder spent the first twelve years wandering with her parents in search of a better life until the family finally filed a homestead claim in Dakota Territory.

Her childhood, as depicted in her books, was happy but hard. She began teaching at the age of fifteen and in this capacity met and married Almanzo Wilder, a homesteader from New York. The couple settled permanently in the Missouri Ozarks, but endured many of the same hardships she had experienced as a child.

At her journalist daughter's suggestion, using school tablets and pencil, Laura created eight loosely autobiographical novels, known collectively as the Little House Books (1932–1943). They have been praised as vividly detailing frontier domestic life, seen through the eyes of a young girl. (08-008)

ANDREW JOHNSON'S IMPEACHMENT, 1868

Tennessee Senator Andrew Johnson remained loyal to the Union after 1861 and then ran with Abraham Lincoln on the National Union Party ticket in 1864. (Republicans adopted the Union Party label that year to enhance their chances.) They won, but shortly thereafter the president was assassinated.

Johnson wished to implement Lincoln's easy readmission plan for the defeated South. Lincoln, as the exalted war leader, might have been able to pull off such a plan, but the stubborn and irascible Johnson was ill-equipped to do the same. For two years, he was at loggerheads with radical Republicans who controlled Congress.

Strengthened by the 1866 congressional elections, the radical Republicans passed tough reconstruction acts and the Tenure of Office law, which forbade the president to remove civil officers without the Senate's consent. Later repealed and declared unconstitutional, the Tenure of Office Act was designed to prevent the president from removing radical allies from the executive branch.

The Tenure of Office Act was a trap into which Johnson stepped. In summer 1867, Johnson fired Secretary of War Edwin McMasters Stanton. On February 24, 1868, the House impeached Johnson for violation of the act. The case was legally weak but politically strong, and after a Senate trial in May, Johnson was saved from removal by a single vote. Politically, he was damaged goods. He could not prevent the radicals from inflicting another decade of reconstruction on the Deep South, thus extending the bitterness of the war for many generations. (03-193, 03-194, 03-195)

BIG FOUR OF THE
CENTRAL PACIFIC I

Theodore Dehone Judah had a vision: to span the continental
United States with a railroad. After brilliant success as an
engineer in New York, Judah had been lured to California to build
the first railroad on the West Coast. In doing so, he fell under
the spell of the Sierra Nevada Mountains that piled up just east
of his work site in the Sacramento Valley. By November 1860, he
had found what he thought was the best way across, established
a company, and issued stock. But then he found he could hardly
give the shares away.

One evening in early January 1861, he gave a speech at the
St. Charles Hotel on Sacramento's K Street. After the crowd
dwindled down, he was approached by two shopkeepers who
owned a hardware business just down the street. They invited him
to meet with them and their associates a few nights later. And so
it was above the hardware store that Judah met the Big Four who
would realize his dream, which he never realized himself. Judah
died in 1863. (01-077, 01-166)

1400   1450   1500   1550   1600   1650   1700

BIG FOUR OF THE
CENTRAL PACIFIC II

The founders of the Central Pacific Railroad were a study in contrast.

Collis Huntington was thirty-nine, weighed 250 pounds, and, as a stalwart Republican, believed the Pacific Railroad would tie Californians to the Union.

Mark Hopkins Jr., forty-seven, was the opposite of Huntington's enthusiastic personality. He would handle the entire bookkeeping system of the huge railroad enterprise.

Leland Stanford was also a large man physically but was not by nature a businessman; he was a politician. He made a fortune in the goldfields and used it to open a large wholesale grocery operation. He drove headlong into politics and became the first Republican governor of California in 1861. The founder of Stanford University, he was an attractive and thoroughly political animal.

Different from his partners in most ways, Charles Crocker, thirty-nine, was a workaholic, typically rising at four in the morning and working until bedtime. Crocker was completely tactless, had huge stamina and physical strength, and was incredibly stubborn. He was the man who was to drive the thousands of workers and the railroad they built through the mountains of California. (01-077, 01-166)

BELLE HUNTINGTON, 1868

After helping build the first transcontinental railroad, Collis Potter Huntington went south to explore investment opportunities. During one of his stays in a Richmond, Virginia, boardinghouse, he fell in love with Arabella, the daughter of the owner who also served as a barmaid. She was vivacious, beautiful, and thirty years his junior. She moved to New York, became his mistress, and bore him a son in 1870.

Though still married, Huntington settled on Arabella and his son an increasingly lavish lifestyle. Often she traveled with him by private train to inspect his far-flung holdings, sometimes introduced as his niece. She was a quick study in languages and art history and developed a refined sense of taste. When his ailing wife died, she married him in 1884.

No longer needing to hide, Arabella began to demonstrate exuberant habits of acquisition. Guiding her son, Archer, and Collis' favorite nephew, Henry Huntington, she accumulated a huge collection of eighteenth- and nineteenth-century paintings. When Collis Huntington's died in 1900, she inherited $150 million, making her perhaps the wealthiest woman in the world—not bad for a barmaid from Shockoe Bottom. (03-121, 03-122)

| 1400 | 1450 | 1500 | 1550 | 1600 | 1650 | 1700 |

SAMUEL TILDEN AND
TAMMANY HALL, 1870

Since the Revolutionary era, the Society of St. Tammany had been a powerful working-class political club in New York City. One of the founders was Aaron Burr, who used its power to further his political aims. As a base for the Democratic Party in New York City and State, Tammany Hall (the group's headquarters) extended political assistance and patronage to immigrants, particularly Irish immigrants, in exchange for loyalty and votes. By the Civil War, the organization was dominated by the Tweed Ring, William Tweed and his associates. The Ring used its power to get government contracts for its allies in exchange for cash payments. A case in point was the construction of the New York County Courthouse, set to cost $250,000. The Tweed Ring plundered $14 million from the city before it was complete.

Samuel J. Tilden rose to prominence as one of the first great corporation lawyers in America. In 1870, Tweed, recognizing the growing power of his former ally, Sam Tilden, tried to bribe him by offering him the Ring's legal business. Tilden refused. When, in 1871, the *New York Times* began to expose the corruption of Tammany Hall, Tilden pressed the investigation. By this he secured a reputation as incorruptible, was elected governor, and nearly won the presidency in 1876. Boss Tweed went to prison, and the corrupt and arrogant empire of Tammany Hall gradually collapsed. (02-071, 02-072)

| 1700 | 1750 | 1800 | 1850 | 1900 | 1950 | PRESENT |

Era of Innovation and Technology

NEW YORK'S FIRST SUBWAY, 1870

By 1870, the streets of New York were clogged with pedestrians, horse-drawn vehicles, and locomotives. Alfred Ely Beach, editor of *Scientific American*, had been experimenting with pneumatic propulsion, the use of air pressure to force a cylinder through a tightly sealed tube. Beach needed permission from the city to start a pneumatic subway but was blocked by Tammany Hall and William M. "Boss" Tweed. Tweed wanted no competition with a proposed elevated railroad in which he was a prospective investor. The inventor did an end around, avoiding the Boss and getting legislative authorization for a demonstration project.

Deep below the surface from the corner of Warren Street and Broadway, the Beach Pneumatic Transit ran one hundred yards westward to Murray Street. Beginning in 1870, passengers descended to the splendidly appointed waiting room, boarded a cylindrical car and were propelled back and forth through the brick-lined tunnel on a stream of air generated by a one-hundred horsepower pump. It was a publicity triumph, but Tweed recovered and again blocked Beach from further construction. In the financial panic of 1873, New York's enthusiasm receded and the city did not get its first subway until after 1900. (03-183)

1400   1450   1500   1550   1600   1650   1700

GREAT CHICAGO FIRE OF 1871

On Sunday evening, October 7, 1871, in a small stable in the south division of the city of Chicago, a lady went out to milk her cow. It was late, and perhaps her milking technique was less than delicate. The cow kicked over the lady's oil lamp, and soon the little stable was ablaze. Soon other buildings in the area were on fire. Before the fire was extinguished two days later by explosives supplied by the army, 300 people had died, 100,000 were homeless, and $300 million damage had been done.

Observers gave four reasons for Chicago's destruction: First, the majority of its buildings were of wood construction. Second, the weather that summer and fall had been unusually dry. Third, gale-force winds drove the fire for two days. Fourth, despite heroism and great sacrifice on the part of individual firemen, once the fire spread, the fire department lost control. It was demoralized and exhausted from another huge fire the previous Saturday night. The fire was a disaster, but many saw it as a purifying event that led to the rebuilding of a dynamic new city. (01-076)

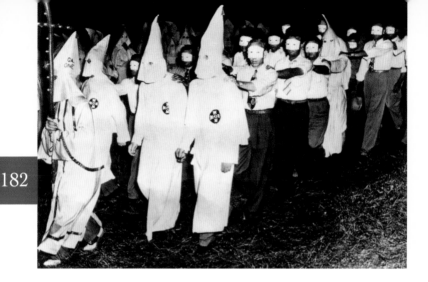

THE KLAN CLAIMS A VICTIM, 1871

During Reconstruction, as black legislators and their white allies controlled state legislatures with backing by federal troops, conservative whites resorted to the Ku Klux Klan to regain power.

Formed in Pulaski, Tennessee, by former Confederate General and slave-trader Nathan Bedford Forrest, the Klan first met in Nashville's Maxwell House Hotel in spring 1867. While publicly a religious and fraternal organization, the Klan and sister groups worked underground, controlling blacks and denying them political power.

By 1870, reports from the South reached a concerned Congress. At a congressional hearing on July 7, 1871, Alberry Bonner told a chilling Klan story:

> They came to my house on Saturday night and said, "Come out."
> . . . I flung out of bed; by that time they had the door bursted
> down . . . and they asked me, "Did you vote the radical ticket?"

| 1400 | 1450 | 1500 | 1550 | 1600 | 1650 | 1700 |

I said I did. He said, "Damn you, what did you do that for?" They wheeled me and jerked a handkerchief out and tied it around my face. . . . They drove me . . . up to the old field and kicked me along the way. When they got me up to the old field, they told me to draw my shirt; they all got hickories, some seven or eight of them, and let in on to whip me. Then they threw me down and whipped me down a while . . . and then raised me and beat me until they had got satisfaction.

When white conservatives regained power legally, Klan popularity waned. But into the twenty-first century in the South and also in some areas of the North, any challenge to white domination found growing Klan activity. (05-106)

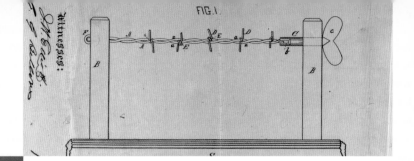

FIG.1.

JOSEPH GLIDDEN AND
BARBED WIRE, 1873

In the 1800s, the grasslands of the American West plains were rich, vast, and inviting, but the immense herds of cattle and sheep had to be tended constantly. There were few trees from which to build fences, no rocky New England soil from which to harvest stone walls.

In 1873, Illinois farmer Joseph Farwell Glidden set out to solve that problem. He first put spikes on smooth fencing wire, but they kept spinning or sliding to the lowest part on the wire. His solution was to twist two wires together and then create a stationary barb every eight inches or so.

He and his friend Isaac Leonard Ellwood suggested that they go into business together. The Barb Fence Company of De Kalb began to manufacture the wire, and Glidden applied for a patent. Though he sold his interests to Ellwood and others, he became one of the richest men in America. Glidden Barbed Wire and its competitors brought fencing and rational development to the American West. (09-015)

1400   1450   1500   1550   1600   1650   1700

TRIAL OF HENRY WARD BEECHER, 1875

During the 1800s, members of the Beecher clan were great moral leaders. Harriet Beecher Stowe wrote *Uncle Tom's Cabin*, enflaming both sides on the slavery question. Henry Ward Beecher was perhaps the most famous American clergyman. For twenty-five years, he was minister of the Plymouth Church in Brooklyn. Employing a casual-yet-emotional, animated, near-sensual preaching style, he supported liberal causes: prohibition, abolition, and women's rights. In the early 1870s, he was accused of having an affair with Elizabeth Tilton, a member of his congregation. Elizabeth allegedly confessed to her husband, Theodore, that Beecher had been giving her a bit more than spiritual guidance.

Both Beecher and Tilton tried to cover up the affair but failed. Tilton was thrown out of the congregation. During the church's investigation, Elizabeth denied the affair, and Beecher was exonerated. Tilton then sued, but Beecher was acquitted during a subsequent trial. The widespread interest in the trial demonstrates the grip religion and religious leaders had on America in the nineteenth century. (02-074, 02-075)

GEORGE WESTINGHOUSE, 1875

By 1870, 50,000 miles of rail stretched across the United States, but the brakes on the trains were too weak and too slow to stop trains in time to avoid sometimes-fatal accidents.

After service in the Civil War and a try at college, George Westinghouse discovered that he had the curious inclination of an inventor. On a trip to Troy, New York, in the late 1860s, he was reminded of the braking problem when his train was delayed by a head-on collision between two trains ahead. Westinghouse started experimenting on a way to bring safety to the rails.

He first tried to use the steam of the locomotive to close brakes on the cars, but that did not work. The steam cooled as it went further from its source, resulting in loss of braking power. Using an idea from European tunnel construction, he built a system that used compressed air generated by the locomotive to force the brakes. He solved the problem of leaks or breaks in the pressure line by installing an air tank on each car. The engineer slowed the train by releasing air from the tanks, which closed the brakes. The system then restored air pressure to the tanks so as to be ready for the next stop. A small railroad in Pittsburgh gave the system a try, and during an emergency the system proved itself. Westinghouse's brake system revolutionized railroading, allowing trains to carry more cargo and passengers at even greater speeds. (03-175, 03-176)

| 1400 | 1450 | 1500 | 1550 | 1600 | 1650 | 1700 |

BUFFALO SOLDIERS, 1875

Over 180,000 blacks served in volunteer regiments fighting with the US Army during the Civil War. Despite valiant and faithful service, no African American troops were allowed to serve in regular army units. In summer of 1866, four infantry and two cavalry regiments were created by Congress made up exclusively of black enlisted men. Most of their service was on the frontier. Native American opponents nicknamed them buffalo soldiers as a designation of respect for their color, which resembled the animal that sustained American Indian life.

They got the worst supplies, rotted food, cast-off horses, and surplus equipment. Their white officers were usually of poor quality and considered their duty to be professional exile. They often abused their men. Both inside the army and outside, in the local communities the troopers were sent to protect, these African Americans were often physically assaulted and even killed, while the army did nothing. Even in such deplorable conditions, they served with courage and dispatch. (05-030, 05-031)

DEMISE OF GEORGE
ARMSTRONG CUSTER, 1876

In fall 1851, a council of plains American Indians met with government agents near Fort Laramie, Wyoming, to discuss the safety of wagon trains traveling west, which crossed the traditional home of the Native Americans. The government thought that if the American Indians would just stop wandering and act like civilized white men, then the pioneers would be safe. But Native Americans disliked this idea and years later went off the reservation. They gathered for protection in a great village on the banks of the Little Bighorn River in southern Montana in summer 1876.

George Armstrong Custer, a vain and ambitious man whose record of so-called victories stretched unblemished, but undistinguished, back to First Bull Run in the Civil War, wanted to be president of the United States. Perhaps his ambition overcame his judgment. The Democratic Convention was just about to begin in St. Louis. News that Custer had scattered or defeated history's largest American Indian encampment might have secured him the nomination.

Custer was significantly outnumbered. The Seventh Cavalry with fewer than 700 troopers faced perhaps the largest concentration of hostile native Americans ever to assemble in one place.

Instead of following his orders to find the Native Americans and then await the rest of the army, on June 25, 1876, Custer lit into them on his own. He foolishly divided his already small unit, attempting what would have been hardly possible for the entire army. Not unlike a man who disturbs a giant hornet's nest, he attacked thousands of Sioux, Cheyenne, and their allies defending their homes and children. Neither he nor any of the men in his personal command survived. The demise of George Armstrong Custer was the high water mark of resistance by Native Americans to the onslaught of white civilization. (02-016, 02-017, 02-018, 02-019)

ELECTION CRISIS OF 1876

In 1876, the Democratic Presidential candidate, Samuel J. Tilden, won the popular vote by 250,000 and had 184 votes in the Electoral College, one vote shy of election. Tilden's opponent, Governor Rutherford B. Hayes of Ohio, had 165 votes and needed the votes of three disputed Republican-controlled southern states to win. The action then shifted to the Congress. Democrats controlled the House, Republicans the Senate. There was no consensus, so an Electoral Commission was appointed to settle the votes from the disputed states: five members each from the Senate and the House and five Supreme Court justices. The election would rest on the decision of the fifth justice, David Davis, an Independent from Illinois.

At the last minute, Davis was elected to the Senate by the Illinois legislature and another Justice, a Republican, took his place. All votes in the commission were decided on a party-line basis and Hayes got every disputed vote. Congress upheld the commission because a large number of southern Democrats joined the Republicans and voted for Hayes. Led by Wade Hampton of South Carolina, southerners extracted from Hayes a promise to withdraw all federal troops from the South, to help rebuild the South's shattered economy with federal money, and to allow the South a free hand with its black citizens. Not surprisingly, Hayes and Jim Crow won. (02-037, 02-038)

EDISON'S PHONOGRAPH, 1877

M ost of Thomas Edison's inventions were either improvements on other ideas or adaptations of existing technology. His incandescent lamp was vastly more efficient than any before, making home lighting economically viable. His kinetoscope laid the foundation for the modern motion picture. It was with the phonograph, however, that Edison made his most creative contribution to modern life, and its discovery was by accident.

During the summer of 1877, Edison was trying to figure a way of sending audio signals along telegraph wires so that telegraph companies could deliver oral messages instead of written ones. He was using a stylus attached to a carbon transmitter. Each sound would reproduce itself on paper covered with paraffin. He was surprised to discover that the sound could be reproduced by dragging the paper back under the stylus. At that point, the basic principle of the phonograph had been determined. The medium of preservation was to be a tinfoil or wax cylinder, vinyl record, magnetic tape, and the laser-interpreted compact disc, but the principle had been the same: sound produces an imprint that can be reproduced. (05-037)

NEZ PERCE WAR, 1877

Considered to be cooperative and adaptable, the Nez Perce Native Americans changed in 1877. For many years, the tribe had inhabited homelands in eastern Oregon and Washington and western Idaho. Under the pressure from white ranchers and miners, their hunting and grazing lands reserved by treaty with the United States had been shrinking. Chief Joseph, leader of a clan yet to participate in a treaty whose ancestral home in Eastern Oregon was about to disappear, had at last reluctantly agreed to move his people to the reservation in Idaho.

Naturally, the move was resented, and it took little to set off the Nez Perce. Three young warriors killed Richard Devine, a white who earlier with impunity had killed a helpless and crippled Nez Perce tribesman. Soon others joined in the murderous spree. Joseph and the other tribal chiefs faced an agonizing choice—join the insurrection or abandon their fellow clansmen.

Thus began one of the most fascinating campaigns in American military history. Employing classic guerrilla tactics, the Nez Perce clans won a series of running defensive battles with the army and civilian volunteers. Their cause was, of course, hopeless. The army regrouped and ran the Nez Perce to the ground in north central Montana after a chase lasting nearly 1,500 miles. Total casualties on both sides were nearly 300 killed and 250 wounded. Because other tribal leaders had escaped or been killed, Joseph was left to surrender. He said, "Our chiefs are killed. The little children are freezing to death. . . . I am tired; my heart is sick and sad. From where the sun now stands, I will fight no more forever." (01-141, 01-142)

WILLIAM CULLEN BRYANT, 1878

When William Bryant migrated to New York from rural Massachusetts in 1825, he already had a reputation as a man of letters. As a youth, he penned *Thanatopsis*, which some consider the first great American poem. In New York, he found company and intellectual stimulation among the artists, essayists, and professors of Columbia College. Bryant became editor the famed *New York Evening Post* in 1829.

The city in 1840 was a hot, noisy, and smoky commercial center of over 300,000 souls, with badly lit, garbage-strewn streets; numerous brothels; and very few open spaces. On a hot July day in 1844 he went for a walk in largely uninhabited central Manhattan and found what he thought was a perfect place for a large park. He wrote an editorial suggesting such an undertaking. Fourteen years later, dream became real in Frederick Law Olmsted's Central Park, a place of recreation and rest in the heart of the city.

Bryant's 1878 death followed an accidental fall in his beloved Central Park. His passing anticipated in the words he wrote as a teenager:

> So live, that when thy summons comes to join
> The innumerable caravan, which moves
> To that mysterious realm, where each shall take
> His chamber in the silent halls of death,
> Thou go not, like the quarry-slave at night,
> Scourged to his dungeon, but, sustained and soothed
> By an unfaltering trust, approach thy grave,
> Like one who wraps the drapery of his couch
> About him, and lies down to pleasant dreams.

(02-181)

CARRY NATION, 1880

Carry Amelia Moore was born in Garrard County, Kentucky, in 1846. She left her first marriage because of her husband's alcoholism and soon married David Nation, a lawyer, journalist, and minister. Religious convictions drove her deeper and deeper into opposition to the sale and consumption of alcohol.

In 1880, Kansas passed a law against the sale of liquor. Carry began hurling verbal abuse in the street at bar owners and patrons alike. Once she and another woman, whose husband was a heavy drinker, went into a local saloon, dropped to their knees, and began praying. As the prayers grew in volume and intensity, the number of patrons shrank. Her campaign was symbolized by the hatchet, which she would not hesitate to use as she invaded drinking establishments, chopping up tables and bars.

Nation was a strong advocate for women's right to vote. She was frequently arrested and often physically assaulted. She financed her crusade and paid her fines with large lecture fees. Her tactics helped lay the groundwork for Prohibition. (05-003)

PHINEAS TAYLOR BARNUM
AND JUMBOMANIA, 1882

For decades in the nineteenth century, Americans were entertained, fooled, and separated from their hard-earned livings by P. T. Barnum, a part naturalist, part huckster, all showman. The public loved his shows, and a few actually believed his attractions were real. In 1882, Barnum scored a coup when he acquired, for $10,000 from the London Zoological Society, the extraordinarily popular African elephant, Jumbo.

At the time, Jumbo was twenty-one years old—an exuberant adolescent as elephants go—weighed six tons, and stood eleven feet at the shoulders. The zoo was anxious to sell him because he becoming too hard to handle. The British public, however, which loved the zoo's giant resident, was not amused by the prospect of transfer to America. Petitions, debate in the House of Commons, and a reported audience with the queen by zoo officials were just a part the resulting uproar. When the elephant lay down in the street and refused to budge in the direction of the ship, the showman cabled, "Let him lie there a week. . . . It is the best advertisement in the world." America also fell into Jumbomania, and for four years the elephant was the star of the "Greatest Show on Earth." He died after a train accident in 1885, and for years his skeleton toured with Barnum's circus. (01-157, 01-158)

ANATOMY OF A
PRESIDENTIAL SCANDAL, 1884

194

A fter being nominated for president by the Democrats in the summer of 1884, Grover Cleveland was publicly accused of fathering an illegitimate child. Cleveland was able to negotiate the shoals of scandal for several reasons.

First, from the beginning, he told the truth. Maria Halpin came to Buffalo in 1871, where she found work in the retail clothing trade. She was a tall, stunning beauty and spoke French; soon, she was seen in the company of several men, one of whom was Grover Cleveland. Their relationship was intimate and sexual. Cleveland provided for both mother and child and confided the truth to a number of prominent clergy and political leaders.

Second, in the 1880s, political parties had real power. Probably Cleveland would not have gotten the nomination had this story broken before the convention, but once he was the nominee, after soul searching and a little hand-wringing, the party stuck with him.

Third, the thing was seen as a private matter. The real issue was public integrity and the capacity of the two candidates. Private conduct was considered irrelevant.

Finally, the reach of the media was relatively small. The Republican papers, of course, kept the pot boiling, but the Democratic papers were hardly interested in pursuing the matter. Cleveland went on to sterling service, elected twice president of the United States. (04-079, 04-081)

| 1700 | 1750 | 1800 | 1850 | 1900 | 1950 | PRESENT |

Era of Innovation and Technology

Laying the Electrical Tubes

EDISON VS. WESTINGHOUSE, 1885

Electricity as a means of lighting homes, businesses, and streets was in its infancy in the early 1880s. Thomas Edison had improved the incandescent light bulb and was constructing the power system for the City of New York. He was using direct current (DC), which can be compared to water flowing in a pipe. Power goes in one direction at low voltage over expensive wiring so as to not blow out the light bulbs.

On a trip from New York to Boston, George Westinghouse had a chance conversation with William Stanley, who had perfected a new type of electrical system. He called it alternating current (AC). Electricity moves back and forth along two lines at very high voltage. To solve the voltage differential, Westinghouse used transformers. Power would leave the station at 500 volts, hit transformers, and be reduced to 100 volts, sufficient for home use.

Edison struck back with a propaganda campaign amplifying some unfortunate early accidents with his rival's system. Eventually, however, the Electric Light Association determined that AC was no more dangerous than DC. By the 1890s, Westinghouse had won the battle. Even New York had converted to AC. (02-009)

1400   1450   1500   1550   1600   1650   1700

In early May 1886 in Chicago's Haymarket, violence erupted at a peaceful rally called to protest an attack by police on strikers at the McCormick reaper factory the previous day. At the end, someone tossed a bomb into police ranks and they started firing, killing civilians and some of their own men as well.

Angry voices crowded out rational discussion, and for months the country was in the grip of hysteria. In Chicago, the police never caught the bomber. Hoping to distract attention away from their fatal lack of discipline that night, they began arresting even labor leaders who had nothing to do with the rally.

Eventually, eight Chicago radicals were brought to trial, and in proceedings that all have condemned as a travesty of justice, they were convicted of murder. After appeal, four were hanged, one committed suicide, and three were sentenced to long jail terms. Six years later, Governor John Peter Altgeld reviewed the case and pardoned the survivors. He vigorously criticized the judge and found that the evidence showed that none of the eight had been involved in the bombing.

The Haymarket Incident divided the nation. It provoked bitter reaction against radicalism, the huge influx of so-called foreign immigrants, and the efforts of labor unions to level the opportunities for American workers. (01-147, 01-148)

JOHNSTOWN FLOOD, 1889

Fourteen miles above Johnstown in western Pennsylvania lay Lake Conemaugh, an exclusive private recreational lake created by a dam built across the south fork of the Little Conemaugh River. The dam had long fallen into serious disrepair, and its owners at the time, the wealthy families of the South Fork Fishing and Hunting Club, had increased the threat by raising the water to dangerous levels.

Early in the morning of May 31, 1889, after hours of torrential rains, the lake overwhelmed the spillway at the center of the dam. Weakened, it began to disintegrate. Water spilling over the top ate away at the earth on the face, which released more water that took more dirt, and so on. The dam gave way at 3:10 p.m., and 4.5 billion gallons of water, an inland tidal wave thirty-five feet high, smashed its way down the valley at forty miles per hour, carrying with it everything in its path. Fifty-ton locomotives were snapped up like toys. People on the roofs of houses floated downstream on their way to certain death.

When the torrent reached Johnstown, it slammed into a new stone railroad bridge and got stuck. All the debris then piled up at the bridge. Later that night, the huge pile caught fire and the screams of trapped victims could be heard for hours. A total of 2,209 people were killed, including one man whose body washed up downstream in Ohio. Many saw the tragedy in class terms: the callous disregard of the rich lake owners for the poor people of Johnstown. (05-073, 05-074)

MASSACRE AT
WOUNDED KNEE, 1890

In the cold early morning hours of December 29, 1890, elements of the 7th and 9th United States Cavalry surrounded approximately 350 Miniconjou Sioux led by Big Foot and camped at Wounded Knee, twenty miles from the Pine Ridge Indian Reservation in southwestern South Dakota. Within a brief time, over 150 Sioux had been killed with another 44 wounded; more would later die of exposure. About half the casualties were women and children. Army casualties were not small: over sixty troopers were wounded or killed. The episode made little sense.

By the late 1880s, the Sioux confederation had largely been beaten into submission. The Sioux were starving, disillusioned, and without hope. They found hope in the teachings of a Paiute named Wovoka. This thirty-year-old had a vision in which he promised salvation to American Indians if they would stop fighting, lead a good life, and dance the Ghost Dance. Fearful that this cultic ceremony was a pretext for a general American Indian uprising, whites put pressure on the army to reign in the Sioux. One of the results was the massacre at Wounded Knee.

Public opinion rose against the army's tactics, but the damage to the Sioux was irreversible. (05-119, 05-120)

1700	1750	1800	1850	1900	1950	PRESENT

FLYING WEDGE, 1892

As it emerged in the late nineteenth century, the new American sport of football combined features of English rugby and soccer. From the beginning, football had a reputation for rough, even brutal, competition. In 1890, Boston businessman Lorin F. Deland, a student of Napoleon, thought that if teams would concentrate force they could score spectacularly.

During the Harvard–Yale game in November 1892, the Harvard team was arranged in two lines at 45-degree angles, shaped like a V from the ball toward the sidelines. The ball was given to Art Brewer, who stepped inside the wedge now moving straight toward Yale's Alex Wallis. The lone lineman never had a chance. Three-quarters of a ton of mass momentum blew through the Yale line. Eventually, unified-momentum plays such as the flying wedge had to be outlawed. In 1905 alone, twenty-two players were killed playing college football, but the memory of the almost unstoppable flying wedge is a reminder of football's vigorous adolescence.

(03-135)

1400   1450   1500   1550   1600   1650   1700

JOHN PIERPONT MORGAN BAILS OUT US GOVERNMENT, 1895

Before the Federal Reserve System, many people would only trust paper money if they could go into a bank and convert it to precious metal, gold, or silver. US law required that $100 million of gold be kept in reserve, but by 1895 the reserves were down to less than $50 million. President Grover Cleveland tried to borrow gold from the London-based House of Rothschild, but the Rothschilds feared nativist resentment if it were known that a Jewish banking house was bailing out the United States.

J. P. Morgan, a prominent Wall Street banker, was chosen to put together the loan. At first, he insisted that the loan be for $100 million in gold, but the president would go no higher than $65 million. It took until early 1896 for the loan brokered by Morgan to calm the markets, but it worked. It was sweet loan. Some estimate Morgan and others pocketed $16 million. Morgan's reputation was made. He occupied a preeminent place in US financial circles until his death before the First World War. (02-039)

WILLIAM JENNINGS BRYAN AND THE CROSS OF GOLD, 1896

In 1893, the United States sank into the worst financial depression the nation had yet experienced. Banks failed, and farmers lost their holdings. The burning issue of the campaign of 1896 was money. There were very few banks, and many of them were thought to be shady operations. Even paper money was considered suspect; real money was gold and silver.

Many farmers believed that if more dollars were in circulation, the price of their wheat would go up, and the price of their farm tools would go down. They wanted the government to buy silver and mint more dollars. Whatever the economic value of such an argument, these people believed it, and at the Democratic Convention in Chicago they found a champion, William Jennings Bryan of Nebraska. He thundered, "You shall not press down upon the brow of labor this crown of thorns. You shall not crucify mankind upon a cross of gold." Three times the Democrats nominated Bryan and three times followed him to electoral disaster. They responded to a man whose use of rhetoric and personality have led many scholars to conclude that he was the first modern American politician. (05-103, 05-104)

| 1400 | 1450 | 1500 | 1550 | 1600 | 1650 | 1700 |

GEORGE WASHINGTON CARVER, 1896

In 1896, agricultural scientist George Washington Carver received a unique invitation. Hey had just been appointed to the faculty of Iowa State College—the school's first black faculty member. Carver already had a national reputation in the field of agricultural research. Booker T. Washington asked Carver to come to Alabama to create the agriculture program at Tuskegee Institute. Carver headed south and spent the rest of his life there.

Carver devoted his career to improving the lives of southern sharecroppers, mostly African Americans, many of whom were in debt due to failure of cotton. Between the deterioration of the soil and the boll weevil, life was hard. Carver promoted crop rotation and planting legumes, peas, and peanuts, which infused the soil with nitrogen and helped nurse the ailing soil back to health. Carver developed 325 uses for the peanut, from cooking oil to shampoo. He also developed over a hundred uses for the sweet potato and other plants native to the South. He died in 1943.

(07-076, 07-077)

SOUSA'S GREATEST MARCH, 1896

On May 14, 1897, John Philip Sousa stood at the podium of the Philadelphia Academy of Music, lifted his baton, and began leading his greatest march. Two encores later, the crowd was still on its feet.

Sousa grew up in Washington, DC, around military band music. His father played trombone in the Marine Band. The boy's musical study began at the age of six. Work with voice, violin, piano, flute, cornet, trombone, and the alto horn demonstrated his prodigious ability, and he was soon taking engagements as an orchestral violinist, doing some conducting, and turning out primitive compositions.

In 1880, he became the conductor of the Marine Band and raised it to the highest standards of technical execution and performance. Sousa conducted the president's own, as the band is affectionately known, for Presidents Hayes, Garfield, Arthur, Cleveland, and Harrison. While returning from a European vacation in 1896 on the liner *Teutonic*, he received the inspiration for a new march. Soon he was playing it at every concert. Until his death in 1932, no audience would permit him to leave the stage without playing it. It was the last piece he conducted: "The Stars and Stripes Forever." (04-070)

HOMER PLESSY AND
SEPARATE BUT EQUAL, 1896

Homer A. Plessy was born a month before the Union Navy took New Orleans out of the Civil War in 1862. His parents were free, French-speaking, Roman Catholic blacks, part of a racial and social mix that lent that port city such a rich cosmopolitan flavor. In the years following the end of Reconstruction, the white majority began to reacquire the privilege denied them by a victorious North. Gone were the federal troops that protected and registered black voters. Disappearing also was the consensus in the North that had help forge the Union victory. Weary of war and the expense of Reconstruction, northerners were losing interest in civil rights of blacks.

With no force to deter it, the white-dominated Louisiana legislature passed the Separate Car Act in 1890, decreeing "separate but equal accommodations for the white and colored races on Louisiana railway cars." On June 8, 1892, Homer Plessy refused to remove himself from a white-only passenger car. He was arrested and appealed the ruling of Judge John Howard Ferguson, who upheld the separate but equal doctrine. The appeal slowly wound its way through the federal court system; in the spring of 1896, the US Supreme Court with only a single dissenter upheld the doctrine. Though he lost in his own lifetime, the cause Homer Plessy championed eventually prevailed fifty-eight years later. In 1954 in *Brown v. Board of Education of Topeka, Kansas*, the Supreme Court reversed itself and declared separate but equal facilities to be unconstitutional. (01-182)

| 1700 | 1750 | 1800 | 1850 | 1900 | 1950 | PRESENT |

REVOLUTION IN PARADISE— HAWAII, 1898

In January 1891, David Kalākaua, the last king of the Hawaiians, died while on a trip to California. Toward the end of his life, he was forced by public opinion aroused by influential Americans to surrender many of his personal powers to the legislature by agreeing to what his successor called the "bayonet constitution." Kalākaua was succeeded by his sister Queen Liliuokalani. She was London-educated and highly skeptical of growing American influence in the Islands. Two years later, she set out to dump the "bayonet constitution," restoring the powers of the monarch and the influence of native Hawaiians. They only would be able to vote, and their property would be exempt from taxation.

Opponents formed a Committee of Safety and offered the presidency to native-born Sanford B. Dole. Queen Liliuokalani under protest was forced to abdicate. In summer 1898, the infant Republic of Hawaii became a territory of the United States. Revolution had come to paradise. (01-128)

1400   1450   1500   1550   1600   1650   1700

On September 9, 1900, the people occupying the colorful streets and sandy white beaches of the resort town of Galveston, Texas, were assaulted in the worst natural disaster in US history. A category 4 hurricane with 145-mph winds pushing an overwhelming storm surge inundated Galveston and then turned northeast, doing great damage as far north as Canada.

The night before landfall, waves became stronger; heavy swells pounded the beach where sand dunes had once protected the city. There had been talk of reconstructing the protective seawall, but many were opposed, thinking it would detract from the city's appearance. The following day, some went to the beach as usual. One local said, "For a while, even ladies were wading in the water, thinking it was fun. The children had a great time." The fun ended abruptly when the bathhouse collapsed and people began to flee the pounding waves. Heavy rains pelted the area, wind raged through the streets, and the barometer plunged to a record low.

Soon debris, telephone wires, and bricks were picked up as if by some giant in a temper tantrum. The next day brought an eerie silence to Galveston. It was now mostly rubble. Eight thousand died, most by the effects of the hurricane's storm surge. Water whipped up by the wind slammed into the low-lying town. Galveston pulled together after the Great Hurricane of 1900, and the city was rebuilt. Not surprisingly, one of the first things they constructed was a protective seawall. (06-025, 06-026)

SUSAN BROWNELL ANTHONY, 1906

Susan Anthony was involved in issues of morality during most of her life. Early on, Anthony was a temperance advocate. She became a popular speaker, encouraging restriction on the manufacture and distribution of spirits. She soon added an antislavery message to her standard speech against alcohol. Anthony helped organize the Seneca Falls Convention, which some mark as the beginning of the women's rights movement.

Her experience with discrimination by men against women in the temperance movement concerned her. By the mid-1850s she was barnstorming New York as a vigorous advocate for women's control of their personal belongings, guardianship over their children, equal pay, and the vote.

After the Civil War, Anthony and her friend Elizabeth Cady Stanton expanded their campaign with renewed vigor, and she and Stanton wrote *History of Woman Suffrage* (1901). For the remainder of her life, Susan B. Anthony toured the country, giving lectures on expanded rights for women. She died in 1906, fourteen years before the Nineteenth Amendment to the Constitution realized the dream of her lifetime. (02-067, 02-068)

1400   1450   1500   1550   1600   1650   1700

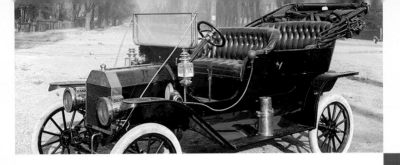

MODEL T, 1908

The Model T Ford was a triumph of engineering and marketing. Through extensive use of light alloy steel and mass production, Ford brought the automobile within the reach of middle-class America. From its introduction in 1908, it was an immediate hit. Because of its large-bore, short-stroke engine, it had enough power to wrench itself out of most mudholes, take the family to town on Saturday in relative style, and still serve as a work vehicle around the farm.

Yet, from the beginning, other manufacturers took the lead in technological innovation. By 1916, most American cars had all-electric starting, ignition, and lighting. Electric starting was not standard on the Model T Ford until 1926. Other companies abandoned the inefficient planetary transmission; Ford held on for years. And until 1925, rear and front tires on the Model T were of different size. At a time when tires had to be changed a lot, drivers had to take two different sets of spares.

Nevertheless, well into the 1920s, the Model T was the best-selling car in America—not through innovation designed to make driving more pleasant, but by dropping the price. In 1908, the runabout cost $825. In 1927, it cost $260. (04-057, 04-058)

SAGA OF LEO FRANK I, 1913

Leo Frank came to Atlanta from New York in the years after the Civil War to open the National Pencil Company. He was an outsider—a Yankee—but most of all Leo Frank was a Jew. On April 26, 1913, Mary Phagan, one of his employees, stopped by Frank's factory to collect her paycheck. She was brutally murdered—choked with her undergarments, with her skull crushed. When asked to identify the body, Frank appeared suspiciously nervous. The police, already under fire for a series of unsolved Atlanta murders, focused on Frank. Two days later he was arrested.

Newspapers fed the rumor mill. Visions of Jewish men taking advantage of gentile girls whipped the public into a frenzy. Four weeks later, the grand jury gave Solicitor General Hugh Dorsey the indictment he sought, but he failed to mention there was another suspect. Jim Conley, a black janitor from the factory, had been seen washing blood from a shirt soon after the murder and admitted writing two nearly unintelligible notes found near the body, which attempted to shift the blame. (03-168, 03-169, 03-0170)

1400   1450   1500   1550   1600   1650   1700

The trial of Leo Frank began at the end of July 1913. Prosecutors based their case almost completely on the testimony of black janitor Jim Conley, who was clearly guilty but who knew that if Frank was acquitted, he was next in line. The irony is that during this era no white, Christian southerner would have been indicted, much less convicted, on the testimony of a black man, but Frank was a Jew. In an era of rampant anti-Semitism, that changed the equation.

On appeal, Governor Slaton commuted Frank's sentence, but tensions were running high, and eventually a lynch mob got to Frank out at the prison farm in Marietta. None of the lynching party was even arrested, though their identities were widely known. In 1986, Georgia pardoned Leo Frank, not because he was judged innocent, but for the technical reason that the state had abridged his civil rights by failing to prevent his lynching. His case was a fascinating snapshot of race and religious sentiment in early twentieth-century America. (03-168, 03-169, 03-0170)

HENRY FORD AND THE $5 WORKDAY

Despite a new factory, new machines, and carefully planned efficiency programs, Henry Ford still had problem: turnover. The pay was low, and men had little incentive to stick around. In 1914, 963 men had to be hired for each one hundred jobs in the plant. With orders for 100,000 cars he could not fill, Ford and his associates met to come up with a solution. First, he expanded the workday. For a half century, workers had been agitating for an eight-hour day. Ford divided the day into equal parts: three eight-hour shifts.

The addition of another shift meant Ford needed 5,000 more workers. One of the managers suggested that the company share its profits year-round. Ford started paying $5 a day, an unheard of salary for regular work. The resulting flood of job seekers meant Ford could pick and choose the best.

Ford workers at last had a decent living, but the program had a downside. Ford's goal was a quiet, docile, obedient, sober, and sup-posedly happy workforce. He established a sociology department that investigated his workers lives, marriages, drinking habits, and finances. Ironically, women, who were prevented from working the assembly line because of the notion that they might be absent too much, were not included in the $5 a day program. They were usually stable, good workers, and unlikely to drink and miss work, thereford Ford saw no need to offer them work with a huge daily salary. (01-199, 01-200)

| 1400 | 1450 | 1500 | 1550 | 1600 | 1650 | 1700 |

BE BLAKMAN ORTER
EDDIKATED
HE KIN VOTE AFORE
US WITES.
WITH
MR. SOLID SOUT

EDUCATION UNDER JIM CROW

Gradually, the South began to climb out of the devastation of the Civil War. By 1900, even public education was making progress, but that was only for white students.

Educational philanthropic foundations such the Peabody Fund, the Slater Fund, and the General Education Board had made some progress in jump-starting public education in the South. They offered challenge grants to communities willing to commit resources to the construction and maintenance of public schools, but these were white schools. It was the era of Jim Crow, and white political leaders were in the business of suppressing the aspirations of black Americans. Schools that elevated their status hardly fit into the plan.

From 1910 to 1925, Julius Rosenwald was president of Sears, Roebuck and Company, the giant catalog retailer. He was also a trustee of Tuskegee Institute, and in the years before World War I, Tuskegee President Booker T. Washington convinced him to give money for the construction of several black schools in rural Alabama. In 1917, he created the Rosenwald Fund to encourage black education, but private money began to dry up during the Great Depression. African Americans then turned to the federal government and courts to get their children's education being denied them by white-dominated state and local governments.

(07-088, 07-089)

FLU EPIDEMIC OF 1918

Experts believe the flu virus makes is way through the air to its victim's respiratory system. It is a swift, clever, and sometimes deadly agent, a survivor of great tenacity. Influenza requires little more than a population weakened by hunger, disease, or war to transform itself from a localized irritant to an epidemic of global proportions. After four years of almost continuous conflict, the nations of the world were exhausted. In addition to nearly 10 million soldiers killed in combat and over twice as many wounded, civilian casualties due to submarine warfare, bombing, dislocation, and famine were enormous. In 1918, the world was ripe for the picking.

In March 1918 at US Army Camp Funston in Kansas, the first troops came down with the symptoms of flu. By April, the American soldiers had spread it to Europe. By July, the flu pandemic had moved into Poland. Outbreaks of the disease occurred all over the world, spreading along transportation arteries out of ports and from city to city. By the end of 1919, over 20 million people had died from this the so-called Spanish Influenza—or, more accurately, the American Flu—including a half million Americans.

(03-144, 03-145)

1400   1450   1500   1550   1600   1650   1700

WILSON AND THE LEAGUE OF NATIONS, 1919

To secure support for the treaty ending World War I and the League of Nations—for him its most important provision—President Woodrow Wilson had to overcome resistance in the United States Senate.

In the Senate, the chief strategist of the resistance was Massachusetts Senator Henry Cabot Lodge. Lodge felt the president was a dangerous radical and nursed a personal animosity that made it impossible for him to cooperate with Wilson. He first employed delaying tactics, hoping that enthusiasm for the treaty would wane. Then he offered a series of amendments (the Lodge reservations) that would require Congressional approval before the United States could be forced to go along with League decisions.

Wilson, frustrated over Senate resistance, began a national speaking tour to whip up support for League, but on September 25, 1919, in Pueblo, Colorado, the president suffered a nervous collapse. For seven vital months, he lived in seclusion. The treaty came up for a vote twice during that period. Each time, Wilson, perhaps with his normal reluctance to compromise exacerbated by his illness, refused to allow his supporters to vote for the treaty with what he considered Lodge's overly restrictive reservations. The Senate rejected it both times. (02-219, 02-220)

THE PALMER RAIDS, 1919

In June 1919, the house of US Attorney General A. Mitchell Palmer was bombed. In the wake of the Mitchell bombing, a wave of anti-immigrant fever spread across this country of immigrants. Palmer assigned twenty-four-year-old former librarian J. Edgar Hoover with the task of keeping up with radical movements. Hoover began cataloging radical individuals and groups to prepare for government action against them. The problem was that there was no federal law making it a crime to be a socialist, communist, or radical.

Using Hoover's documentation, Attorney General Palmer conducted a series of raids in late 1919, arresting radical and communist leaders in twelve cities around the country. They seized literature, books, papers, and membership lists. The arrested radicals were often roughed up and denied access to lawyers.

The government's aggressive tactics produced public revulsion and backlash against the campaign's anti-immigrant orientation. But when the immigrant hostility and backlash were over, J. Edgar Hoover's career had become firmly established. He was soon chosen to head the Bureau of Investigation, the predecessor of the FBI. For more than forty-seven years, he led the agency and continued to amass data on persons he thought threatened national security—and on many individuals about whom he was simply curious. (02-043, 02-044)

BLACK SOX SCANDAL, 1919

In 1919, the Chicago White Sox was one of the finest teams in the history of baseball. In left field was Joe Jackson, one of the game's great hitters. On the mound was spitball specialist Eddie Cicotte. Although favored to win the World Series, the White Sox lost to Cincinnati, in one of baseball's most sensational reverses.

Rumors flew for a year, finally reaching the ear of Charles A. McDonald, Cook County Chief Justice. He convened a grand jury. In September 1920, it indicted eight players.

Apparently, in September 1919, Cicotte met Philadelphia gambler Billy Maharg in a New York hotel room. The price was $100,000 to throw the series, but the plan began to fall apart almost immediately. This crew was incredibly talented, but not that smart. Their poor performance was transparently obvious. An enlivened Cincinnati team won the series 5–3. Despite their later acquittal for lack of evidence, the eight players were banished for life from the major leagues. Desperate to restore its damaged reputation, baseball appointed a powerful commissioner. Judge Kenesaw Mountain Landis ruled the sport with an iron hand for two decades. (04-033, 04-034)

BOOKER T. WASHINGTON
VS. W. E. B. DU BOIS, 1920

At the Cotton States Exposition in Atlanta (1895), ex-slave Booker T. Washington outlined for a multiracial crowd a program for economic and racial progress. He decried racial antagonism. Whites should moderate their hostility and use blacks to get rich. Blacks should temper their quest for social and political equality and concentrate on economic progress. Not unexpectedly, the white establishment, North and South, hailed Washington's program. Honors, invitations to speak, and support for his creation, the Tuskegee Institute, multiplied, but his program of accommodation was not supported by all.

Chief among Washington's critics was W. E. Burghardt Du Bois. Born a child of blacks free for generations in Massachusetts, Du Bois lacked experience with overt racial prejudice until later in life. He studied at Fisk University and the University of Berlin in Germany, and he held a PhD from Harvard. He felt that Washington was calling for accommodation just at the point that the growth of Jim Crow laws was crushing civil rights for blacks. Industrial education caused funds to be drawn away from black academic education. He advocated that "a talented tenth" must have advanced education or African Americans would be relegated to second-class intellectual status. In hindsight, it seems that Washington's call for accommodation was a distasteful compromise with white supremacy. Yet, his call for concentration on economic gains might also be seen as legitimate strategy for a people under siege, waiting for a brighter future in which to mount another campaign for equality. (04-033)

1400   1450   1500   1550   1600   1650   1700

TEAPOT DOME SCANDAL, 1922

In 1920, voters elected as president an Ohio newspaperman-turned-politician, Senator Warren Harding. Inexperienced in high executive office, Harding formed personal attachments he was deeply reluctant to break. His worst appointments were Interior Secretary Albert B. Fall and Director of Veterans Affairs Charles Forbes. Forbes charmed the future president during a poker game in Hawaii when the two first met during Senator Harding's inspection tour. He was soon deeply discounting government medical supplies to contractors for a cut. President Harding finally confronted Forbes, shook him "like a dog would a rat," and obscenely demanded his resignation. Forbes left the country.

In that era, the US Navy ran ships on oil, often taken from government land. To protect these reserves, Navy oil was legally pumped out and resold to the government for storage. Albert Fall in spring 1922 began giving private oil leases in exchange for cash, interest-free loans, and bonds. The Wyoming reserves, on property called Teapot Dome because of the unique shape of the huge oil cavity, were made available to Harry Sinclair of Mammoth Oil Company. Rumors of the deal had circulated for months, but the president could not believe his poker buddy was a crook. Significantly, shortly after he issued the private leases to Sinclair, Fall's ranch in New Mexico doubled in size and acquired a new hydroelectric dam.

Harding died on a tour of the West in 1923, perhaps, as much as anything else, broken by his friends' faithlessness. Both Fall and Sinclair denied everything, but they went to jail. Until the modern era, the Harding administration was considered the most scandal-plagued in American history. (02-023, 02-024, 02-025)

Sui funerei silenziamenti della reazione sorge
e matura l'uragano plebeo che lava ed espia

La persecuzione non placa il rancore dei re-
ietti, ma irrobustisce ed accelera il ritmo delle

SACCO AND VANZETTI, 1923

On April 15, 1920, F. A. Parmenter, paymaster of a shoe factory in South Braintree, Massachusetts, and his twenty-eight-year-old security guard, Alessandro Berardelli, were robbed and murdered during a routine transfer of payroll funds. Nicola Sacco and Bartolomeo Vanzetti were arrested, tried, convicted, and eventually executed for the crime.

The 1920s were a time of great change for Americans. The certainties of religion, patriotism, and family values were perceived as under heavy attack from all quarters. The First World War had also unleashed powerful new ideologies that were thought to threaten the very survival of democracy. Communism had taken root in Russia, but even more menacing was anarchism, whose followers advocated the destruction of all political, economic, and religious authority. Sacco and Vanzetti both subscribed to an anarchist publication.

When brought to trial, evidence against them was largely circumstantial. Their attorneys mounted a largely incompetent defense. Judge Webster Thayer was clearly prejudiced in favor of the prosecution. There was contradictory testimony, and no witness to the event. In 1925, another felon confessed to the crime, but Judge Thayer denied the pair's appeal for a retrial. For years, thoughtful observers have considered this a travesty of justice, a snapshot of a nation coming to grips with a changing world. (05-043, 05-044, 05-045)

"RHAPSODY IN BLUE" – GEORGE GERSHWIN, 1924

At the age of fifteen, Jacob, the son of Rose and Morris Gershovitz, dropped out of high school to work in tin-pan alley as a piano-playing song plugger. Actually, Jacob's brother Ira was supposed to be the family musician, but Jacob, who later took the name George Gershwin, took over the house piano. In 1919, he wrote a couple of songs for the *Capitol Review*, one with a lyric by Irving Caesar that received little notice until Al Jolson used it in his new show *Sinbad*. "Swanee" was an extraordinary success. Gershwin began turning out a series of high-quality Broadway musicals: *Oh, Kay, Strike Up the Band*; *Girl Crazy*; and *Of Thee I Sing*, the first musical to win a Pulitzer Prize in Drama. In *Lady, Be Good*, George and lyricist brother Ira Gershwin, instead of simply inserting a group of unrelated songs into the story, made the music an integral part of character and plot development.

On February 12, 1924, at Aeolian Hall in New York City, Gershwin debuted a work of classical jazz, "Rhapsody in Blue," an immediate success. Gershwin's music was sophisticated and risky. His form, structure, and syncopated rhythms eluded conventional categories. By the time he produced *Porgy and Bess* in 1935, he was helping to expand the boundaries of music with new, exuberant, completely American, wholly Gershwin music.

George Gershwin died out of time after a brain tumor operation at the age of thirty-seven. (05-001, 05-002)

SCOPES'S MONKEY TRIAL, 1925

In May 1925, John Thomas Scopes, a popular biology teacher, was invited to Fred Robinson's drugstore in Dayton, Tennessee. There, several town citizens suggested he challenge the Butler Act, which made teaching any theory about human origins deemed contrary to the Bible illegal. The two sides recruited prominent lawyers for the defense and prosecution, so the trial would be no footnote.

The two lawyers, friends and progressives, represented divergent approaches to life, religion, and law. William Jennings Bryan had been nominated for president by the Democrats. A dynamic speaker and former secretary of state, he was a Protestant fundamentalist very popular with small-town people who valued his stand against urban industrial change. Clarence Darrow had defended labor leaders and people on the fringe. A religious skeptic inclined toward socialism, Darrow vigorously supported progress and believed in evolution.

The trial, begun on a steamy July 10, was a media circus. Reporters, the curious, and ideologues of all types descended on the little mining town. From the beginning, the fix was in. The judge ruled the Butler Act constitutional. The only question was whether Scopes had violated the law. Bryan spent most of his

1400   1450   1500   1550   1600   1650   1700

time denouncing life without God. Denied the opportunity to defend evolution, Darrow called Bryan to the stand as a Bible expert. Under intense questioning, Bryan's scripture knowledge was exposed as shallow. He even admitted he was unsure how long days of creation lasted, twenty-four hours or millions of years; the literalist considered modern interpretation. Scopes was fined, but his conviction was overturned on appeal. Humiliated, Bryan died within a week. The Scopes trial was an early marker in America's continuing culture wars. (02-030, 02-031, 02-032)

EUGENICS, 1925

Sir Francis Galton (1822–1911) confessed to having had a happy childhood. His upper-class parents gave him a Cambridge education and left him sufficient inherited funds to indulge his great love of travel. From 1845 to 1853, Galton explored parts of the Middle East and Africa, but he is best known for advocating selective parenting, a process he called eugenics. He was a cousin of Charles Darwin and suggested that, just as species of plants and animals had been improved through selective breeding for centuries, humanity could be improved if parents would seek partners of superior intellect, ability, and strength. Galton's upper-class British prejudices have opened him to the charge of racism, but his interests focused primarily on improving the entire human race rather than a racial subdivision.

Problematically, eugenics focused primarily on inborn characteristics and almost completely disregarded social, environmental, educational, and physical factors. If society is to improve itself, according to the theory, it must eliminate genetic threats to racial purity. In the sad history of eugenics, many groups have been singled out for elimination: the mentally ill, habitual criminals, sexual predators, blacks, Native Americans, and any nonwhite people. Jews, gypsies, and even evangelical Christians failed to make the eugenic cut.

Beginning in 1926, the American Eugenics Society advanced the notion that the white race was superior to all others and that the Nordic race was superior to any other white grouping. It was not a gigantic leap from such repulsive racial and genetic profiling to the gas ovens of Auschwitz. (10-007, 10-008)

| 1400 | 1450 | 1500 | 1550 | 1600 | 1650 | 1700 |

COURT-MARTIAL OF
BILLY MITCHELL, 1925

In the 1920s, the US military was hampered by severe budget cutbacks and a debate on the airplane's future. One persistent and prophetic voice belonged to Brigadier William "Billy" Mitchell. His father and grandfather were congressmen, so he grew up around power and expected people to listen when he spoke. His confrontational—even hectoring—style, his unwillingness to defer to higher authority, and his increasing tendency to publicly mock perceived military incompetence made him many enemies.

Mitchell's experience as head of army air combat forces in Europe during World War I led him to conclude the warplane was key to victory in future conflicts, and he crusaded for that idea. He was particularly adept at using the press to further his ideas. He arranged a series of highly publicized tests in which his bombers spectacularly sank several surplus battleships, thus proving their vulnerability and increasing obsolescence.

Mitchell had many supporters, but his style won him disdain of others who considered him insubordinate and a source of embarrassment; among those was President Calvin Coolidge. When demotion and banishment to an obscure post in San Antonio failed to quiet him, in 1925 he was brought up on charges of "bringing discredit on the military service." He was found guilty, suspended from duty and pay. He resigned and until his death in 1936 promoted his ideas about the airplane, which proved to be all too accurate. Likewise, his warnings of the growing Japanese threat in the Pacific were accurate, and fatally so. (11-039, 11-040)

FOOD AND DRUG ADMINISTRATION, 1927

Until the twentieth century, most people in the United States grew up on farms or in the small towns of rural America. Most of the food or medical remedies there consumed were prepared and concocted at home or bought close to home. If you did not make your own, you usually knew the person who did make it. Food was raised or cured fresh and either eaten on the spot, canned for the basement, or stored in the smokehouse. Home remedies were fashioned from herbs and roots from adjacent fields. Neighborliness, community discipline, and face-to-face bargaining usually prevented outright fraud.

The coming of industrialization transformed American society. Working in factories and living in large cities, the growing number of urban consumers found themselves personally disconnected from the source of the prepared and canned foods becoming staples of their diet. Not surprisingly, unhealthy and dishonest practices in manufacturing, packaging, and long-distance shipping of medicine and food provoked increasing public pressure for reform.

Spurred by this pressure and muckraking exposes such as *The Jungle*, Upton Sinclair's pungent novel about the Chicago meatpacking industry, Congress passed the Pure Food and Drugs Bill. This and several similar laws were consolidated and assigned for enforcement under the Food and Drug Administration established in 1927. Today, the FDA is the nation's first line of protection against fraudulent and deceptive product labeling and contaminated food and ensures the correct development and appropriate use of prescription drugs. (09-040)

MAKING PICTURES TALK, 1927

Twelve years after recording his own voice reading "Mary Had a Little Lamb" on a wax cylinder in 1877, Thomas Alva Edison tackled recording and reproducing moving photographs. In 1894, Edison unveiled the kinetoscope, enabling patrons to see minute-long silent film loops of boxing matches and performers like Buffalo Bill and Annie Oakley.

1400   1450   1500   1550   1600   1650   1700

Eventually, sound and moving photography combined in the motion picture, but not without great difficulty. Edison solved the first problem, getting still pictures to move. Others would solve the second problem, synchronization. Without synchronization, the audience would see the mouth move and hear the word several seconds later or vice versa. By 1910, Alexander Graham Bell's telephone showed sound could be converted into an electric signal. Then Lee de Forest developed the audion, a vacuum tube that amplified and manipulated recorded sound. By 1920, processed by his audion, light was shone through a slit and recorded on film at the right time; therefore, speaking lips matched spoken words.

In the early 1920s, Sam Warner and later his brother Harry, of the small studio Warner Brothers, worked with Western Electric to develop the vitaphone, a synchronized phonograph and camera with one motor driving both. The first vitaphone film, *Don Juan*, premiered on August 6, 1926, featuring silent film star John Barrymore. The film had sound effects and a musical score; synchronized dialogue would not arrive for another year. *The Jazz Singer*, starring Al Jolson, was the first film to integrate synchronized dialogue and music with the story line. Eventually, a sound-on-film process similar to that developed by de Forest replaced the vitaphone. Movies had found their voice. (02-098, 02-099)

CAUSES OF THE GREAT
DEPRESSION I, 1929

Harry Truman once complained that what the world needed was a one-handed economist: "On one hand . . . and then on the other." During the decade of the 1920s, the United States enjoyed unprecedented prosperity, but little-understood economic weaknesses set the stage for the Great Depression of the 1930s.

Any economic phenomenon is complex and resists simple description, but economists have settled on a few highly significant factors that led to this long period of economic contraction and social distress, discussed here and in the next two sections.

FACTOR #1: OVERPRODUCTION
AND UNDERCONSUMPTION

During the 1920s, modern laborsaving machinery greatly increased the manufacturing output of factories and resulted in an oversupply of goods. Factory output had increased 43 percent during the decade, but workers' real wages had poked along at an increase of only 11 percent. Little of the tremendous economic boom went into the hands of the workers who were making it possible. Most benefits from increased productivity went into plant expansion, corporate profits, and stock dividends. (08-055, 08-056, 08-057)

| 1400 | 1450 | 1500 | 1550 | 1600 | 1650 | 1700 |

CAUSES OF THE GREAT
DEPRESSION II, 1929

FACTOR #2: TREMENDOUS INCOME GAP
BETWEEN WEALTHY AND WORKING CLASS

Among those who did not prosper in during the 1920s were farmers. After World War I, the demand for grain and other agricultural products abruptly declined. Having mortgaged their farms to buy modern agricultural equipment, farmers were able to turn out huge surpluses. Farm prices dropped 40 percent between 1920 and 1921. This agricultural slump continued throughout the 1920s. The inability of farmers to pay off their debts led to bank failures. Farmers, who still constituted a large part of the population, slowly lost their purchasing power, which compounded the problem factory workers were facing.

In America, the annual income of the top 30,000 families was equal to the income of the bottom 11 million families. Lower and middle classes could not buy goods and services fast enough or in quantities great enough to support the ever-expanding industrial base. For a while, they bought on credit. Installment plans seemed to make it possible for millions of people to enjoy the good life, but gradually they stopped spending to hold down their debts. Contraction in spending lowered demand for new goods, which slowed down business. In 1929, the house of cards collapsed. Then came the killer tariff. (08-055, 08-056, 08-057)

CAUSES OF THE GREAT DEPRESSION III—THE KILLER TARIFF, 1930

Taxes on imported or exported goods have been around for a long time. Governments have not only always raised money with tariffs but also used them to protect native industries from foreign competition.

FACTOR #3: TARIFFS

In 1922, the United States Congress, fearing a flood of European imports after the war, passed the Fordney–McCumber Tariff Act, which raised taxes on agricultural and foreign-made goods, to protect US farmers and businesses. It helped neither.

In 1930, working with President Hoover, Congress passed the Smoot–Hawley Tariff—the killer tariff. This draconian legislation placed a duty as high as 50 percent on some goods coming into the country. A thousand economists signed a petition urging that Congress not pass Smoot–Hawley, but one should never expect a politician to consider consequences when faced with an easy solution. It passed. It was a disaster.

Other nations responded by imposing tariffs on US goods. The resulting trade war hammered the United States deeper and deeper into the Depression. European nations, already devastated by years of war and further weakened by debts and reparations, began experiencing economic and political disintegration. Tariff-driven policies virtually destroyed world trade for nearly a decade—and in the case of Germany, helped bring on World War II.

The ill-advised tariffs, together with the other factors, led to catastrophe. The signal came on October 24, 1929, when the New York Stock Exchange fell faster and further than ever before. Except for occasional brief upturns, not until World War II did the United States emerge from the Great Depression. (01-025)

AL CAPONE AND THE ST. VALENTINE'S DAY MASSACRE, 1929

New England puritans came to Massachusetts in the 1620s searching for a place to worship and build a godly society. These two often conflicting goals, freedom and societal godliness, have profoundly influenced the way America has developed. By the middle of 1800s, a highly vocal segment of American Protestantism had concluded that liquor must be eradicated. In 1920, the Eighteenth Amendment to the Constitution, or Prohibition, began to restrict the flow of liquor. Prohibition advocates failed to reckon with the law of unintended consequences. Not only did Prohibition fail, ultimately increasing the consumption of liquor, but also it created an underclass of criminal entrepreneurs such as Al Capone willing to supply liquor illegally.

Capone began his career in New York working with John Torrio. By 1925, they moved to Chicago where they supplied Chicago's eager and thirsty public with liquor, gambling, and prostitution. After Torrio's retirement, Capone set out to take over the whole city. His biggest impediment was George "Bugs" Moran. On St. Valentine's Day, 1929, Capone's men allegedly murdered seven members of Moran's gang, thus securing Capone's control over Chicago.

Eventually, Capone was convicted of income tax evasion in 1931 and served part of his eleven-year sentence. By the time of his release, he was in the advanced stages of neurosyphilis, having contracted the disease as teenager in a gangland brothel. He spent his last years at his Miami estate. In late January 1947, Alphonse Capone had a stroke then contracted pneumonia. On January 25, he died of cardiac arrest. (04-011, 04-012, 04-013)

BABE RUTH—SULTAN OF SWAT, 1932

George Herman Ruth Jr. was born the son of a Baltimore saloonkeeper in 1895. Even as a child, he was loud, brash, and pushy. He was such trouble that his parents finally sent him to St. Mary's School, part reform school for boys. The students there excelled mostly in baseball, and Ruth could catch, pitch, and hit.

He was so good he caught the attention of the Baltimore Orioles, then a minor-league team. They signed him, and in his first outing at spring training, Ruth hit a home run. He was known as Babe, called that by his fellow players because of his youth. In two decades of professional baseball, Ruth set record after record, many of which stood for decades.

One famous incident was the "called shot." By 1932, time was taking its toll on the Yankee slugger. In the World Series against Chicago, he played every game. The Cub fans and players were taunting the Babe when he came to bat in Game Three. Legend has it that he stared the crowd down and pointed to a spot in the center-field stands, and promising to hit the ball there. It was typical Ruth bravado, but it worked; that was the longest home run at Wrigley Field to that point. He probably didn't actually point, but as he rounded the bases he said to himself, "You lucky bum, you lucky, lucky bum." Ruth retired after a disappointing final year with the Boston Braves in 1935. He died in 1948. (02-105, 02-106)

HYBRID SEED CORN, 1933

Corn, native to the Americas, is today exceeded only by marijuana as the number one cash crop in the United States, with a value over $23 billion per year. Most is grown in the Corn Belt—Iowa, Ohio, Illinois, Indiana, Missouri, Kansas, and Nebraska. The United States grows half the world's crop, with most of that going to feed livestock. Until hybrid seed corn was commercially available beginning in 1933, most varieties of corn grown were inbred, self-pollinated, and weak, with low yields. Hybridization was a long time coming.

In 1812, Pennsylvania farmer John Lorain pioneered advanced corn breeding by crossing dent corn and flint corn. He discovered that such yielded a dramatic increase in bushels per acre. In 1876, Charles Darwin, best known for his theory of evolution, published his findings of how inbred lines of plants were often weak, but vigor could be restored through cross-breeding.

Most of the corn grown in the United States today is first generation grown from seeds produced by crossing carefully selected unrelated parent stocks. The yield of hybrid corn is 25–30 percent higher than inbred corn. Hybrids are better yielding, more resistant to disease, and more vigorous, but each generation must be bred anew. Through hybridization and improved agricultural practices, corn production in the United States tripled during the second half of the twentieth century. (07-051)

CIVILIAN CONSERVATION CORPS—
BUILDING DURABILITY, 1933

Unemployment, hunger, fear—America was in the grips of the Great Depression. In record time, the new Roosevelt administration created the Civilian Conservation Corps (CCC).

The Corps was designed to put many young men with bleak employment prospects to work on public improvement projects. By July 1933, nearly 300,000 men worked in 1,300 camps. Qualifications were that a man must be between seventeen and twenty-eight years old, single, without a job, in good physical condition, and in need. All participants were volunteers and signed up for a minimum of six months. The men were paid $30 per month, with most of it sent home to their families. In its nine years of existence, nearly 3 million served in the Corps.

The camps were primitive. Usually they consisted of a recreation hall, mess hall, several long barracks, and nearby latrines and bathhouses. Some of the jobs were ordinary road construction, but others were unusual. The masonry dam and bridge near Crossville, Tennessee, has the appearance of a Roman aqueduct. A state-park amphitheater in California has several stones weighing over two tons scattered throughout its graceful rows.

Many Americans considered the CCC a make-work scheme bordering on socialism, but for those involved, the Corps provided a hand up in perilous times. In many areas of the country, it provided public improvements that remain to this day an important part of the nation's infrastructure. The legacy of the Civilian Conservation Corps is a collection of well-constructed bridges, watercourses, buildings, roads, and conservation and renewal projects built to last. (02-116)

TENNESSEE VALLEY AUTHORITY, 1933

The Tennessee River, covering the heartland of southern America, meanders through seven states and from ancient times has brought riches, topsoil, and a steady supply of fresh mountain water to the area. But the river also brought the curse of severe periodic flooding. Navigation to the upper river was blocked by a series of sandbars and rapids at Muscle Shoals, Alabama. As early as 1824, John C. Calhoun proposed to President James Monroe that the blockage at Muscle Shoals be removed. Attempts to win support for improvements on the Tennessee were unsuccessful, until Franklin D. Roosevelt brought together a determined coalition of progressive Republicans and southern Democrats, who devised a massive plan for the uplift of states along the 650-mile river. The Tennessee Valley Authority (TVA) drew great resistance but is one of FDR's greatest achievements.

First, 75,000 men were put to work reforesting the hillsides all along the Tennessee and its tributaries. Soil erosion had blighted the region. Then, the blockage at Muscle Shoals was cleared, enabling barge traffic to the upper reaches of the valley. Next, dams were built to create flood-control basins in the river's watershed. Then, power plants used the water behind those dams to generate cheap electricity for homes and farms, but more importantly the presence of power helped attract industry to an area that had hardly recovered from Civil War destruction. (04-042, 04-043)

The enormous potential for aviation was compromised by the inability to fly at night and during bad weather. Often, aviators would become disoriented, lose control of their aircraft, and crash, more often than not with fatal consequences.

The solution would require pilots to suspend reliance on their own senses and trust the readings of a whole new class of instruments based on the gyroscope. Invented in the nineteenth century and used primarily at sea, the gyroscope, like a spinning top, holds the same position no matter how its supporting structure moves.

The Sperry family of inventors first developed a gyroscopic turn indicator. With unvarying accuracy, the instrument would tell the unbelieving pilot that the plane was turning in the middle of a cloud. On his record-breaking solo flight to Paris in 1927, Charles Lindbergh twice started to fall off into a spin; both times, he trusted his turn indicator and recovered.

Test pilot and future war hero James H. Doolittle, working with the Sperry Corporation, helped develop an artificial horizon that showed the pilot his correct position relative to the ground and a gyroscopic compass that helped determine the direction of flight. Finally, in 1933, the first reliable autopilot was installed in Wiley Post's Lockheed Vega *Winnie Mae* and helped him complete the first solo round-the-world flight in eight days. (02-127)

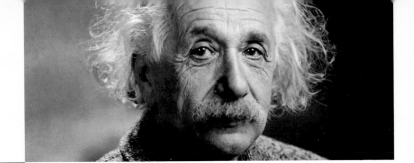

ALBERT EINSTEIN, 1935

Born in 1879, Albert Einstein, though fascinated with mathematics and science, showed no particular academic gift early on in his German schools. He did study music and became a more-than-competent violinist. After completing his education, he became an examiner in the Swiss patent office in Bern. In 1905, he published a series of scholarly articles, one of which he began as a teenager. The articles' content was later expressed mathematically as the Special Theory of Relativity: energy within a piece of matter is equal to the mass of the matter, multiplied by the speed of light, squared: $E=mc^2$.

His work challenged classical physics as described by Isaac Newton and denied that gravitation was a force. Rather, Einstein said, it is a curved field created by the presence of matter and could be confirmed by measuring starlight as it passed the sun on the way to the earth during a total solar eclipse. In 1919, a group of British astronomers confirmed Einstein's calculations.

Soon, Einstein was a household name. Few understood his ideas, which added to his mystery and charisma. In the wake of Adolf Hitler's electoral victory, he left Germany and became one of the early scholars at the Institute of Advanced Study in Princeton, New Jersey. His letter to President Roosevelt describing atomic research helped set in motion the process leading to the first nuclear weapon. (03-045, 03-046, 03-047)

SOCIAL SECURITY, 1935

Following the stock market crash in late 1929, the economy of the United States contracted by almost 50 percent. Unemployment soared to unprecedented levels, and radical demands for relief began to counterbalance traditional American reluctance to go on welfare. Townsendites, technocrats, Huey Long, and Father Coughlin were advancing very radical schemes for the time.

Franklin Delano Roosevelt, in his second year as president and with his carefully tuned political receptors, needed a dramatic move to ward off those ideas. He commissioned a task force, led by Labor Secretary Frances Perkins, to devise a system of general relief. They chose as a model the European concept of social insurance. First adopted in imperial Germany at the urging of Chancellor Otto von Bismarck in the 1880s, social insurance meant that society was responsible for organizing the relief structure. Workers and employers would pay for it through a payroll tax. The plan would be governed according to accepted business practices driven by actuarial tables and would insure people against defined risk.

Social Security, contrary to the assertion of its Republican critics, was not the end of the American way of life. It was a very conservative response to what Roosevelt called "crackpot ideas" arising from the public's demand for relief from economic devastation, unemployment, and disability. The system was signed into law in August 1935. The first monthly retirement check was issued to Ida May Fuller of Ludlow, Vermont, on January 31, 1940, in the amount of $22.54. (08-002, 08-003)

DILLINGER AND HOOVER, 1935

John Herbert Dillinger, raised on a farm in Mooresville, Indiana, was perhaps America's most famous bank robber. After a turn in the Navy, from which he deserted, Dillinger was caught after a botched holdup and served eight years in various state prisons. While incarcerated, he learned the craft of bank robbery from professionals and shortly after his release began a reign of bank heists—five in four months. Captured, Dillinger escaped twice and eluded the FBI twice more. But he was finally betrayed by a lady friend and was shot on the street outside the Biograph Theater in Chicago on July 22, 1934.

FBI Director John Edgar Hoover used Dillinger to create favorable publicity for the FBI and for himself. Over the years, he transformed the agency. Agents were recruited on the basis of merit, the world's largest fingerprint file assisted in catching criminals, the FBI labs provided world-class forensic assistance, and the FBI Academy trained top cops from around the country. Yet, Hoover had a dark side. He had an obsession with radical groups and pursued them with only token regard for First Amendment rights. (09-021, 09-022)

1400   1450   1500   1550   1600   1650   1700

FDR AND THE COURT-PACKING PLAN, 1937

During the Depression, Franklin Roosevelt and his allies in Congress passed a series of laws they hoped would ease the suffering gripping the country. Soon, powerful corporations and well-entrenched special interests brought suit to undo these laws. One New Deal law after another fell under the judicial ax of a Supreme Court majority deeply skeptical of Roosevelt's expansive view of federal power. Between 1789 and 1865, the court had declared only two acts of Congress unconstitutional. Between 1934 and 1936 it had struck down thirteen.

President Roosevelt began to consider how he might circumvent the "nine old men" on the court. Three months after his enormous landslide in November 1936, Roosevelt brought a plan to Congress, probably his most serious political error as president. The political reaction was swift and negative.

His plan was to add an additional judge to every federal bench whenever a judge reached the age of seventy and failed to retire. That way, he could appoint up to six new Supreme Court justices who would vote his way. By the summer of 1937, Roosevelt had to admit that he was attempting "to save the court from itself."

Actually, the court was beginning to save itself. Probably under pressure from the election and the court-packing plan, the justices began to uphold Roosevelt's New Deal laws, provoking the famous appellation, "a switch in time saves nine." Soon, through death and retirement, Roosevelt was appointing his own, more sympathetic, "nine old men." (02-010, 02-011, 02-012, 02-013)

CRASH OF THE *HINDENBURG*, 1937

The success of the Wright brothers proved the feasibility of heavier-than-air craft. They were relatively small and fast but could not carry heavy loads. The German military had begun to combine the lifting power of balloons with the forward motion of airplanes. Giant sealed bags of gas were placed inside a rigid metal frame, aircraft engines were attached, and fairly large loads could be carried over long distances. The ideal lifting substance was helium, but the United States controlled the source and means of production of most of the world's helium supplies. It was not about to help Germany send aloft a fleet of bomber dirigibles. Therefore, the Germans had to use highly flammable hydrogen.

The pride of the German airship fleet was the *Hindenburg*. Launched in early 1936, *Hindenburg* ferried passengers to North and South America. Traveling at close to 80 mph, hydrogen-lifted dirigibles cut the transatlantic trip nearly by two-thirds. Passengers rode in quiet, plush luxury high above the sea-lanes in an enormous Nazi flying billboard.

In May 1937, *Hindenburg* exploded on its approach to Lakehurst, New Jersey. The official investigation lay the blame for this spectacular disaster on an atmospheric charge of static electricity, but speculation remains that the crash was the result of anti-Nazi sabotage. Thirty-six persons died that day, as did the reputation of the passenger airships. (02-052, 02-053, 02-054, 02-056)

PEGGY MARSH WRITES HER BOOK, 1937

Peggy Marsh was an unreconstructed southerner. She held the Old South and its legends almost in reverence. In her view, white slave owners were noble cavaliers, and slaves were "servants" who mostly loved their enforced servitude. In the mid-1920s, she started a novel that would tell the neo-Confederate story of the Old South. It took Marsh ten years. The manuscript was slowly collecting dust in odd corners of the Marsh's small Atlanta apartment. At one point, part of the narrative was used to prop up a collapsing sofa.

In the mid-1930s, Harold Latham, New York agent for the publisher Macmillan, asked to see her novel. At first Peggy refused, but at the last minute got Latham huge piles of envelopes containing the unedited manuscript. He settled into his green Pullman chair and began to read. He was hooked. Months of extensive revision preceded its release and suddenly to her horror, the shy and reclusive Peggy Marsh was a celebrity.

They struggled with a title. The publisher didn't like *Another Day*, so Peggy called it *Tomorrow Is Another Day*, and then *Tomorrow and Tomorrow*, and then *Tomorrow Will Be Fair*. Finally, they settled on the name under which title the book sold more than 25 million copies and made the names Scarlett O'Hara and Rhett Butler household words. Peggy Marsh (Margaret Mitchell) had finally published her book: *Gone with the Wind*. (02-117)

PANIC BROADCAST, 1938

On Halloween Eve, 1938, invaders from Mars landed on a truck farm east of Princeton, New Jersey. Well, at least that's what they said on the radio. The invasion, of course, was fictional, one of the CBS Sunday night broadcasts of the Mercury Theater on the Air, a dramatic retelling of Herbert George Wells's novel *The War of the Worlds*.

Orson Welles, the young director, devised a broadcast within a broadcast. News reports and live on-the-scene accounts breaking into what seemed to be an ordinary evening of musical entertainment created vivid realism. Many listeners believed earth was really being invaded.

Welles began with an eerie monologue: The earth for years had been watched, "across an immense ethereal gulf. . . . Beings drew their plans against us." By 8:15, the 6 million in the audience had been hooked.

Part of the story featured a live on-the-scene report from Grover's Mill, New Jersey. "Wait! . . . A humped shape is rising out of the pit. I can make out a small beam of light against a mirror. . . . There's a jet of flame. . . . Good Lord, the men . . . are turning into flame! It's coming this way. About twenty yards to my right—" Silence.

A man in Pittsburgh returned in midbroadcast to find his wife just about to drink poison. The network was overwhelmed with calls, complaints, and congratulations. Orson Welles's career was made. The evening helped demonstrate the awesome power of mass communication, for good or ill. (03-070, 03-071)

1400   1450   1500   1550   1600   1650   1700

LOUIS–SCHMELING FIGHT:
SECOND VICTORY 1938

I t was rematch time. Joe Louis got his revenge.

Joseph Louis Barrow was a stalker. Whereas Jack Dempsey won through sheer aggression and, later, Muhammad Ali through his speed and agility, Joe Louis patiently pursued his opponent until the opening came, and he connected with a knockout. He began his boxing career in Detroit and was a Golden Gloves titleholder and an AAU champion in 1934. Louis went professional that same year, and within twelve months knocked out the first of eight heavyweight champions that were to fall victim to his style. One of those was Max Schmeling, but not before Schmeling, the German heavyweight, humiliated Louis in their first meeting on June 19, 1936.

As rumors of war closed in on an anxious world, Joe Louis had retaken the heavyweight title and was prepared to defend it in a rematch with his old nemesis. Maximilian Schmeling was never a follower of Adolf Hitler, though his prospective victory was hyped by Nazi propagandists as proof of white superiority. Joe Louis was African American and he disappointed the Führer. It happened in a single round in Yankee Stadium, June 22, 1938.

Video and audio links to the fight can be found in Bibliographic Appendix. (05-051)

JOHN STEINBECK AND
THE GRAPES OF WRATH, 1939

John Ernst Steinbeck was born in Salinas, California, a rural community one hundred miles south of San Francisco. As a child, he observed the hard life of itinerant and migrant farm workers. His boyhood home became the setting of much of his work. Beginning in 1935 with *Tortilla Flat*, and later with *In Dubious Battle* and *Of Mice and Men*, Steinbeck proved himself an acute observer of social conflict and pain. Yet it was with *The Grapes of Wrath* that he reached the pinnacle his literary craft. Much of the material in the novel came from a series of investigative articles the author wrote for the *San Francisco News* on the plight of the Oakies, those moving from the midwestern dust bowl in Oklahoma, Missouri, and Kansas. In *The Grapes of Wrath*, Steinbeck wove an elegant, semidocumentary narrative telling the story of the Joads, a 1930s Depression-era farm family from Oklahoma. Seeking a better life, they migrated to California only to find themselves caught in the same cycle of poverty and hopelessness left behind.

The book was censored and banned from some libraries and school curricula because of its vivid and pungent descriptions. Some called it obscene, but many believed the novel to be realistic fiction at its finest.

Steinbeck was awarded a Pulitzer Prize in 1940 and the Nobel Prize for literature in 1962. (07-063)

| 1400 | 1450 | 1500 | 1550 | 1600 | 1650 | 1700 |

The son of German immigrants, Henry Louis Gehrig grew up in New York City and as a young boy was not very good at baseball. He dropped the ball and was a terrible hitter, but when he got into school he improved.

In his second year at Columbia University, playing football and baseball, Gehrig felt the irresistible pull of the pros. In 1923, he signed with the Yankees farm team in Hartford, Connecticut. Called up to the Yankees in the fall, he batted over .400 in twenty-six at-bats. After another brief turn with Hartford the following year, he returned to the Yankees as first baseman. In the middle of the 1925 season, he became a regular at first base, and there he remained until 1939, appearing in 2,130 consecutive games, a record that stood until broken by Cal Ripken Jr. in 1995.

In 1927 and 1928, Babe Ruth was on top of the baseball world, but close behind him was Lou Gehrig. In those years they were a part of Murderers' Row, a batting dynasty that dominated the sport. Gehrig's best years were in the mid-1930s, but by 1938 something was wrong. His power and strength ebbing, he was diagnosed with amyotrophic lateral sclerosis, a rare disease of the nervous system, which in later years bore his name. On Lou Gehrig's Day, July 4, 1939, in Yankee Stadium, he demonstrated some of the character that endeared him to millions of admirers.

A link to the video of the Lou Gehrig's Day ceremony can be found in Bibliographic Appendix. (05-026)

THE WIT OF FRANKLIN
DELANO ROOSEVELT, 1940

F DR had endured hardships, especially poliomyelitis. His supreme confidence in the face of adversity and his humor encouraged those enduring the Great Depression.

In 1940, Roosevelt ran for a third term, which no president had attempted. To deflect attention, he eviscerated reactionary Republicans opposing his social programs, as he did here:

> Of course we [Republicans] believe . . . in Social Security . . . in work for the unemployed . . . in saving homes, cross our hearts and hope to die. . . . But we don't like the way the current administration is doing them. Just turn them over to us. . . . We will do more of them. We will do them better. And most important of all, the doing of them will not cost anyone anything.

When he ran in 1944, he attacked Republicans for creating a false rumor about his dog, Fala:

1400   1450   1500   1550   1600   1650   1700

These Republican leaders have not been content with attacks on me or on my wife or on my sons. . . . They now include my little dog, Fala. Now, of course, I don't resent attacks, and my family [doesn't] resent attacks. But Fala does . . . When he heard that the Republican fiction writers . . . had concocted a story that I had left him behind on the Aleutian Islands and sent a destroyer back to find him at a cost of 2 or 3 or 8 or 20 million dollars . . . his Scotch soul was furious. . . . He has not been the same dog since.

Roosevelt's humor endeared him to millions. They laughed, and they voted. (05-021)

THE PROBLEM WITH
CHARLES LINDBERGH, 1941

Charles Augustus Lindbergh, the "Lone Eagle," inspired the world with his solo Atlantic flight in 1927 and was nearly everyone's hero. An intensely shy man, he moved his family to rural New Jersey. Their son was kidnapped and murdered in the early 1930s. After the trial and execution of the killer, the Lindberghs spent extended time in Europe, where Lindbergh witnessed the growing power of Nazi Germany. He accepted a decoration from Hermann Goering, Hitler's close associate and chief of the German Air Force. As the clouds of war gathered over Europe, he returned to America a vehement isolationist, suspected of Nazi sympathies.

Lindbergh was recruited by the isolationist America First Committee, a group of powerful conservative businessmen opposed to US involvement in the European war. As America First's poster boy, he spoke extensively against President Roosevelt's support for Britain.

After Pearl Harbor, America First was humiliated. The committee dissolved and urged its members to support the war. Lindbergh answered the nation's call. He flew fifty combat missions in the Pacific, but he could never quite shake off his suspected Nazi associations. The Lone Eagle died in obscurity in 1974. (04-073, 04-074)

| 1400 | 1450 | 1500 | 1550 | 1600 | 1650 | 1700 |

Opana Mountain rises majestically on the northwest part of the island. Signal Corps Sergeant George E. Elliott Jr. and Private Joseph Lockard had been at the station since noon the previous day. They were there to guard the apparatus, but each day from 4:00 to 7:00 a.m., they practiced on the then state-of-the-art SCR-270-B radar unit.

At 7:02, a large number of objects popped up on the radar screen—airplanes, flying about 136 miles out. Both of the men were new to the operation of the equipment, and they had never seen such a large number of targets. Quickly, however, they plotted the course and contacted the early warning information center. Unable to get through on the tactical line, they tried the regular administrative telephone line. No one at the information center knew exactly what to do with this information. Two or three minutes later, a lieutenant (whose identity will thankfully forever remain unknown) came on the line. Elliott and Lockard reported to the lieutenant the approximate number of approaching planes and the distance. The lieutenant said to forget about it.

But Elliott was not convinced, so he spent the next forty-five minutes watching the planes approach. At twenty miles out, they disappeared from the radar screen. The two shut down the unit and headed back to the barracks. Later, George Elliott would learn he had witnessed the approach of death: the lead flight of Japanese planes on the way to Pearl Harbor. It was December 7, 1941. (01-046)

DOOLITTLE RAID, 1942

Up to the middle of 1942, nearly everywhere American forces were on the defensive, reeling from repeated defeats. Under orders from President Roosevelt, legendary air ace Lieutenant Colonel James Doolittle assembled a volunteer force, which began practice-flying B-25 Mitchell bombers off the deck of the USS *Hornet*. The plan was for the ship to close to within 500 miles of Japan, but, during the mission, the crew encountered Japanese picket boats 600 miles out; one of them got off a message before it was destroyed. Doolittle decided to continue anyway. At 8:20 a.m., April 18, 1942, sixteen B-25 bombers lumbered down the breathlessly short deck of the *Hornet* and clawed their way into the air.

Despite the warning, the force surprised the Japanese, who had miscalculated their arrival time. All planes dropped their bombs and headed out over the Sea of Japan for bases in Nationalist China. Several of the raiders were killed when their planes crashed. Some were captured and executed. But most returned to active duty and combat. The Doolittle raid accomplished very little actual damage. The B-25s only could carry four 500-pound bombs. The real effect was psychological. Americans felt that at last someone had done something. (03-053, 03-054)

| 1400 | 1450 | 1500 | 1550 | 1600 | 1650 | 1700 |

BATTLE OF MIDWAY, 1942

In late spring 1942, two great naval armadas met off the Midway Islands. Japanese Admiral Isoroku Yamamoto was back in the Central Pacific to take out US aircraft carriers he had missed at Pearl Harbor. Chester William Nimitz, commander in chief of the US Pacific fleet, intended to thwart Yamamoto. His code breakers had revealed the Japanese plan, so Nimitz prepared an ambush.

In the early morning hours of June 4, 1942, the Japanese launched an air attack against Midway Island, and the planes returned and were about to launch again when torpedo bombers from the US carriers *Enterprise*, *Yorktown*, and *Hornet* made their appearance over Japanese decks littered with aviation fuel and bombs ready for loading. The American torpedo bombers were almost wiped out by Japanese fighters, but their sacrifice drew Japanese defensive aircraft down to the sea. They were unable to counter a wave of American dive-bombers. In five minutes, three Japanese carriers were on their way to the bottom, and a fourth was mortally wounded. These loses, combined with those it suffered at the Battle of the Coral Sea earlier in May, meant that Japan was unable to mount an effective offense for the rest of the war. (03-150, 03-151, 03-152)

1700	1750	1800	1850	1900	1950	PRESENT

Era of Economic Struggle

JAPANESE AMERICAN CONCENTRATION CAMPS, 1942

During World War II, the United States incarcerated over 100,000 Japanese American citizens. The "detention centers" were spartan and, at first, barely livable, but gradually conditions improved for these American citizens—men, women, and children who had been shipped from their homes on the Pacific coast to the ten inland concentration camps.

In the wake of Japan's sudden attack on December 7, 1941, there was an explosion of patriotic sentiment and anger against all things Japanese. Newspapers fed the feelings of hurt and betrayal with often-inaccurate stories about possible Japanese American complicity. The US military had been unprepared by the attack and demanded the removal of ethnic Japanese, despite their citizenship.

President Franklin Roosevelt promulgated Executive Order 9066, permitting the removal, despite a warning by Attorney General Francis Biddle that such a removal was unnecessary and unconstitutional.

Not until 1944 did the Supreme Court effectively close the camps, ruling that citizens could not be indefinitely detained. Not until the 1990s did the US Congress acknowledge, in word and financial restitution, what some have called the biggest wartime mistake of the United States. (08-007, 08-008)

1400   1450   1500   1550   1600   1650   1700

PT BOATS, 1943

Patrol torpedo boats were often the first allied line of offense in the Southwest Pacific during the dark early days of World War II. They were powerful, boasting three Packard V-12 power plants; swift and sleek at 40 knots per hour; and weaponized, with two 50-caliber machine guns, an antiaircraft weapon, and four torpedo launchers. The little boats packed a punch out of proportion to their size.

Life on the PT boats was pretty spartan. The diet was monotony itself—canned everything punctuated by occasional ice cream deliveries.

The boats were typically stationed far forward of the main base areas on the bright edge of contact with the enemy. By 1943, the Japanese navy had been so decimated that it had to supply island troops with barges that ran down the coastline at night. PT boat captains would hide in the shallows under the cover of the shoreline and pounce with deadly surprise. Small and often unheralded, the PT boats nevertheless played an indispensable role in the allied victory in the Pacific during World War II. (05-091, 05-092)

ARMED SERVICES RADIO, 1943

In 1942, allied forces began to assemble for the Normandy invasion in bases throughout the English countryside. The GIs missed their American radio. Their only choice was the British Broadcasting Company, which was in its heyday. All over the world, people tuned in to hear news that was clear, accurate, and largely free from the disheartening propaganda that poured out of Berlin, Rome, and Tokyo. To the American ear, however, the BBC was excruciatingly dull—the music boring, the humor dry and out of context, the announcers starchy and pretentious.

To keep up morale, General Eisenhower wanted to start a GI network to bring news and commentary, variety shows, music, and comedy direct from home. The BBC bureaucrats began intensive guerrilla warfare in the halls of power to stop it. Probably the real reason was the fear that the BBC's once-captive audience would start listening to GI radio. They were right. By the end of the war, 5 million Britons were regular listeners. Despite opposition and under severe restrictions, American Forces Network went on the air on July 4, 1943. (05-032, 05-033)

ROSIE THE RIVETER, 1943

For generations, American women had been told their place was in the home. That had to change if the allies were going to meet the threat of Japan and Germany. World War II, more than any prior war, was a battle of production. Victory would go to the side that produced the most airplanes, battleships, guns, and ammunition. With 15 million men in uniform, who was going to build the tanks and guns? The answer, of course, was their wives, girlfriends, sisters, and mothers.

The New Deal propaganda machine kicked into high gear, and the American press joined the war effort. Women in overalls appeared in advertisements, films, and posters. They were the new heroes of the war. On Memorial Day 1943, Norman Rockwell contributed the great symbol of women in the war effort: Rosie the Riveter—young and pretty, with powerful arms and shoulders. She had a riveting gun resting on her lap and copy of Adolf Hitler's *Mein Kampf* under her feet. By 1946, a million more women were in American factories than there were in 1940. Rosie had helped change forever American attitudes about women in the workforce.

(06-003)

GI BILL OF RIGHTS, 1944

Fearful of GI unemployment facing returning veterans, Congress passed the Servicemen's Readjustment Act (1944). Almost as an afterthought, it added a section guaranteeing any qualified veteran college tuition for forty-eight months in part at least, at government expense.

The first vets were in the program by the summer of 1944, and twelve months later their number had risen to over a million. The first veteran to sign up for the education benefits was Don Balfour of Washington, DC, a student at George Washington University who went on to become an insurance executive.

The most astounding result of the GI Bill was the change it made on college campuses. College in the 1930s was a destination of the children of the elite, teachers, and preachers. Suddenly, college was available for people who never expected to be able to go. Stanford, for instance, more than doubled its enrollment in a single year. The first GI Bill cost over $5 billion, but it was well worth it, as newly educated professionals flooded into the workplace. (02-145)

D-DAY 1944

Gradually, the tide had begun to turn in favor of the allies in World War II. After the Battle of Stalingrad, Soviet forces were taking back territory lost to Germany earlier in the war. Soviet leader Joseph Stalin constantly badgered the western allies to open a second front in France. After long preparations, a million troops were staging in southern England for that assault, planned for late spring 1944.

A clever deception campaign focused German attention on the area around Calais, while Supreme Allied Commander Dwight D. Eisenhower had determined Normandy the better location. Bad weather delayed the invasion, but on June 6, with heavy naval and aerial bombardment and then paratroop landings behind German lines, the largest seaborne landings in history occurred. By the end of June, just short of a million men had fought their way off transport ships onto French soil.

Operation Overlord succeeded because the Germans had completed only a fraction of their defensive preparations, were defending a huge stretch of territory, and suffered from complexity and indecisiveness that ran through the German command structure all the way up to Adolf Hitler. The destructive combination of French Resistance attacks on German infrastructure and allied air superiority meant the troops that landed at the five Normandy beachheads were able to hammer their way slowly inland. It would be many long months until VE Day, but D-Day was the beginning of the end.

JACKIE ROBINSON STAYS PUT, 1944

As much anything, having to sit at the back of the bus was a constant reminder to African Americans of their second-class citizenship. Long before Rosa Park's experience in Alabama in 1955, while on active duty in the United States Army during World War II, future Brooklyn Dodger star Jackie Robinson struck a small blow for equality.

Post rules at Camp Hood stated that there would be no segregation on base buses. On a summer night in 1944, Robinson and the light-skinned wife of one of his friends were riding about halfway back on a post bus. Robinson suddenly realized that the bus had stopped and the driver was shouting at him to go to the back of the bus. Robinson thought the driver might have been irritated, thinking the girl was white. Robinson refused to move, and at the gate MPs arrested him. Lieutenant Robinson was within his full rights, but in the world of white bigotry he could not expect fair treatment. The black lieutenant, a teetotaler, was accused of public drunkenness and disobedience. Fellow officers at Hood alerted the NAACP, which put pressure on the army. At his court-martial, Robinson was acquitted.

Robinson's small victory at Camp Hood and his later baseball exploits were an inspiration to many, but for millions of African Americans suffering under a regime of petty segregation, relief was years away. (05-110)

USS INDIANAPOLIS—
VOYAGE OF DEATH, 1945

Having delivered components of the first atomic bomb to Tinian Island, USS *Indianapolis* sailed west, at 9:00 a.m., July 29, 1945, after refueling at Guam. About midnight, the Japanese submarine I-58 put two torpedoes squarely into its side. The ship's radio was damaged, so no SOS signal got sent. The ship sank in less than thirty minutes, with several hundred sailors suddenly in the ocean.

When the *Indianapolis* failed to reach the Philippines, it was assumed some emergency could have caused a delay, so no one reported its tardiness. The men of the *Indianapolis* were abandoned for five long days. As the wounded continued to bleed, shark attacks overwhelmed survivors clinging for life in the ocean. Lack of drinking water, coupled with exposure to the sun and exhaustion, had created a mass of delirious men, trapped in a horrifying world of fantasy. Almost by accident, a routine air patrol mission discovered the sea of floating bodies and reported the loss. About 1,100 sailors and officers had departed Guam; just over 300 survived, most dying in the water.

In the aftermath, Captain McVay was court-martialed on two counts, but it soon became clear the Navy needed a scapegoat for its greatest loss of the war. After his trial, the sentence was remitted, and he was restored to active duty. In the 1990s by act of Congress, McVay was completely exonerated, but this action was a bit too late. Retired Rear Admiral Charles B. McVay III became the last victim of the disaster. He committed suicide in 1968.

(02-120, 02-121, 02-122)

ATOMIC DAWN, 1945

By the mid-1930s, scientists had determined that a nucleus consisted of protons and neutrons. Enrico Fermi concluded that bombarding a nucleus with neutrons from another element would create another lighter element. The experiments of Otto Hahn and Lise Meitner confirmed Fermi's theory by splitting uranium atoms, which resulted in an extraordinary release of energy. Scientists needed little imagination to realize the potential for creating a weapon of terrible power.

1400   1450   1500   1550   1600   1650   1700

In a letter to President Roosevelt in August 1939, Albert Einstein highlighted recent atomic research and warned that "extremely powerful bombs" might be constructed—and possibly by Germany. Roosevelt then initiated the billion-dollar Manhattan Project to ensure the United States would first build these weapons. Under the leadership of General Leslie Groves and physicist J. Robert Oppenheimer, the United States constructed two types of bombs.

The first utilized uranium-235 created by using Fermi's splitting technique and a "gun mechanism" to achieve critical mass and an atomic explosion. This bomb, "Little Boy," was dropped on August 6, 1945. Hiroshima, Japan, incinerated in a blinding bluish flame. Within a year, 90,000 to 166,000 residents had died in the blast or from injury or radiation.

The second bomb utilized plutonium, derived from uranium-238, and required an extraordinarily complex implosion mechanism to explode. This bomb, "Fat Man," was dropped on Nagasaki, Japan, on August 9, 1945. It inflicted lesser damage than that at Hiroshima, due to the uneven terrain. Still, at least initially 30,000 people were killed. Japan surrendered on September 2, 1945, fearing future attacks and recognizing the atomic dawn. (02-150, 02-151, 02-152, 02-153, 02-154)

CREATION OF THE
UNITED NATIONS, 1945

Determined to avoid past mistakes, the founding countries of the United Nations, a name coined by Franklin Roosevelt, met to draft a charter in San Francisco in spring of 1945. Preliminary conferences struggled with security and how the great powers—the United States, Britain, the Soviet Union, China, and later France—would maintain their predominance and protect their own interests. The principal agency of that concern became the Security Council. Its five permanent members could veto actions of the fifteen-member Council, and hence the United Nations, but they could not stifle debate.

At the charter conference, issues governing admission of disputed states, the role of smaller nations, the disposition of colonies and territories held in trust by large nations, and, importantly, the ultimate responsibilities of the secretary-general and the role of the General Assembly were discussed. In the end, the UN that emerged reflected great power consensus. It would change over the years in complexion and approach, but that would come as a result of Cold War conflict and enormous growth in the number of member states. (11-009, 11-010)

| 1400 | 1450 | 1500 | 1550 | 1600 | 1650 | 1700 |

CHURCHILL'S IRON-CURTAIN SPEECH, 1946

After World War II, US public opinion moved against the Soviet Union. Secretary of Defense James Forrestal and other military leaders were fearful of Soviet power and expansionism. Key Republicans, such as Senator Arthur Vandenberg, and journalists like Henry R. Luce, publisher of *Time Magazine*, and the editors of the *New York Times* echoed this concern.

By early 1946, President Truman was becoming alarmed at Soviet leader Stalin's aggressive actions in southern Europe and the Middle East. At about that time, Winston Churchill received an invitation to speak at the small Presbyterian Westminster College in Fulton, Missouri. Churchill and Truman met in Washington on February 10, 1946, and agreed on the speech's substance. Truman accompanied Churchill to Fulton and introduced him on March 5. Churchill described a descending "iron curtain" of Communist domination over Eastern Europe. He called for an Anglo-American alliance to combat this Soviet aggression.

Reaction to the speech was predictable. The left wing of American politics disapproved, and the right supported his ideas. But Churchill proved to accurately predict the postwar landscape. The Cold War had begun. (02-027, 02-028)

COLE PORTER'S
BREAKTHROUGH, 1948

In the 1930s, his music and lyrics were the epitome of sophistication and wit, but during the war decade Cole Porter sank into a long period of depression. Much of this grew out of a severe riding accident in the summer of 1937. He was riding with friends at an estate on Long Island when his high-spirited horse tripped and fell on one of Porter's legs and then reared up and fell again on the other. Months of painful therapy followed; when he finally returned to work, despite a quick series of musical hits, his creative edge seemed to have dulled.

When the possibility of creating a musical based on Shakespeare's *The Taming of the Shrew* came late in the 1940s, he was not very enthusiastic. He tried it, however, and *Kiss Me Kate* became his greatest hit. It was a play within a play, depicting the lives of a theater couple, Fred and Lilly, who, though divorced, were still romantically attached. After a rocky start, the show opened at the new Century Theatre in New York on December 30, 1948. It was a smash, the longest running play in Cole Porter's career. Many of its songs became standards, such as "Too Darn Hot," "Another Op'nin', Another Show," "So in Love," and "Wunderbar." (01-024)

HARRY TRUMAN'S 1948 DILEMMA

In 1948, the president seemed on the way to defeat. No longer would the old South be the Democratic solid base. Conservatives under Governor Strom Thurmond of South Carolina had split off because of the aggressive civil rights plank in the Democratic platform. Harry Truman's advisors told him he needed the northern city vote, which necessitated support of African Americans. But they were particularly vexed at continued segregation in the armed forces.

This was a twentieth-century phenomenon. Even in the late 1880s, there was a fully integrated navy. Yet, with the rise of overt legal racism beginning in the 1890s, military leadership insisted on full segregation.

By 1940, blacks comprised less than 2 percent of the army and the navy. During World War II, desperate for men to fill the ranks, generals reluctantly allowed African American service. The results were impressive. Studies indicated that segregation reduced the efficiency of the armed forces and that black units performed very well in combat.

Truman was in trouble. Governor Tom Dewey was running on a Republican platform pledged to integrate the military. Unless he moved quickly to placate blacks, he was going to lose, but if he did so too publicly he would lessen his remaining support among whites in the South. On July 26, 1948, he issued Executive Order 9981, calling for equal treatment for everyone in the armed services without regard to race, color, religion, or national origin. Integration of the armed services did not happen overnight, but because of a politician in trouble, one of the most conservative American institutions ended up guaranteeing equality for black Americans. (01-037)

1700	1750	1800	1850	1900	1950	PRESENT

Era of Economic Struggle

BERLIN AIRLIFT, 1948

Since the fall of Nazi Germany in 1945, Berlin had remained a source of bitter contention between East and West. By 1948, the United States, Britain, and France were moving to unify West Germany and West Berlin. Russia felt threatened by these moves, and on July 24, 1948, it cut off West Berlin from outside contact and vital supplies of electricity, coal, and food. The city had only thirty-five days of food to feed its 2.5 million.

At first, the allies considered forcing through the blockade but instead settled on an amazing rescue plan. The idea was known as a *Luftbrüke*, or "air bridge." Denied the right of surface passage, they supplied the needs of a great city by air. At the height of the mission, courageous allied pilots were ferrying 13,000 tons of food, fuel, and medical supplies on 1,000 flights per day. Inclement weather and occasional Soviet harassment increased the danger and brought about sixty-five accidental deaths, but for eleven months the Berlin airlift was a triumph of ingenuity, hard work, sacrifice, and determination. It hastened the creation of NATO and delivered to the Soviets a humiliating blow to their prestige. (03-191, 03-192)

1400   1450   1500   1550   1600   1650   1700

ED SULLIVAN, 1948

Born in the age of ragtime and coming to maturity in the frenetic jazzy 1920s, Ed Sullivan helped establish rock and roll as the medium of expression for a generation of restless baby boomers. He got his start in the newspaper business, eventually hired by the *New York Daily News* to write his "Little Old New York" strip. These notes on New York society life would continue for the rest of his life.

In 1947, ad man Marlo Lewis, who was creating a variety show for the new medium of television, noted his special abilities. From the first show in July 1948, *Toast of the Town*, was a hit. Sponsors were skeptical, critics were vicious, but viewers loved it. One critic said that Sullivan "was the only man who brightens up a room by leaving it." They called him "Stone Face" and the "Toast of the Tomb" and giggled at his bungled introductions, which on live television could not be redone. He once introduced Delores Gray as "now starving on Broadway" and said, "Let's hear it reeally big fer singer Jose Feliciano! He's blind—and he's Puerto Rican."

Nevertheless, Sullivan had an uncanny connection to his audience. For each show, the success formula was the same: open big, keep it clean, and stick in something for the kids. Another critic described the twenty-three year reign of Ed Sullivan: "Never before and never again . . . would so many gather so loyally, for so long, in the thrall of one man's taste." (04-071)

TRUMAN AND MACARTHUR, 1951

During the Korean War, the allies were pushing hard into North Korea in the fall of 1950, recovering from nearly being thrown off the peninsula the previous summer. Then thousands of Chinese troops entered the war, which forced a standoff. Soon, the opponents faced each other across the 38th parallel. President Harry Truman felt that it was time for a cease-fire.

Theater commander General Douglas MacArthur strongly disagreed. He told Congress that if the United States was not in Korea to win, the administration should be indicted for the murder of American boys. MacArthur was playing politics. With the unanimous support of the Joint Chiefs of Staff, Truman fired him.

Public support for MacArthur was enormous and turned against the president, but Truman knew he had done the right thing. Douglas MacArthur had strayed beyond the bounds permitted the military in the Constitution. He had to go. (01-001)

| 1400 | 1450 | 1500 | 1550 | 1600 | 1650 | 1700 |

BROWN V. BOARD OF EDUCATION, 1954

Each morning, Linda Brown would rise early, dress in her warmest coat, and wait for the bus in her low-income neighborhood of Topeka, Kansas. The bus would take her twenty-one blocks to a school only for African American children. An hour after Linda left, the white girl across the street would take the bus waiting just out front, which took her to her segregated school only seven blocks away. Linda's father sued.

The local board was on good legal grounds. In *Plessy v. Ferguson* (1896), the Supreme Court had ruled that separate but equal facilities were permitted. Brown's attorneys argued that segregated schools were almost always unequal. Black schools had difficult access, unsatisfactory building and equipment quality, and poor academic programs. White schools were much better.

Newly confirmed Chief Justice Earl Warren insisted that in such sensitive civil-rights cases the court should speak with a firm and united voice. On May 17, 1954, the Court unanimously reversed *Plessy*, stating that segregated schools were "inherently unequal" and declared them unconstitutional. Thus began one of the most wrenching American social struggles since the Civil War, in which many parts of the country only grudgingly came to bend before the idea of equal justice under law. *Brown v. Board of Education* highlighted the enduring architecture of legal racism in American society and attempted to remove at least one part of that structure. (04-059, 04-060, 04-061)

JOSEPH MCCARTHY, 1954

In the early 1950s, Joseph Raymond McCarthy, a lackluster Republican senator from Wisconsin, enlivened his bid for a second term by alleging a vast communist conspiracy undermining American government and universities. He was reelected in 1952, and because the Republicans were in the majority in the Senate he used investigation and subpoena to pursue his crusade.

For two years, as chairman of the Senate's Committee on Government Operations, he was unable to prove a single creditable case of sedition. By his strategy of insinuation, he was able to drive some people from their jobs and bring others under public censure and humiliation.

He began to strike out in an increasingly irresponsible manner, accusing Republican and Democratic leaders, including President Dwight D. Eisenhower, of complicity in the communist conspiracy. Finally, Ike had enough and began to work quietly to crush McCarthy.

The senator's fall came when he took on the US Army. In thirty-six days of sensational televised hearings in spring 1954, little evidence was presented, but McCarthy's bullying tactics were exposed for all to see. The climax to the hearings came when the senator accused Fred Fisher, a young lawyer in the firm of Army counsel Joseph Welch, of being communist. In a dramatic confrontation, Welch summarized the growing national revulsion over McCarthy and his tactics: "Have you no sense of decency, sir?"

Nearly overnight, McCarthy's political and popular support collapsed. His name is used to this day when politicians engage in vicious personal attacks having little basis in fact. (05-081, 05-082, 05-083)

| 1400 | 1450 | 1500 | 1550 | 1600 | 1650 | 1700 |

By the late 1920s, most technical problems of TV broadcasting were solved. Frozen images were scanned by the camera, converted to electricity, and then sent to the TV set, which then reconverted the signal into a picture with sound. The simpler way of scanning was to shine light through a spinning disk, which then would be converted. A clearer picture was produced by a more complicated electronic system with an electron gun firing a signal across a photosensitive background before conversion.

NBC favored the latter method and began broadcasting in black and white. CBS worked with the spinning disk, which could allow them to jump to color broadcasts but required an expensive converter to display its black-and-white programming.

By 1950, CBS had secured FCC approval for its system but had not sold a single color set. Eventually, CBS surrendered to the NBC all-electronic system for all broadcasts. It would still be 1954 before the first color sets went on the market. They cost $1,000, more than a quarter of the average worker's salary. NBC's parent company, RCA, didn't make a profit on color television until 1960, but the battle over color TV was over. NBC had won.

But the spinning disk was not completely dead. The RCA system was very bulky. When NASA wanted to send a color camera to the moon with Apollo 12, it had to be very light; therefore, the agency never considered the all-electronic RCA system. The camera chosen, which sent the first color TV pictures from the moon surface, had a spinning tricolor disk. (03-184, 03-185)

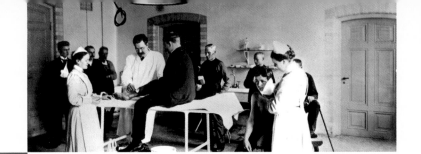

POLIO, 1955

Poliomyelitis is a viral infection of the intestinal tract. In most cases of polio, the patient recovers within three or four days. In more serious cases, the virus attacks the motor nerve cells of the spinal cord; if nerve damage is severe, the result may be paralysis.

Prior to the modern era, most people lived in filth—particularly fecal matter—so young children were exposed to and acquired immunity to the virus. The disease reached epidemic levels in the United States in the first half of the twentieth century, ironically, because of improved sanitation conditions. Modern children living in relatively cleaner conditions did not acquire immunity. Exposure later in life, such as in the case of Franklin Roosevelt, was more likely to result in infection, often resulting in paralysis.

With the United States averaging 21,000 annual paralytic cases of polio, the country declared war on the disease. In 1949, scientists identified and grew the poliovirus in a lab culture. In 1955, physician researcher Jonas Salk developed a polio vaccine that utilized killed viruses to immunize patients. Six years later, Albert Sabin's oral vaccine containing a weakened poliovirus was approved and eventually supplanted the Salk vaccine. Polio continues to be a threat in less developed parts of the world, but is extremely rare where the vaccine is routinely administered. (07-032, 07-033)

| 1400 | 1450 | 1500 | 1550 | 1600 | 1650 | 1700 |

It was unseasonably warm that December night in 1955. Four thousand people overflowed out of Montgomery's packed Holt Street Baptist Church. A prayer was said, a scripture passage was read, and then a young man began speaking from the pulpit. As a kid, the young man was known as Mike. He came up in a sophisticated church family in Atlanta and was well educated, rejecting medicine and gravitating toward theology before eventually holding a PhD from Boston University. There he met his wife, and they were married in summer 1953.

Just over a year after he moved to Montgomery, the city became embroiled in a boycott of the segregated bus system. The combination of his education, leadership skills, and eloquence—but mostly because he had not been in town long enough to make enemies—compelled him to lead the crusade. That night from the pulpit, he articulated the real reasons for the boycott:

> There comes a time when people get tired. We are here this evening to say to those who have mistreated us so long that we are tired—tired of being segregated and humiliated, tired of being kicked about by the brutal feet of oppression. For many years, we have shown amazing patience. We have sometimes given people the feeling that we liked the way we were being treated. But we come here tonight to be saved from that patience that makes us patient with anything less than freedom and justice.

Martin Luther "Mike" King Jr. had found his calling. (01-060)

MALCOLM MCLEAN—
CONTAINER KING, 1957

Malcolm McLean's first truck went on the road in 1931. Years of hard work and innovation enlarged that truck into a fleet of many hundreds. As the decades passed, he grew adept at devising ways of getting around transportation bottlenecks. One of the most severe impediments occurred when products changed from one mode of transportation to another: wagon to railroad, railroad to barge, barge to truck, truck to ship.

In 1937, he was patiently waiting at dockside in Hoboken, New Jersey, while one of his tractor-trailers was being unloaded so that the goods could be reloaded onto a waiting ship. The process was tedious, labor intensive, time-consuming, and very expensive. He reasoned that if the trailer could be transferred from truck to ship and vice versa the shipping business would be transformed. By 1956, he had the resources to pioneer the process. His first "container ship" was *Ideal* X; with its sailing, the bottleneck was broken.

By the twenty-first century, a huge percentage of goods shipped between continents are carried in containers loaded by cranes and kept organized by codes scanned into computers. Containerization is considered one of the modern era's most important innovations in commerce. (02-149)

| 1400 | 1450 | 1500 | 1550 | 1600 | 1650 | 1700 |

INTEGRATION COMES
TO LITTLE ROCK, 1957

In 1954, the US Supreme Court declared that separate but equal schools were unconstitutional. In subsequent decrees, it instructed states and localities to desegregate with "all deliberate speed." The Little Rock, Arkansas, school board, a fairly progressive body at that time, started desegregating its schools, but very slowly. The black community in Little Rock, frustrated with the incremental pace of the school board's efforts, sued to achieve immediate compliance. A federal court took jurisdiction and ordered desegregation by the fall of 1957; as the date approached, local feelings escalated.

At that point, Governor Orval E. Faubus intervened for a variety of reasons. He was genuinely concerned that should any black children enter Central High School they might be harmed. Faubus also was in big political trouble. He was considered by die-hard segregationists to be a liberal, and his reelection was in serious jeopardy. At 9:00 p.m. on September 2, 1957, under orders from the governor, the Arkansas National Guard surrounded Little Rock Central High School, supposedly to keep peace. For three weeks, Faubus and the Guard blocked black students from entering. Those who attempted were subjected to verbal abuse and near physical violence, sometimes directly in front of the soldiers supposedly there protect them.

Desegregation did come to Central High School but only after President Dwight D. Eisenhower sent the troops from 101st Airborne Division and federalized the Arkansas National Guard to secure the school and enforce the court order. The decades-long difficult road to racial peace and cooperation had begun. (01-067)

| 1700 | 1750 | 1800 | 1850 | 1900 | 1950 | PRESENT |

MASSIVE RESISTANCE I, 1958

The Rev. Dr. Martin Luther King Jr. wrote from the Birmingham jail in 1963 that "privileged groups rarely give up their privileges voluntarily." This was clearly demonstrated by Virginia's reaction to the 1954 Supreme Court desegregation order.

The response was called massive resistance and was the inspiration of the Byrd machine. Named for and dominated by US Senator and former Governor Harry Flood Byrd Sr. of Winchester, the machine's base of power was a band of counties south of the James River known as the southside. It was tobacco country, with a population split pretty evenly between disenfranchised and poorly educated African Americans and lots of very fearful whites. Through artful design of legislative districts, the southside controlled the Virginia General Assembly. At first, Virginia tried a form of local option in which some districts would be allowed to experiment with integration, but the machine-dominated legislature rejected any compromise that would lead to segregated schools.

The debate was stoked by a series of inflammatory editorials by the editor of the *Richmond News Leader*, James Jackson Kilpatrick, who advocated a novel but not very new theory known as interposition. In it, states could interpose themselves and block federal law. Andrew Jackson in the 1833 nullification crisis and Abraham Lincoln in the Civil War had dispensed with this nonsense, but unfortunately in the 1950s, many of Virginia white citizens were racially biased and in their desire to block African American progress desperately clung to Kilpatrick's imprudent notion. (10-026, 10-027, 10-028, 10-029, 10-030)

| 1400 | 1450 | 1500 | 1550 | 1600 | 1650 | 1700 |

MASSIVE RESISTANCE II, 1958

In 1958, the federal courts ordered Norfolk, Charlottesville, and Warrenton, Virginia had to integrate their schools. When Governor Lindsay Almond closed those schools, finally, the moderates of Virginia reacted. Led by Blair Buck, the Virginia Committee for Public Schools, then with 25,000 members, provided school classes in districts the state had closed. They organized a statewide petition drive that hammered the governor and the General Assembly. By focusing only on the issue of "keeping the schools open," they soon found an ally in the business community, which warned the governor that further resistance would destroy what was left of the commonwealth's already nationally tarnished reputation. Massive resistance collapsed, but not everywhere.

In the little southside county of Prince Edward, defiance festered, fed by incendiary editorials in the *Farmville Herald* by publisher and editor J. Barrye Wall. Masquerading under the always useful but intellectually bereft constitutional banner of states' rights, Wall was actually advocating segregation forever.

The county closed its schools, and white students entered private segregation academies. Blacks were left to fend for themselves for four long years. Free schools were set up in churches and taught by ex-state schoolteachers, parents, and outside volunteers drawn by the unfortunate circumstances of the African American students. Finally in 1964, the US Supreme Court ordered the county to reopen its public schools. Yet, not until the 1990s did white participation in the public schools pass 40 percent in a county with 47 percent white students. (10-026, 10-027, 10-028, 10-029, 10-030)

THE FIRST PRESIDENTIAL
TELEVISION DEBATE, 1960

Neck and neck in the polls, John F. Kennedy and Richard M. Nixon engaged in the first televised presidential debate on September 26, 1960, in Chicago. Television had been a part of presidential elections for a decade but did not yet have the impact it would soon have.

Nixon was by far the better known of the two and had twice been elected to national office. He had considerable experience in foreign affairs and solid support nationally. There was no reason why he should have given the junior senator from Massachusetts a platform in which he would appear to be an equal. Nixon never made that mistake again.

Those who listened to the debate on the radio said the encounter was either a tie or narrowly won by Nixon. On television, the result was different. Nixon had injured his knee, had lost five pounds, and seemed haggard and pale. Kennedy arrived rested and tan, made his points clearly, and listened to Nixon with a slightly amused expression, which reflected his growing disdain for the Republican.

Television magnified their differences, and Kennedy looked better. In an election that was so close that 12,000 votes in strategic precincts nationwide might have changed the result, the first televised debate could very well have given Kennedy the White House. (01-145)

PRESIDENTIAL WIT—
JOHN FITZGERALD KENNEDY, 1961

Jack Kennedy had an image problem. He was perceived as a poor little rich boy who would never have succeeded were it not for daddy's money. He used humor to deflect this perception. He said, "I just received a telegram from my father. He says, 'Don't buy one more vote than you need. I'll be damned if I'll pay for a landslide.'"

He was a Catholic running for president in a Protestant country. He used humor before the Houston Ministerial Association: "I have asked Cardinal Spellman how to deal with the question of the pope's infallibility. And Cardinal Spellman said, 'I don't know what to tell you, senator. All I can say is, he keeps calling me Spillman.'" When criticized of nepotism for appointing brother Bobby as attorney general, he confronted the issue head-on: "I see nothing wrong with giving him a little legal experience before goes out into private practice."

Even the sainted Dwight Eisenhower was not immune to the occasional Kennedy jab. At one of the Gridiron Dinners in the 1950s, Kennedy referred to Ike's often confusing explanations, this time of the current recession: "As I interpret the president, we're now at the end of the beginning of the upturn of the downturn. Every bright spot the White House finds in the economy is like the policeman bending over the body in the alley who says cheerfully, 'Two of his wounds are fatal—but this other one's not so bad.'" Smiling voters usually vote for the author of their smiles. (03-156)

LUNCHEON RACISM, 1961

Perhaps no part of the elaborate structure of white dominance in the era of Jim Crow was more irritating to African Americans than the intricate structure of petty segregation. Separate and usually very unequal sleeping and eating facilities, restrooms, drinking fountains, and public transportation were a constant reminder to blacks of their second-class status.

Late in the afternoon on February 1, 1960, four students from North Carolina Agriculture and Technical College staged the first of many "sit-ins." Carrying their schoolbooks, the students entered the Woolworth's on South Elm Street, Greensboro, purchased a few school supplies, and then proceeded to the "whites only" lunch counter where they politely asked for service. As they anticipated, they were denied. The four sat peacefully, studying, until the store closed. Back on campus that evening, others pledged to help.

During the next several years, the momentum of the sit-in and the sometimes ugly and violent reactions to it helped shift the focus of the civil rights movement toward discrimination in public accommodations. By September 1960, roughly 70,000 people participated in sit-ins, resulting in 3,600 arrests. The combination of such nonviolent protests and later legal actions by the federal government eventually ripped apart the legal discriminatory infrastructure of white rule. This campaign demonstrated that the advancement of true equality is an ongoing feature of the American experience. (09-043, 09-44)

1400   1450   1500   1550   1600   1650   1700

CUBAN MISSILE CRISIS, 1962

Faced with evidence of Soviet missiles in Cuba in fall 1962, President John Kennedy determined to get them out without going to war. At first, an invasion of Cuba or a surgical air strike was considered, but there was little time to mount an invasion and no guarantee that striking by air would be surgical enough. In the end, the administration decided on a blockade, quaintly called a quarantine, to prevent further shipments of missiles.

Russian leader Nikita Khrushchev had miscalculated, thinking Kennedy would not challenge the placement of missiles, but the president and his congressional allies faced an important midterm election. The presence of so visible a threat ninety miles off the Florida coast would have dealt Kennedy a political body blow. The missiles had to go.

As the world faced the possibility of a nuclear exchange, Soviet and American leaders struggled to find some accommodation short of war. On October 28, Khrushchev yielded, but not before getting the United States to promise not to invade Cuba and to pull US missiles out of Turkey. The two nuclear giants had pulled back from the brink. Ironically, the one clear victor of the Cuban Missile Crisis was Fidel Castro. Kennedy's pledge of noninvasion permitted his regime to survive despite its serious weaknesses, at least into the following century. (06-007, 06-008, 06-009)

| 1700 | 1750 | 1800 | 1850 | 1900 | 1950 | PRESENT |

Era of Social and Economic Advance

insect spray

CONTAINING 50% DDT

RE: PATENT NO. 22,922

DDT AND THE MODERN ENVIRONMENTAL MOVEMENT, 1962

At first DDT, dichloro-diphenyl-trichloroethane, seemed a miracle. Modern agricultural practices produced greater crop yields but had opened the way to greater pest infestation. Some chemical insecticides were tried, but not until DDT arrived in the late 1930s did there appear to be a true solution to insect control. As soon as the chemical gained USDA approval, farmers snatched it up, and crop production soared. The grayish white powdered insecticide killed nearly every insect that consumed it by interrupting respiration at the cell level. The insects literally suffocated from the inside out. Then came the problems.

The compound is a very effective poison against not only insects but also, in sufficient quantities, birds, squirrels, the family cat, and sometimes humans. DDT is also biologically persistent, meaning that it decomposes very slowly. It sticks around and is stored in fat. Grasshoppers, dying by the millions in a field, are snatched up by field mice. They in turn are eaten by predatory birds, and so on, up the food chain. Finally, DDT killed all the good nonpest insects, many of which eat the pests. Crop damage from pest infestation actually went up following the adoption of DDT.

In 1962, author and biologist Rachel Carson released her book *Silent Spring*. It was a sensation and provoked calls for reform. Eleven years later in 1973, the USDA cancelled the use of DDT in the United States. The controversy sparked the modern environmental movement. (07-112, 07-113)

| 1400 | 1450 | 1500 | 1550 | 1600 | 1650 | 1700 |

US SUPREME COURT
VS. SCHOOL PRAYER, 1962

In 1962, the Supreme Court ignited a firestorm when it abolished officially endorsed prayer in public schools. That prayer read, "Almighty God, we acknowledge our dependence upon thee, and we beg thy blessing upon us, our parents, our teachers, and our country."

The prayer was little more than tipping one's hat in God's direction, hardly an attempt to inculcate religion. It was an artless compromise between those who believed schools should not be barren of religious expression and those who saw a clear unconstitutional state establishment of religion.

Soon the national discourse erupted with expressions of deep feelings on both sides. One southern congressman observed that the Supreme Court, having put the Negro into the schools, had now driven God out. More responsible opponents feared for the basic moral supports of free democracy. On the other side, some Protestant leaders and many Jewish rabbis believed the decision strengthened the Constitutional wall of separation between church and state.

The school-prayer controversy represents one of the continuing fault lines in American life. The United States is an intensely religious nation, yet a widely diverse one. The court decision reflects the struggle over how citizens of a democracy express their faith without stepping on the faith or lack of faith of others. The Second Amendment's prohibition against establishment of religion in part grew out of Europe's horrible experience with religious warfare in the sixteenth and seventeenth centuries. The founders were determined not to repeat it in the United States. (01-112)

FREEDOM SUMMER, 1964

In the 1960s, civil rights groups worked hard to end segregation and political discrimination in the Deep South, which were deeply entrenched and strongly defended by many whites. In the summer of 1964, a coalition of civil rights organizations led by the Student Nonviolent Coordinating Committee (SNCC) focused their efforts on Mississippi. There, only 6.7 percent of blacks were registered to vote, a number intentionally kept small by institutional obstruction. African Americans had to pay poll taxes and pass various tests, which did not apply to whites.

SNCC was launched in early 1960 in Greensboro, North Carolina, and grew out of the sit-in movement that sought equal service at lunch counters and other public places. Many of the 1,000 SNCC volunteers that summer were upper middle-class white students from northern colleges.

The voting issue attracted national attention, and hundreds of reporters were on hand to cover their voter-registration efforts in Mississippi. Tragically, they also covered violent white resistance. The campaign of white confrontation peaked with the murders of three civil rights workers, James Chaney, Andrew Goodman, and Michael Schwerner, in Neshoba County, as vividly described in the film *Mississippi Burning*.

The violence in Mississippi and other parts of the South galvanized the nation and prodded Congress into passing the Civil Rights Act of 1964 and, the following year, the Voting Rights Act, both of which succeeded in removing much of the legal infrastructure of white supremacy. (08-118)

SELMA, ALABAMA, 1965

Martin Luther King Jr. was convinced that the greatest ally the civil rights movement had lay in the consciences of white people. For too long, the white majority had advanced rhetoric in support of liberty and justice but had acquiesced in the face of white bigotry. Nonviolent tactics were designed to enflame white consciences.

By late winter 1965, King had focused the nation's attention on Selma, Alabama, and black voting rights. On Bloody Sunday, March 7, nearly a hundred protesters attempted to begin a protest march toward the state capital, Montgomery. At the Edmund Pettus Bridge they were run down by club-wielding state troopers and a mounted posse. Alarmed by continued white intransigence, President Lyndon Johnson personally brought a voting rights bill to the floor of Congress, closing his message with the words of the protest song, "we shall overcome."

With the way cleared by federal injunctions and protected by army and nationalized troops from the Alabama National Guard, on March 21, led by King, more than 3,000 marchers began a second march to Montgomery. When they arrived, King spoke to the largest civil rights rally in southern history gathered in front of the state capital. Governor Wallace peered through the blinds of his office at the crowd below, 25,000 strong. Soon, under federal pressure, the states of the Deep South were forced to include thousands of African Americans in the rites of civil life.

(05-006, 05-007, 05-008)

| 1700 | 1750 | 1800 | 1850 | 1900 | 1950 | PRESENT |

Era of Reaction, Social Struggle, and Political Contention

REAGAN VS. BROWN, 1966

In 1966, California Governor Edmund "Pat" Brown, a champion of liberalism, eagerly awaited the election against a political novice from Los Angeles, Ronald Wilson Reagan, a washed-up actor who had become General Electric's corporate spokesman in the 1950s. He was a rising conservative political activist. Brown thought he was a pushover and was soon locked in a real contest.

Unexpectedly, Brown ran into problems in his primary. His opponent, maverick conservative Democratic Los Angeles Mayor Sam Yorty, sounded like Reagan with vigorous rhetoric against free love, student disturbances, the Watts Riots, and big government. Democrats gave Yorty 38 percent. Brown had to prevent Yorty's votes from going to Reagan; otherwise, the governor would lose. Alarm went up in the Brown camp, and they began to attack the former actor for his political extremism. It never took.

Reagan was attractive, humorous, well scripted, and had the smoothest running campaign money could buy. Conservative Republicans had decided to move away from the ideological fringe and instead win elections and govern. That would require compromise and at least moderate-appearing candidates.

Voters buried Brown in a million-vote landslide. Reagan went on to preside over a revolution in state government and then, in two terms as president, the transformation of the national political conversation. (04-081, 04-082)

1400   1450   1500   1550   1600   1650   1700

APOLLO I TRAGEDY, 1967

At the beginning of the space race, the United States was nearly always behind. By 1966, President Kennedy's goal of reaching the moon by decade's end seemed unachievable. Kennedy's successor, Lyndon Johnson, needed a triumph. The Vietnam War, racial unrest, antiwar protests, and budget problems beset him from all sides. He turned up the pressure on NASA, and it responded by changing testing procedure. After bitter internal debate, the space program began employing an "all up" testing mandate for components. Prior to that, every part had to work individually before being put into a system. Now all major systems had to be complete before any testing occurred. This increased speed but also danger.

Soon after the module CSM 012 was delivered, thousands of failures, errors, and omissions were discovered. Late in the afternoon of January 27, 1967, the United States paid the price for haste. Three astronauts, Gus Grissom, Ed White, and Roger Chaffee, were locked in the Apollo command and service module atop a Saturn IB rocket at Cape Kennedy. At 6:31 p.m., all the carelessness and multiple flaws came together. There was fire in the cockpit.

Flight control listened helplessly as the crew reported the fire and screamed before there was silence. In the pure oxygen of the CSM, the lives were finished in fifteen seconds. It would have taken ninety seconds to open the hatch. Corrections were made after the tragedy, so this painful sacrifice probably ensured the success of man's first trip to the moon. (06-045, 06-046)

ASSASSINATION AND NIXON'S
SOUTHERN STRATEGY, 1968

The 1960s marked a significant shift in American party politics, propelled by the assassination of three important leaders in the Democratic Party: President John F. Kennedy in 1963 and, in succession in spring 1968, civil rights leader Dr. Martin Luther King Jr. and Senator Robert Kennedy. The events robbed the Democrats of national leadership, complicated by President Lyndon Johnson's decision not to seek a second term. Yet the most important change in future political direction came in the Republican Party.

That year, Richard Nixon, in an act of political genius, won the presidency by courting southern whites skeptical of African American progress. He made it clear to South Carolina Senator Strom Thurmond that he would tone down federal enforcement of civil rights laws and appoint "strict constructionist" conservative judges to federal courts. Johnson anticipated this shift when he signed the epic 1964 Civil Rights Act. He told aide Bill Moyers, "I may have just turned the South over to the Republican Party for the next generation." Yet the southern strategy had its downside. Republicans abandoned their original moral legacy of support for African Americans.

Such an obvious racist appeal disturbed many prominent Republicans. In summer 1968 during an address to the NAACP, Ken Mehlman, chair of the Republican National Committee, apologized: "Some Republicans gave up on winning the African American vote, looking the other way or trying to benefit politically from racial polarization. . . . I am here to tell you we were wrong." Nevertheless, 1968 marked the beginning of a mass shift in southern, hence national, party politics. (14-040, 14-041, 14-042)

| 1400 | 1450 | 1500 | 1550 | 1600 | 1650 | 1700 |

STONEWALL UPRISING, 1969

A full moon hung over Greenwich Village in lower Manhattan that warm June night in 1969. Near Sheridan Square, at the Stonewall Inn, a small bar catering mostly to homosexuals and their friends, a police raid was in progress. Owned by the Mafia, the Stonewall was serving liquor without a valid license. Normally, the owners had paid off the police but lately had withheld the bribes. The raid on the Stonewall was just another in a pattern of raids on gay establishments in the Village that summer. This time the result was different.

The officers had arrested several drag queens. A crowd began to gather, and soon rocks, cans, and bottles were being thrown at the police. The officers were surprised, as normally no resistance occurred in bars of this type. The gathering crowd forced the squad back into the inn, where they barricaded themselves and called for backup.

For the next four nights the battle of the Stonewall Inn continued with ever-larger police contingents facing swelling crowds of college students, antiwar radicals, and gay-rights proponents. There was no looting, and the riots occasionally took on a theater-of-the-absurd tone, with police tactical squads facing off against a kick-line of dancers baring their way to the inn.

Most Americans have never heard of the events of those June nights, but just as the 1956 Montgomery bus boycott was a milestone for black civil rights, the Stonewall Uprising represents for many homosexuals a watershed event in their resistance to legal discrimination. (01-004)

APOLLO 11, 1969

For millennia, humans have gazed heavenward at our nearest lunar neighbor in curiosity and awe. It became the first extraterrestrial destination set by the United States in its space quest. Following close earth orbits, the Apollo program in gradual stages drew closer to the first manned moon landing.

Apollo 11 would be the attempt. Launched by a Saturn V rocket, it was the fifth manned mission in the program. The trip took three days, and on July 21, 1969, six hours after the lunar module Eagle touched down, astronaut Neil Armstrong set foot on the moon's surface with the historic words "one small step for [a] man, one giant leap for mankind." He was soon joined by Buzz Aldrin. They spent over twenty-one hours on the moon performing a series of scientific experiments before returning to the command module *Columbia*, piloted by Michael Collins. The return journey ended in a splashdown in the Pacific on July 24.

This mission fulfilled the goal set by President John F. Kennedy to land a man on the moon and return him safely to the earth within the decade of the 1960s. It gave a strong boost to space exploration.

The warning of the right to remain silent must be accompanied by the explanation that anything said can and will be used against him in court in order to make the individual aware not only of the fact of his privilege but also of the consequences of foregoing

MIRANDA DECISION, 1972

In 1966, Ernesto Miranda, a confessed rapist and kidnapper in an Arizona state prison, had acknowledged in his confession that he was aware of his legal rights. But during interrogation, he had not specifically been informed of the right to counsel.

When Miranda's conviction was appealed to the Supreme Court, Chief Justice Earl Warren, writing for the majority, insisted prosecutors must provide certain safeguards to defendants before statements taken in custody could be used as trial evidence. Those placed under arrest had to be read their rights, often from a so-called Miranda card: to remain silent, to understand that anything they say may be used as evidence, and to use an attorney.

Defenders of the ruling believed *Miranda* actually made the police's job easier, standardizing arrest procedures and ensuring confessions after rights were read could survive legal scrutiny. Critics charged that the ruling weakened law enforcement.

Miranda was retried, convicted, and, after a prison term, released. He died ten years after the decision that bears his name, stabbed in a bar fight.

Over the years, opponents tried with legislation and litigation to weaken the "Miranda warning," but, generally, courts have upheld requiring disclosure of a defendant's rights as constitutional. Late in the 1990s at the federal appellate level, successful attacks were made on some aspects of the Miranda requirement, including the Supreme Court's decision in *Berghuis v. Thompkins* (2010). The court said that police interrogations do not have to end if an arrested person gives "ambiguous or equivocal" statements or no statements. Some scholars have questioned whether this decision effectively undermined the Miranda policy. (05-042)

WATERGATE AND
THE RESIGNATION OF
RICHARD NIXON, 1974

Within two years of securing one of the most astounding victories in US electoral history, the presidency of Richard Nixon collapsed. The stunning reversal can largely be traced to the president's insecurities: he felt socially, professionally, and personally inadequate. Because much of the political establishment looked down on him, he was so determined to prevail that he skirted the edge of legality. He and his men put together an unofficial team of security operatives known as "the plumbers," originally intended to plug White House leaks to the press. They soon engaged in various illegalities, culminating in an abortive attempt to bug the headquarters of the Democratic National Committee in late spring 1972. The group was caught and arrested.

From the beginning, Nixon covered up the origin, funding source, and extent of the operation. For the next two years, the president denied his participation and that of his White House aides in, what he called the "third-rate burglary." Despite vigorous efforts by the president and his allies to undermine trust in those pursuing him, slowly, fitfully the truth emerged through enterprising efforts of journalists, congressional sleuths, and Justice Department investigators.

Unknown to his visitors and even his staff, Nixon had taped his Oval Office conversations, continuing his predecessors' practice. After an epic legal battle eventually decided by the US Supreme Court, the president had to surrender his tapes, particularly those proving him guilty of obstruction of justice. Within days of the release of the "smoking gun" tape, Nixon's support in his own party collapsed. The US House of Representatives was preparing to impeach him. To avoid this rebuke, he resigned on August 8, 1974.

US LEAVES SAIGON, 1975

Graham Martin, US ambassador to South Vietnam, had been at his post for twenty-one months. America had been involved in Vietnam since President Kennedy sent military advisors in 1962. The toll of the war was billions spent, nearly 60,000 Americans dead, and a mountain of Vietnamese casualties. It had come down to this fateful day with a nation crumbling, a capital surrounded by North Vietnamese tanks, and a US ambassador destroying his papers in the wee dark hours of the morning.

After sending a final message, Martin left his office and with most of the staff went upstairs. They came out onto the roof of the embassy at 4:40 a.m. Soon a CH-46 helicopter inscribed with the words *Lady Ace 09* landed. The ambassador, the flag under his arm, boarded the helicopter. The United States departed Vietnam as the hard, dark eastern sky softened with the dawn of April 30, 1975. (01-004)

1400   1450   1500   1550   1600   1650   1700

For 444 days beginning in November 1979, more than fifty American citizens and diplomatic personnel were held hostage in the US Embassy, Tehran. The immediate cause was the decision of the United States to admit the deposed Shah Mohammad Reza Pahlavi for cancer treatment. This seemed a signal to the followers of the Iranian Revolution led by Ayatollah Ruhollah Khomeini. They feared that perhaps America was reverting to its pattern of lockstep support for the Shah, which stretched back to the coup d'etat that overthrew Prime Minister Mohammad Mosaddegh in 1953 and allowed Pahlavi to assume absolute control of Iran's government.

The students originally intended to take over the embassy for a brief period, but then the Ayatollah publicly supported the action and Iranian public opinion turned strongly supportive of the invasion and hostage-taking. The crisis likewise produced a surge of patriotic feeling in America. President Carter turned up the heat by freezing Iranian assets in the United States and ending oil imports from Iran. He also authorized a high-stakes attempt to rescue the hostages. The mission was aborted when aircraft became disabled. This failure and Carter's acceptance of responsibility weakened his reelection prospects. As a gesture of insult, the hostages' release was timed to coincide with Carter's departure from the presidency on January 20, 1981.

"THERE YOU GO AGAIN"–
FOUR LITTLE WORDS, 1980

Presidential debates have only been around for a short time—prior to 1980, only in 1960 and 1976. After much negotiation and posturing, President Jimmy Carter and Republican candidate Ronald Reagan met on October 28 in Cleveland, Ohio.

The candidates came to Cleveland with separate agendas. Jimmy Carter was the embattled incumbent, distracted by the crisis caused by the Iran hostage crisis and running ever so slightly behind in the polls. Ronald Reagan needed to dispel the impression that he was a washed-up motion picture actor with little experience and prone to recklessness in matters of foreign policy.

They began by discussing the Iran hostages and terrorism, then arms control, the energy problem, and social security. The climax occurred when Jimmy Carter began to attack Reagan on his record on Medicare. Reagan responded to Carter, screwed himself up to his true height, looked at the president, and shaking his head said, "There you go again." As if admonishing a poor student, he seemed to rebuke the president's incorrect information.

Probably on merits the two had come out even, but on image Reagan carried the day. In 1960, Jack Kennedy helped erase the image of his inexperience. In 1980, Reagan dealt with the negative image of immaturity. By lecturing the president of the United States, he appeared himself to be presidential.

1400   1450   1500   1550   1600   1650   1700

WILLIE HORTON AND THE POLITICS OF RACE, 1988

The Republican Party's southern strategy to appeal to disgruntled white southern voters was precarious. Overt racist appeals were unacceptable, but code words and phrases could arouse conservative southerners without offending northern voters' sensibilities.

Lee Atwater, a South Carolina political consultant, was one of the finest practitioners of this dark art. Speaking in a 1981 interview with political scientist Alexander Lamis, Atwater said southern politics in the old days permitted blatant racist appeal with copious use of the N word. By the 1960s, use of racist terms "backfires. So you say stuff like . . . forced busing, states' rights . . . now [even] talking about cutting taxes."

In 1988, Atwater managed George H. W. Bush's presidential campaign. He found the perfect vehicle for activating the racist vote without seeming to do so. With an independent Republican group, Atwater produced national TV ads featuring Willie Horton, a black prisoner convicted of murder and serving a life sentence. While on weekend furlough in Massachusetts, he escaped before committing rape and murder in Maryland. Atwater tied Horton to Bush's opponent, Governor Michael Dukakis, who presided over the furlough program. Many voters concluded Dukakis was weak on crime and criminal justice.

In the early 1990s, Atwater was diagnosed with an aggressive and ultimately fatal brain cancer. Soon after, he converted to Roman Catholicism; to repent, he apologized to those he believed were hurt by his ruthless campaign tactics. Many admired his confessions. Yet, playing to racial prejudice to secure votes remains a potent weapon. As Barry Goldwater, the 1964 candidate who capitalized on racism, said, he wanted to "go hunting where the ducks are."

| 1700 | 1750 | 1800 | 1850 | 1900 | 1950 | PRESENT |

REPUBLICAN REVOLUTION, 1994

In American government, political parties serve a unique function. They recruit and nurture political talent, articulate ideological values in hopes of appealing to a large segment of the electorate, and help organize political institutions when in power. Through history American parties have risen and fallen. Some have disappeared into to a successor party. For example, in the 1850s the Whig Party and the Know-Nothing Party collapsed and were folded into the antislavery Republican Party, which defended the Union during the Civil War and until the Great Depression of the 1930s dominated American politics.

The Democratic Party then led American national politics until the southern strategy of Richard Nixon began the exodus of conservative southerners away from the Democratic coalition to join with the Republicans. The election that signaled the end of the Democratic era was the midterm election in 1994.

During that election, the Republicans developed a two-point strategy. First, they steadily attacked the then occupant of the White House, President Bill Clinton, whose popularity was on the wane. Second, they developed a contract with America, which was a list of goals they would pursue if given the chance in power. This strategy worked: for the first time in forty years, Republicans controlled both houses of Congress. Within the first year, the House of Representatives enacted all pieces of the contract with America.

One of the most fascinating developments in modern American politics is the increasing discussion of a candidate's sexual activity. Prior to this era, the press and voters largely ignored the personal lives of politicians, including possible sexual liaisons. The experience of presidential candidate Gary Hart in the 1988 is instructive and signaled a turning point. Hart, a man immensely rich in political talent, was the front-runner for the Democratic nomination until he was ensnared in rumors of a sexual affair with Donna Rice, an affair both have consistently denied.

In 1998, President Bill Clinton was impeached because he did not tell the truth in sworn testimony about a sexual liaison with a White House intern. He later confessed to having had inappropriate relations with Monica Lewinsky. In his senate trial, he was acquitted.

The previous "rule" that a public figure's private life was out-of-bounds unless it impacted public duties seems in this era to be wishful thinking. Now everything is subject to scrutiny and public revelation. Such is driven in part by hardening political polarization in the electorate and in part by news media caught in a hot competitive environment in pursuit of the revenues secured through sensational speculation and revelation.

BUSH V. GORE, 2000

In 2000, the presidential election was one of the most contentious in US history. Democratic candidate Vice President Al Gore contended with Texas Governor George W. Bush for the White House. Ultimately, Gore won the popular vote nationally by more than 537,000 votes. Nevertheless, Bush won in the Electoral College 271–266, with 270 needed for victory. The key was the results in Florida; the official state count gave Florida to Bush by a 537-vote majority.

The Gore campaign, after first conceding the election to Bush, took that back and began to seek a manual recount of votes in counties such as Broward County, which was a target-rich environment for Democratic voters. The count continued until December 8, when the Florida Supreme Court ordered a statewide manual recount. At that point the US Supreme Court stopped that recount. Seven of nine justices agreed that there was a violation of the Equal Protection Clause of the Fourteenth Amendment because no consistent voting standards existed throughout the state. Five of nine justices said that there was not enough time to establish a statewide vote-counting standard. This effectively stopped the recount and allowed the state-determined Bush victory to proceed. Subsequent studies conducted by news organizations produced a variety of results, some for Gore, some for Bush, based on the vote-counting standards applied.

Bush v. Gore remains was one of the most controversial decisions in Supreme Court history and did little to smooth the deep partisan divide that characterizes modern American electoral politics.

| 1400 | 1450 | 1500 | 1550 | 1600 | 1650 | 1700 |

9/11 AND ASYMMETRIC WARFARE, 2001

On September 11, 2001, four airliners were hijacked by devotees of Osama Bin Laden, leader of Al-Qaida, the militant Sunni Islam multinational organization. Two planes hit the World Trade Center in New York City, one hit the Pentagon, and the fourth crashed in the Pennsylvania countryside after an apparent passenger revolt against the hijackers.

Symmetric warfare is between two enemies whose resources and strengths are generally comparable and whose strategy is similar. The 9/11 attacks exemplified asymmetric or irregular warfare, in which one or more weaker opponents attempt to counterbalance

1700	1750	1800	1850	1900	1950	PRESENT

their weaknesses by exploiting the weaknesses of their stronger opponent or opponents.

The attacks were perpetrated against an international power with a huge population, whose military resources and economic supremacy was unequaled, perhaps in human history. The group carrying out this attack had very few adherents by comparison. The United States had lax airport security, and its intelligence services and law enforcement were dangerously disconnected. Both knew something was afoot but failed to act in concert to thwart the attacks. One factor of the spectacular success of the Trade Center attack was engineer Bin Laden's understanding of its structure. A plane hitting the towers at a quarter of the distance from the top would cause the top floors to collapse and then sheer weight would take the tower down.

To defend against such asymmetric attacks, a strong power must be much more aware of its own weaknesses and prepare to defeat attempts by weaker entities to exploit them.

SMARTPHONES, THE IPHONE, AND THE END OF BOREDOM, 2007

One social commentator has remarked that we may have created a generation whose members will not know boredom. The advent of smartphones, particularly the industry-leading iPhone, has created a social phenomenon in which people stay connected at all times, constantly stimulated by incoming messages from email, text, and social platforms and by information, music, audio, and video instantly available to the user. All of this is driven and often herded by an artificial-intelligence technology that grows increasingly more sophisticated with each passing month.

The smartphone is a breathlessly recent development. Prior to introduction and use, people carried a cell phone and a PDA (personal digital assistant) device. In the mid-1990s, companies began to combine the two into the first primitive smartphones, such as the Pocket PC and Palm Pilot. As each year passed, the technology became more complex, and though the size of these devices remained only marginally smaller, what they could do was enhanced.

The climax of this revolution was the introduction in 2007 of the first generation iPhone by Apple with its multifunction screen and virtual keyboard. It captured the imagination of consumers and immediately leaped to the forefront of sales, setting the standard that other manufacturers imitated and in some cases improved upon. The question about these devices is whether they enhance or smother intellectual development.

| 1700 | 1750 | 1800 | 1850 | 1900 | 1950 | PRESENT |

ELECTION OF THE FIRST AFRICAN AMERICAN PRESIDENT, 2008

From the earliest days of English settlement in Virginia, African Americans have played an important role in America's development. They were first slaves whose forced servitude provided the economic foundation of the plantation economy in southern colonies and then states. After the cataclysmic struggle of the Civil War, which was fought largely to resolve the moral question of slavery, blacks took their place as citizens. The extent of their civic participation depended on which region of the country they lived in. During the era of Jim Crow, black involvement in civic and economic life was repressed in the American South.

Beginning in the 1950s, African Americans and their allies began to break up resistant racist institutions denying them full participation in the American dream. Nevertheless, race remains a factor influencing interpersonal attitudes and actions. Despite this fault line of race, the republic seemed to move beyond it when in 2008 an African American was elected president.

In 2004, at the Democratic National Convention, a little-known state senator from Illinois, Barack Hussein Obama, electrified the convention with a stem-winder keynote address on the possibilities and hopes for America. After a landslide victory in the US Senate race and a spirited primary campaign against Hillary Rodham Clinton, Obama bested Republican candidate Senator John McCain in a runaway election victory. He became the 44th president of the United States on January 20, 2009.

ADVENT OF GENDER-NEUTRAL
MARRIAGE, 2015

Perhaps no social and legal transformation in US history has been as swift as that for LGBT citizens. While there remains a bitterly resistant minority, strong majorities in American society now support unimpeded participation of homosexuals in all social, legal, economic, and even religious parts of life.

Homosexuals have endured spiritual, personal, and professional discrimination for generations. Then, beginning in the early 1980s, due to the unique manner in which the retrovirus HIV-AIDS is transmitted, the LBGT family was ravaged by a vicious pandemic. In addition to having to bear the brunt of AIDS stigma, the community struggled with the loss of hundreds of thousands friends and loved ones as researchers attempted to find medical means of attenuating the progress of the virus.

Despite these agonizing circumstances, there has been substantial statutory relief for homosexuals.

Loving v. Virginia (1967), the Supreme Court decision that struck down laws banning interracial marriage, was a basis for eliminating legal discrimination against homosexuals. Despite *Bowers v. Hardwick* (1986), which upheld Georgia's antisodomy law, the US Supreme Court dismantled the discrimination in three key decisions.

In *Lawrence v. Texas* (2003), the court reversed the *Bowers* decision, striking down antisodomy laws nationwide. Having decided that homosexuals could not be legally impaired from affectional expression, the court, in *United States v. Windsor* (2013), struck down DOMA (Defense of Marriage Act), which it said violated the Fifth Amendment's prohibition against depriving a citizen of life and liberty. The case expanded individual state recognition of same-sex relationships to the entire nation, extending federal marriage benefits to same-gender couples. In *Obergefell v. Hodges* (2015), the court ruled that same-gender couples could marry on the same terms as opposite-gender couples, guaranteed in the Due Process and Equal Protection Clauses of the Fourteenth Amendment.

Dr. Martin Luther King Jr. liked to quote nineteenth-century clergyman Theodore Parker: "The arc of the moral universe is long, but it bends toward justice." The arc for African Americans has been long and still requires heavy effort for bending. The experience of homosexuals shows that legal transformation can be breathtakingly swift. In both cases, transforming attitudes and feelings of a resistant minority takes much, much longer.

BIBLIOGRAPHIC APPENDIX

INTRODUCTION

Morison, Samuel Loring. "Origin of 'Fair Winds and Following Seas.'" Ibiblio
.org, https://www.ibiblio.org/hyperwar/NHC/fairwinds.htm. Naval historian
Samuel Loring Morison says that the goodbye blessing "fair winds and
following seas" probably comes from two older quotes merged into one. "Fair
winds" indicates the well-wisher's desire that a friend will have a safe journey
and good fortune. Nautically, it probably refers to unfurling all sails to aid in a
swift journey home. "Following seas" is when the waves and the surface of the
water go in the direction of the tide and convey the traveler moving swiftly and
pleasingly toward the destination.

The phrase is often used in beginning ceremonies, such as the commissioning
of a vessel or promotion of an individual. It may also be used in farewell
ceremonies. In the case of this book, the reference is to the beginning of a
voyage of discovery.

1. COLUMBUS DID NOT DISCOVER AMERICA

Boorstin, Daniel J., and Gerald Parshall. "History's Hidden Turning Points."
U.S. News and World Report 110 (22 April 1991): 52–66.

Starr, S. Frederick. "So Who Did Discover America?" *History Today* 63
(12 December 2013): 34–39.

Weiner, Eric. "Coming to America: Who Was First?" National Public Radio
(8 October 2007), https://www.npr.org/templates/story/story.php?storyId
=15040888.

2. TRANSATLANTIC COD BRIDGE

Kurlansky, Mark. *The Basque History of the World*. New York: Walker Publishing,
1999.

——. *Cod: A Biography of the Fish That Changed the World*. New York: Penguin
Group, 1997.

Morison, Samuel Eliot. *The Great Explorers: The European Discovery of America*. New
York: Oxford University Press, 1978.

3. JOHN CABOT

Morison, Samuel Eliot. "Cabot, The Mysterious Sailor Who Gave England Rights
to North America." *Smithsonian* 2 (1 April 1971): 12–20.

Williamson, James Alexander. *The Cabot Voyages and Bristol Discovery under Henry VII*. Cambridge: Cambridge University Press, 1962.

4. ANTONIO PIGAFETTA AND THE MISSING DAY

Durant, David N. *Ralegh's Lost Colony*. New York: Atheneum, 1981.

Kupperman, Karen Ordahl. *Roanoke: The Abandoned Colony*. Totowa, NJ: Rowman and Allanheld, 1984.

——. "Roanoke Lost," *American Heritage* 36 (5, 1985): 81–96.

Manchester, William. *A World Lit Only by Fire*. New York: Little, Brown and Company, 1992.

Morison, Samuel Eliot and Mauricio Obregon. *The European Discovery of America: The Southern Voyages*. New York: Oxford University Press, 1974.

——. "Follow Magellan's Wake in His Strait." *Smithsonian* 4 (11 February 1974): 44–52.

Pigafetta, Antonio. *Magellan's Voyage Around the World*, ed. James Alexander Robertson. 2 vols. Cleveland: Arthur C. Clark Company, 1906.

Quinn, David B. *Set Fair for Roanoke: Voyages and Colonies, 1584–1606*. Chapel Hill, NC: University of North Carolina Press, 1985.

Roditi, Edouard. *Magellan of the Pacific*. New York: McGraw-Hill, 1972.

Stick, David. *Roanoke Island: The Beginnings of English America*. Chapel Hill, NC: University of North Carolina Press, 1983.

5. DON LUÍS'S REVENGE

Martinez, Bartolomé. "Relation," in *The Spanish Jesuit Mission in Virginia, 1570–1572*. Clifford M. Lewis and Albert J. Loomie, eds. Chapel Hill, NC: University of North Carolina Press, 1953.

Rountree, Helen C. *Powhatan Foreign Relations: 1500–1722*. Charlottesville, VA: University of Virginia Press. 1993.

Taylor, Alan. *American Colonies*. New York: Viking, 2001.

6–7. THE LOST COLONY I & II

Durant, *Ralegh's Lost Colony*. Full ref. under 4.

Kupperman, *Roanoke: The Abandoned Colony*. Full ref. under 4.

Kupperman, "Roanoke Lost." Full ref. under 4.

Quinn, *Set Fair for Roanoke*. Full ref. under 4.

Stick, *Roanoke Island*. Full ref. under 4.

8. BRITAIN AND VIRGINIA

Bridenbaugh, Carl. *Jamestown: 1544–1699*. New York: Oxford University Press, 1980.

Bucholz, Robert, and Newton Key. *Modern England: 1485–1714*. Oxford: Blackwell Publishing, 2004.

Divine, Robert A., et al. *America: Past and Present*. New York: Addison-Wesley Longman, 1998.

Taylor, *American Colonies*. Full ref. under 5.

Wright, Louis Booker. *The American Heritage History of the Thirteen Colonies*. New York: American Heritage Publishing Company, 1967.

9. FOUNDING JAMESTOWN

Barbour, Philip L. *The Jamestown Voyages 1606–1609*. London: Cambridge University Press, 1968.

Bridenbaugh, Jamestown. Full ref. under 8.

Craven, Wesley Frank. *The Virginia Company of London, 1606–1624*. Williamsburg, VA: Virginia 350th Anniversary Celebration Corporation, 1957.

Davis, Jane Eliza. *Round about Jamestown*. Hampton, VA: J. E. Davis, 1907.

Hall-Quest, Olga W. *Jamestown Adventure*. New York: E. P. Dutton and Co., 1950.

Kelso, William M., Nicholas M. Luccketti, and Beverly A. Straube. *Jamestown Discovery III*. Richmond, VA: APVA, 1997.

LeMay, J. A. Leo. *The American Dream of Captain John Smith*. Charlottesville, VA: University Press of Virginia, 1991.

Vaughan, Alden T. *American Genesis, Captain John Smith and the Founding of Virginia*. Boston: Little, Brown and Company, 1975.

The World Book Encyclopedia. Vol. 9. Chicago: World Book-Childcraft International, 1980.

Warton, Henry. *The Life of John Smith*. Chapel Hill, NC: University of North Carolina Press, 1957.

10. POCAHONTAS

Edmunds, Pocahontas Wight. *The Pocahontas–John Smith Story*. Richmond, VA: Dietz Press, 1956.

Mossiker, Frances. *Pocahontas: The Life and the Legend*. New York: Alfred A. Knopf, 1976.

Rountree, Helen C. *Pocahontas's People: The Powhatan Indians of Virginia through Four Centuries*. Norman, OK: University of Oklahoma Press, 1944.

Smith, Bradford. *Captain John Smith, His Life and Legend*. Philadelphia: Lippincott Publishing, 1953.

Smith, John. *Captain John Smith: Works 1608–1631*. Edited by E. Arber. Edinburgh: John Grant, 1910.

Tilton, R.S. *Pocahontas, The Evolution of an American Narrative*. Cambridge: Cambridge University Press, 1994.

11. JOHN SMITH

Barbour, Philip. *Three Worlds of Captain John Smith*. Boston: Houghton Mifflin, 1964.

Smith, John. *Complete Works of Captain John Smith*. Edited by Philip Barbour. Chapel Hill, NC: University of North Carolina Press, 1986.

Vaughan, *American Genesis*. Full ref. under 9.

12. BARON DE LA WARE

Coward, Barry. *The Stuart Age: England, 1603–1714*. London: Longman, 1994.

Morrill, John, ed. *The Oxford Illustrated History of Tudor & Stuart Britain*. Oxford: Oxford University Press, 1996.

Palliser, D. M. *The Age of Elizabeth: England under the Later Tudors, 1547–1603*. London: Longman, 1983.

Smith, Lacey Baldwin. *The Horizon Book of the Elizabethan World*. New York: American Heritage Publishing Company, 1967.

13. JOHN ROLFE

Price, David. *Love and Hate in Jamestown*. New York: Alfred A. Knopf, 2003.

Rolfe, John. *A True Relation of the State of Virginia . . . 1616*. Charlottesville, VA: University Press of Virginia, 1971. See especially the biographical sketch by John Melville Jennings.

Rountree, *Pocahontas's People*. Full ref. under 10.

Rountree, Helen. *Young Pocahontas in the Indian World*. Yorktown, VA: J & R Graphic Services, 1995.

Townsend, Camilla. *Pocahontas and the Powhatan Dilemma*. New York: Hill and Wang, 2004.

14. SLAVES COME TO VIRGINIA

Bennett, Lerone. *Before the Mayflower: A History of Black America*. Whitefish, MT: Literary Licensing, 2012.

Foner, Philip S. *History of Black Americans: From Africa to the Emergence of the Cotton Kingdom*. Westport, CT: Greenwood Press, 1975.

Franklin, John Hope. *From Slavery to Freedom: A History of Negro Americans*. New York: Alfred A. Knopf, 1967.

Roeder, Bill. *Jackie Robinson*. New York: A. S. Barnes and Company, 1950.

Toppin, Edgar A. *The Black American in United States History*. Boston: Allyn and Bacon, 1973.

15. MAYFLOWER COMPACT

Bradford, William. *Of Plymouth Plantation*. Edited by Samuel Eliot Morrison. New York: Alfred A. Knopf, 1952.

Langdon, George D., Jr. "The Franchise and Political Democracy in Plymouth Colony." *William and Mary Quarterly, 3rd Series* 20 (4 October 1963): 513–526.

Marsh, Daniel L. *The American Canon*. New York: Abingdon-Cokesbury Press, 1939.

Morison, Samuel Eliot. "New Light Wanted on the Old Colony." *William and Mary Quarterly, 3rd Series* 15 (2 July, 1958): 359–364.

Osgood, Herbert L. *The American Colonies in the Seventeenth Century.* London: Macmillan and Company, 1904.

Sargent, Mark L. "The Conservative Covenant: The Rise of the Mayflower Compact in American Myth." *New England Quarterly* 61 (2 June, 1988): 233–251.

Smith, Lacy Baldwin. *This Realm of England 1399–1688*, 8th ed. Boston: Houghton Mifflin Company, 2001.

Yale Law School, Avalon Project. "The Mayflower Compact: 1620," http://avalon .law.yale.edu/17th_century/mayflower.asp.

16. TOBACCO

Bridenbraugh, Carl. *Jamestown: 1544–1699*. New York: Oxford University Press, 1980.

Taylor, *American Colonies*. Full ref. under 5.

Wright, *The American Heritage History of the Thirteen Colonies*. Full ref. under 8.

17. VIRGINIA COMPANY'S DEMISE

Canny, Nicholas, ed. *The Origins of Empire: British Overseas Enterprise to the Close of the Seventeenth Century*. Vol. 1 of *The Oxford History of the British Empire*. New York: Oxford University Press, 1998.

Rountree, Helen. *The Powhatan Indians*. Full ref. under 13.

Taylor, *American Colonies*. Full ref. under 5.

18. ANNE HUTCHINSON

Anticaglia, Elizabeth. *Twelve American Women*. Chicago: Nelson-Hall, 1975.

Devine, Robert A., et al. *America Past and Present*. New York: Longman, 1998.

Foster, Warren Dunham, ed. *Heroines of Modern Religion*. Freeport, NY: Books for the Libraries Press, 1970.

"Hutchinson, Anne." Encyclopedia Britannica, https://www.britannica.com /biography/Anne-Hutchinson.

Lang, Amy Schrager. *Prophetic Woman: Anne Hutchinson and the Problem of Dissent in the Literature of New England*. Berkeley: University of California Press, 1987.

Tobin, Lad. "A Radically Different Voice: Gender and Language in the Trials of Anne Hutchinson." *Early American Literature* 25 (3, 1990): 253–270.

19. ROGER WILLIAMS AND RHODE ISLAND

Gaustad, Edwin S. *Liberty of Conscience: Roger Williams in America*. Valley Forge, PA: Judson Press, 1999.

Keary, Anne. "Retelling the History of the Settlement of Providence: Speech,

Writing, and Cultural Interaction on Narragansett Bay." *New England Quarterly* 69 (2, 1996): 250–86.

Settle, Mary Lee. *I, Roger Williams*. New York: W. W. Norton, 2001.

Skaggs, Donald. *Roger Williams' Dream for America*. New York: P. Lang, 1993.

"Williams, Roger." Encyclopedia Britannica, http://www.britannica.com.

20. ALGONQUIAN ANNIHILATION

Axtell, James. "The Rise and Fall of the Powhatan Empire." In *After Columbus: Essays in the Ethnohistory of Colonial North America*. New York: Oxford University Press, 1988.

Rountree, *Pocahontas's People*. Full ref. under 10.

Taylor, *American Colonies*. Full ref. under 5.

21. CAROLINA COLONY

Devine, Robert A., et al. *America Past and Present*. New York: Longman, 1998.

Edgar, Walter. *South Carolina: A History*. Columbia, SC: University of South Carolina Press, 1998.

"Historical Highlights of North Carolina: Colonial Period." North Carolina Encyclopedia, http://statelbirary.dcr.state.nc.us/nc/history/history.htm.

"North Carolina." Encyclopedia Britannica, http://www.britannica.com/eb/article?eu=12129.

22. BACON'S REBELLION

Billings, Warren M., John E. Selby, and Thad W. Tate. *Colonial Virginia: A History*. White Plains, NY: KTO Press, 1986.

Oberg, Michael Leroy. *Samuel Wiseman's Book of Record: The Official Account of Bacon's Rebellion in Virginia, 1676–1677*. New York: Lexington Books, 2005.

Washburn, Wilcomb E. *The Governor and the Rebel: A History of Bacon's Rebellion in Virginia*. New York: Norton, 1972.

23. WILLIAM PENN'S HOLY EXPERIMENT

Bronner, Edwin B. *William Penn's Holy Experiment: The Founding of Pennsylvania, 1681–1701*. New York: Temple University Publications, 1962.

"Friends, Society of." Encyclopædia Britannica, https://www.britannica.com/topic/Society-of-Friends.

Hudson, Patricia. *Penning a Legacy*. New York: Gale Group, 1999.

Wildes, Harry Emerson. *William Penn*. New York: Macmillan, 1974.

24-25. WITCHCRAFT IN MASSACHUSETTS I & II

Hansen, Chadwick. *Witchcraft at Salem*. New York: G. Braziller Publishing Company, 1969.

Mappen, Marc. *Witches and Historians: Interpretations of Salem.* Huntington, NY: R. E. Krieger Publishing Company, 1980.

Starkey, Marion Lena. *The Devil in Massachusetts: A Modern Inquiry into the Salem Witch Trials.* London: R. Hale Publishers, 1962.

Upham, Charles Wentworth. *Salem Witchcraft.* New York: F. Ungar Publishing Company, 1959.

Williams, Salem R. *Riding the Nightmare: Women and Witchcraft from the Old World to Colonial Salem.* New York: Harper/Perennial, 1992.

26. JOHN LAW AND THE MISSISSIPPI BUBBLE

Law, John. *Money and Trade Considered, with a Proposal for Supplying the Nation with Money* (1705).

Minton, Robert W. "John Law's Bubble: Bigger . . . Bigger and then Bust." *Smithsonian* 6 (10 January 1976): 92–98.

27. JAMES OGLETHORPE AND THE FOUNDING OF GEORGIA

Baine, Rodney M., ed. *The Publications of James Edward Oglethorpe.* Athens, GA: Georgia University Press, 1994.

Ettinger, Amos Aschbach. *James Edward Oglethorpe: Imperial Idealist, 1936.* Oxford: Oxford University Press, 1968.

Wright, Edmond. "Rev. of Some Account of the Design of the Trustees for Establishing Colonys in America, by James Edward Oglethorpe." *English Historical Review* (June 1994): 737.

28. TRIAL OF JOHN PETER ZENGER

Alexander, James. *A Brief Narrative of the Case and Trial of John Peter Zenger, Printer of the New York Weekly Journal.* Edited by Stanley Katz. Cambridge, MA: Harvard University Press, 1963.

Buranelli, Vincent, ed. *The Trial of Peter Zenger.* New York: New York University Press, 1957.

Finkleman, Paul. "The Zenger Case: Prototype of a Political Trial." In *American Political Trials*, Michael R. Belknap, ed. Westport, CT: Greenwood Press, 1982.

Hamburger, Philip. "The Development of the Law of Seditious Libel and the Control of the Press." *Stanford Law Review* 661 (1985).

Smolla, Rodney A. *Smolla and Nimmer on Freedom of Speech.* St. Paul, MN: Westgroup, 63rd ed., 1998.

"The Trial of Mr. John Peter Zenger." *17 Howell's State Trials* 675 (1735). London: T. C. Hansard, 1813.

29. GREAT AWAKENING

Davidson, Edward D. *Jonathan Edwards, The Narrative of a Puritan Mind.* Cambridge, MA: Harvard University Press, 1968.

Gaustad, Edwin S. *The Great Awakening in New England*. Gloucester, MA: Peter Smith, 1965.

Miller, Perry. *Jonathan Edwards*. Toronto: William Sloane Associates, 1949.

30. GILBERT TENNENT

Coalter, Milton. *Gilbert Tennent: Son of Thunder*. Westport, CT: Greenwood Press, 1986.

Fisgburn, Janet F. "Gilbert Tennent, Established 'Dissenter.'" *Church History* 63 (1, 1994): 31–49.

Gaustad, Edwin S. *Religious Issues in American History*. New York: Harper and Row Publishers, 1968.

Tennent, Gilbert. "The Danger of an Unconverted Ministry." Ligonier Ministries, https://www.ligonier.org/learn/articles/the-danger-of-an-unconverted-ministry.

Westerkamp, Marilyn. "Division, Dissension, and Compromise: The Presbyterian Church during the Great Awakening." *Journal of Presbyterian History* 31 (October 2003).

31. SCOTTISH SETTLEMENT IN NORTH CAROLINA

Bailyn, Bernard. *Voyagers to the West*. New York: Vintage, 1986.

MacDonell, Margaret. *The Emigrant Experience*. Toronto: University of Toronto Press, 1982.

Murdoch, Alexander. "A Scottish Document Concerning Emigration to North Carolina in 1772." North Carolina Office of Archives and History, 1990, http://www.ncpublications.com/colonial/nchr/subjects/murdoch.htm.

Newton, Michael. *We're Indians Sure Enough: The Legacy of the Scottish Highlanders in the United States*. Richmond, VA: Saorsa Media, 2001.

32. FLORA MACDONALD

Kerber, Linda K. *Women of the Republic: Intellect and Ideology in Revolutionary America*. Chapel Hill, NC: University of North Carolina Press, 1980.

Ryan, Mary P. *Womanhood in America: From Colonial Times to the Present*. New York: New Viewpoints Publishing, 1975.

Spruill, Julia Cherry. *Women's Life and Work in the Southern Colonies*. Chapel Hill, NC: University of North Carolina Press, 1938.

Young, Philip. *Revolutionary Ladies*. New York: Alfred K. Knopf, 1977.

33. WHITEFIELD AND FRANKLIN

Cray, Robert E., Jr. "Memorialization and Enshrinement: George Whitefield and Popular Religious Culture, 1770–1850." *Journal of the Early Republic* 10 (3, Fall 1990): 339–362.

Lambert, Frank. "Subscribing for Profits and Piety." *William and Mary Quarterly, Third Series* 50 (3 July 1993): 531–548.

34. GEORGE WASHINGTON ON THE FRONTIER

"George Washington: The Soldier through the French and Indian War."
USHistory.org, www.ushistory.org/valleyforge/washington/george1.html.

Lengel, Edward G. *General George Washington: A Military Life*. New York: Random House, 2005.

Wall, Charles Cecil. *George Washington: Citizen-Soldier*. Charlottesville, VA: University Press of Virginia, 1980.

35. PATRICK HENRY AND THE PARSON'S CAUSE

Axelrad, Jacob. *Patrick Henry: The Voice of Freedom*. New York: Random House, 1947.

Beenman, Richard R. *Patrick Henry: A Biography*. New York: McGraw-Hill, 1974.

Campbell, Norine Dickson. *Patrick Henry: Patriot and Statesman*. New York: Devin-Adair Company, 1969.

Meade, Robert D. *Patrick Henry: Patriot in the Making*. Philadelphia: J. B. Lippincott Company, 1957.

Red Hill Patrick Henry Memorial Foundation, http://www.redhill.org.

Scott, Arthur P. "The Constitutional Aspects of the 'Parson's Cause.'" *Political Science Quarterly* 31 (December 1916): 558-577.

36. THE MASON-DIXON LINE

Bode, Carl. D. *A Bicentennial History*. New York: Norton Publishing Company, 1978.

Brugger, Robert J., ed. *Maryland: A Middle Temperament, 1634-1980*. Baltimore: Johns Hopkins University Press and the Maryland Historical Society, 1988.

Land, Aubrey. *Colonial Maryland: A History*. Millwood, NY: KTO Press, 1981.

Leach, Charles D. "Placing the Post Mark'd West," *Pennsylvania Heritage* 8 (4, 1982): 8-12.

Wainwright, Nicholas B. "Mason and Dixon's Map." *Princeton University Library Chronicle* 45 (1, 1983): 28-32.

Walsh, Richard. *Maryland: A History, 1632-1974*. Baltimore: Maryland Historical Society, 1974.

37. MONTICELLO

Bear, James, and Frederick Nichols. *Monticello*. Charlottesville, VA: Thomas Jefferson Memorial Foundation, 1993.

Fisher, Leonard. *Monticello*. New York: Holiday House, 1988.

Guney, Clare, and Gene Gurney. *Monticello*. New York: Franklin Watts, 1966.

McLaughlin, John. *Jefferson and Monticello: The Biography of a Builder*. New York: Henry Holt and Company, 1988.

38-39. BOSTON MASSACRE I & II

Wemms, William. *The Trial of the British Soldiers, of the 29th Regiment of Foot for* the Murder of Crispus Attucks, Samuel Gray, Samuel Maverick, James Caldwell, and Patrick Carr, on Monday Evening, March 5, 1770. Boston: Belcher and Armstrong, 1807. Reprinted, Miami, FL: Mnemosyne Publishing, 1969.

Zobel, Hiller B. *The Boston Massacre*. New York: W. W. Norton and Company, 1970.

40. CRISPUS ATTUCKS

Bennett, *Before the Mayflower*. Full ref. under 14.

Foner, *History of Black Americans*. Full ref. under 14.

Franklin, *From Slavery to Freedom*. Full ref. under 14.

Toppin, *The Black American*. Full ref. under 14.

41. BOSTON TEA PARTY

Christie, Ian R. *Crisis of Empire: Great Britain and the American Colonies, 1754–1783*. New York: Norton, 1966.

Johanson, Bruce E. "Mohawks, Axes, and Taxes: Images of the American Revolution." *History Today* 35 (April 1985): 10–16.

Larabee, Benjamin Woods. *The Boston Tea Party*. New York: Oxford University Press, 1964.

Olson, Alison G. "The Virginia Merchants of London: A Study in Eighteenth-Century Interest-Group Politics." *William and Mary Quarterly* 40 (3, 1983): 363–388.

Thomas, Peter David Garner. *Tea Party to Independence: The Third Phase of the American Revolution*. New York: Oxford University Press, 1991.

Ward, Harry M. *The American Revolution: Nationhood Achieved, 1763–1788*. New York: St. Martin's Press, 1995.

42. FIRST CONTINENTAL CONGRESS

Inguaanzo, Anthony P. "Continental Congress." In *The American Revolution 1775–1783, An Enyclopedia*. New York: Garland Publishers, 1993.

Tindall, George Brown. *America, A Narrative History*. New York: Norton and Company, 1996.

43. PATRICK HENRY'S PERSONAL TRAUMA

Beeman, Richard. *Patrick Henry: A Biography*. New York: McGraw-Hill Publishing Company, 1974.

Campbell, Norine Dickson. *Patrick Henry: Patriot and Statesman*. New York: Devin-Adair Publishers, 1979.

Meade, Robert D. *Patrick Henry: Patriot in the Making*. Philadelphia: Lippincott, 1957.

Mayer, Henry. *A Son of Thunder: Patrick Henry and the American Republic*. New York: F. Watts Publishing Company, 1986.

44. DANIEL BOONE IN BOONESBOROUGH

Faragher, John Mack. *Daniel Boone: The Life and Legend of an American Pioneer.* New York: Henry Holt and Company, 1992.

Filson, John. *The Discovery and Settlement of Kentucky.* Ann Arbor, MI: University Microfilms, 1966.

Lofaro, Michael A. *The Life and Adventures of Daniel Boone.* Lexington, KY: University Press of Kentucky, 1986.

45. PAUL REVERE'S RIDE

Arvin, Newton. *Longfellow: His Life and Work.* Boston: Little, Brown and Company, 1963.

Fischer, David Hackett. *Paul Revere's Ride.* New York: Oxford University Press, 1994.

O'Connell, Richard W. "'On the Eighteenth of April, in Seventy-Five . . .' Longfellow Didn't Know the Half of It." *Smithsonian* 4 (1 April 1973): 72–78.

46. VIRGINIA DECLARATION OF RELIGIOUS FREEDOM

Buckley, Thomas E. *Church and State in Revolutionary Virginia, 1776–1787.* Charlottesville, VA: University of Virginia Press, 1977.

Peterson, Merrill D., and Robert C. Vaughan, eds. *The Virginia Statute for Religious Freedom: Its Evolution and Consequences in American History.* Cambridge: Cambridge University Press, 1988.

Miller, William. *The First Liberty: Religion and the American Republic.* New York: Alfred A. Knopf, 1985.

47. LEE-DEANE CONFLICT

Allison, Robert, ed. *American Eras: The Revolutionary Era, 1754–1783.* London: Gale Publishing, 1997.

Nagel, Paul C. *The Lees of Virginia: Seven Generations of an American Family.* New York: Oxford University Press, 1985.

Rakove, Jack N. *The Beginnings of National Politics: An Interpretive History of the Continental Congress.* New York: Alfred A. Knopf, 1979.

Roberts, Carey, and Rebecca Seely. *Tidewater Dynasty: The Lees of Stratford Hall.* New York: Harcourt Brace and Company, 1982.

Wood, Gordon S. *The Creation of the American Republic, 1776–1787.* Chapel Hill, NC: University of North Carolina Press, 1990.

48-49. BENJAMIN FRANKLIN I & II

Franklin, Benjamin. "Franklin's Kite Experiment, as Described by Franklin Himself in a Letter to a Colleague in London." Reprint, *Weatherwise* 50 (Oct–Nov 1997): 23.

Giblin, James Cross. *The Amazing Life of Benjamin Franklin.* New York: Scholastic Press, 2000.

Issacson, Walter. "Benjamin Franklin Joins the Revolution." *Smithsonian* 14 (5 August 2003): 80–89.

Lawson, Robert. *Ben and Me.* Boston: Little, Brown and Company, 1939.

Mulford, Carla. "Figuring Benjamin Franklin in American Cultural Memory." *New England Quarterly* 72 (9, 1999): 415.

Middlekauff, Robert. *Benjamin Franklin and His Enemies.* Berkeley: University of California Press, 1996.

Nuechterlein, James. "American Dreaming." *First Things: A Monthly Journal of Religion and Public Life* (1, 2000): 11.

Stevens, Bryna. *Ben Franklin's Glass Armonica.* Minneapolis, MN: Carolrhoda Books, 1983.

Wright, Esmond, ed. *Benjamin Franklin: His Life as He Wrote It.* Cambridge, MA: Harvard University Press, 1990.

Wright, Esmond. "The Papers of Benjamin Franklin, Volume 31, November 1, 1779–February 29, 1780." *English Historical Review* 113 (6, 1998): 755

Zall, Paul M. *Franklin's Autobiography: A Model Life.* Boston: Twayne, 1989.

50. BATTLE OF SARATOGA

Troiani, Don. "Battles of the Revolution: Saratoga." *American Heritage*, December 1975.

Wood, William J., and John S. D. Eisenhower, eds. *Battles of the Revolutionary War, 1775–1781.* New York: Da Capo Press, 1995.

51. MOLLY CORBIN

Hall, Edward. *Margaret Corbin: Heroine of the Battle of Fort Washington, 16 November 1776.* New York: The American Scenic and Historic Preservation Society, 1932.

Pierce, Grace M. "Three American Women Pensioned for Military Service." *Daughters of the American Revolution Magazine* 51 (1917): 140–145; 222–228.

Ward, Harry M. "Margaret Cochran Corbin and Mary Ludwig Hays McCauley." In *Women in World History*, Annie Commire and Deborah Klezmer, eds. Waterford, CT: Yorkin Publications, 1999–2002.

52. BENEDICT ARNOLD

"Arnold, Benedict." Encyclopedia Britannica, http://www.britannica.com.

"Battles of Saratoga." Encyclopedia Britannica, http://www.britannica.com.

Brandt, Clare. *The Man in the Mirror: A Life of Benedict Arnold.* New York: Random House, 1994.

Devine, Robert A., et al. *America Past and Present.* New York: Longman, 1998.

Martin, James Kirby. *Benedict Arnold, Revolutionary Hero: An American Reconsidered.* New York: New York University Press, 1997.

53. MAJOR ANDRÉ

Hatch, Robert McConnell. *Major John Andre: A Gallant in Spy's Clothing*. Boston: Houghton Mifflin Company, 1986.

54-55. FRANCIS MARION I & II

Heider, Karl. G. "The Gamecock, the Swamp Fox, and the Wizard Owl: The Development of Good Form in an American Totemic Set." *Journal of American Folklore* 93 (1980): 9-15.

McCrady, Edward. *The History of South Carolina in the Revolution, 1775-1780*. New York: Russell and Russell, 1969.

Nadelhaft, Jerome Joshua. *The Disorders of War: The Revolution in South Carolina*. Orono, ME: University of Maine at Orono Press, 1981.

Pancake, John S. *This Destructive War: The British Campaign in the Carolinas, 1780-1782*. Tuscaloosa, AL: University of Alabama Press, 1985.

56. JAMES CALDWELL

Ford, Harry P. "A Revolutionary Hero, James Caldwell." *The Journal of the Presbyterian Historical Society* 6 (September 1912): 260-266.

Murray, Nicholas. "A Memoir of the Rev. James Caldwell of Elizabethtown." *Proceedings of the New Jersey Historical Society* 3, (2, 1848): 77-89.

Sweetser, Kate D. "The 'Fighting Parson' of New Jersey." *Daughters of the American Revolution Magazine* 54, (March 1920): 140-145.

57-58. BATTLE OF KING'S MOUNTAIN I & II

Alden, John Richard. *The South in the Revolution: 1763-1789*. Baton Rouge, LA: Louisiana State University Press, 1957.

Allaire, Anthony. *Diary of Lieutenant Anthony Allaire*. New York: New York Times and Arno Press, 1968.

Hilborn, Nathaniel, and Samuel Hilborn. *Battleground of Freedom: South Carolina in the Revolution*. Columbia, SC: Sandlapper Press, 1970.

Lambert, Robert Stansbury. *South Carolina Loyalists in the American Revolution*. Columbia, SC: University of South Carolina Press, 1987.

Lumpkin, Henry. *From Savannah to Yorktown: The American Revolution in the South*. Columbia, SC: University of South Carolina Press, 1981.

Malgee, David George. *A Frontier Biography: William Campbell of King's Mountain*. MA thesis, University of Richmond, 1983.

59. ELIZABETH ZANE

Booth, Sally Smith. *The Women of '76*. New York: Hastings House Publishing Company, 1973.

Cole, Adelaide M. "Did Betty Zane Save Fort Henry?" *Daughters of the American Revolution Magazine* 114 (1980): 672-675.

Fowler, William Worthington. *Women on the American Frontier*. New York: Source Book Press, 1970.

Grey, Zane. *Betty Zane*. New York: Grosset and Dunlap, 1933.

Van Every, Dale. *A Company of Heroes: The American Frontier, 1775–1783*. New York: Arno Press, 1977.

60. AMERICANS AND TAXES

Break, George. *Taxation Myths and Realities*. Menlo Park, CA: Addison, 1978.

Groves, Harold M. *Trouble Spots in Taxation*. Princeton, NJ: Princeton University Press, 1948.

Leef, George. "Some Thoughts on Taxation." Foundation for Economic Education, http://www.fee.org/articles/some-thoughts-on-taxation/.

Steinmo, Sven. *Taxation and Democracy*. New Haven, CT: Yale University, 1993.

Wang, N. T. *Taxation and Development*. New York: Praeger, 1976.

Webber, Carolyn, and Aaron Wildavsky. *A History of Taxation and Expenditure in the Western World*. New York: Simon and Schuster, 1986.

61. YORKTOWN AND THE TREATY OF PARIS

Davis, Burke. *The Campaign That Won America*. New York: HarperCollins, 2007.

Grainger, John. *The Battle of Yorktown, 1781: A Reassessment*. Woodbridge, England: Boydell Press, 2005.

Greene, Jerome A. *The Guns of Independence: The Siege of Yorktown, 1781*. New York: Savas Beattie, 2005.

Middlekauff, Robert. *The Glorious Cause: The American Revolution, 1763–1789*. Vol. 3 of *The Oxford History of the United States*. Edited by C. Vann Woodward. New York: Oxford University Press, 1982.

Morrissey, Brendan. *Yorktown 1781: The World Turned Upside Down*. London: Osprey, 1997.

Wickwire, Franklin, and Mary Wickwire. *Cornwallis: The American Adventure*. Boston: Houghton Mifflin, 1970.

62–63. SHAYS' REBELLION I & II

Minot, George Richards. *History of the Insurrections in Massachusetts in 1786 and of the Rebellion Consequent Thereon*. New York: Da Capo Press, 1971.

Szatmary, David P. *Shay's Rebellion: The Making of an Agrarian Insurrection*. Amherst, MA: University of Massachusetts Press, 1980.

64–65. JAMES MADISON AND THE CONSTITUTION I & II

Adair, Douglas. "The Tenth Federalist Revisited." *William and Mary Quarterly, Third Series* 8 (January 1951): 48–67.

Banning, Lance. "Madison, James." American National Biography, http://www

.anb.org/view/10.1093/anb/9780198606697.001.0001/anb-9780198606697-e-0300303?rskey=uX0896&result=2.

Bums, Edward McNall. *James Madison: Philosopher of the Constitution*. Rutgers University Studies in History, Volume I. New Brunswick, NJ: Rutgers University Press, 1938.

"Constitution of the United States of America." Encyclopedia Britannica, http://www.britannica.com/topic/Constitution-of-the-United-States-of-America.

Madison, James. *James Madison: Writings*. Edited by Jack N. Rakove. New York: Literary Classics of the United States, 1999.

Madison, James, Alexander Hamilton, and John Jay. *The Federalists Papers*, 1788. Edited by Gary Wills. New York: Bantam Books, 1982.

Meyers, Marvin, ed. *The Mind of the Founder: Sources of the Political Thought of James Madison*. American Heritage Series. Indianapolis: Bobbs-Merrill, 1973.

Phillips, Donald T. "Compromise and Create the Culture," chap. 14; and "Stick Around and Follow Through" chap. 15 in *The Founding Fathers on Leadership: Classic Teamwork in Changing Times*. New York: Warner Books, 1997.

Rakove, Jack N. *James Madison and the Creation of the American Republic*. Edited by Oscar Handlin. New York: Longman, 1990.

Rutland, Robert A. *James Madison: The Founding Father*. New York: Macmillan Publishing Company, 1987.

Sheldon, Garrett Ward. *The Political Philosophy of James Madison*. Baltimore: Johns Hopkins University Press, 2001.

Watson, Paul Barron. *Our Constitution: As Adopted by the Constitutional Convention and Ratified by the Thirteen Original States*. Cambridge, MA: University Press, 1946.

66. COMPROMISE OF SHAME

Bowen, Ezra. "Constitutional Convention, Philadelphia, 1787." *Smithsonian* 18 (14, 1987): 32–43.

Collier, Christopher, and James Lincoln Collier. *Decision in Philadelphia: The Constitutional Convention of 1787*. New York: Random House, 1986.

Finkelman, Paul R."A Covenant with Death: Slavery and the U.S. Constitution." *American Visions* 1 (3, 1986): 21–27.

Peters, William. *A More Perfect Union*. New York: Crown Publishers, 1987.

Rakore, Jack N. "Philadelphia Story." *Wilson Quarterly* 11 (2, 1987): 105–121.

67. WHISKEY REBELLION

Baldwin, Leland Dewitt. *Whiskey Rebels: The Story of a Frontier Uprising*. Pittsburgh: University of Pittsburgh Press, 1968.

Parker, Iola B., "Whiskey Creek Keeps Running, but Only with Water." *Smithsonian* 5 (3 June 1974): 82–89.

Slaughter, Thomas Paul. *The Whiskey Rebellion: Frontier Epilogue to the American Revolution*. New York: Oxford University Press, 1986.

68. PIERRE L'ENFANT

Kite, Elizabeth Sarah. *L'Enfant and Washington, 1791–1792*. Baltimore: The Johns Hopkins Press, 1929.

Lewis, David L. *District of Columbia: A Bicentennial History*. New York: W. W. Norton and Company, 1976.

Stevenson, Richard W. *A Plan Wholly New: Pierre Charles L'Enfant's Plan for the City of Washington*. Washington, DC: Library of Congress, 1993.

69–70. XYZ AFFAIR I & II

Halperin, Teri Diane. *The Alien and Sedition Acts of 1798*. Baltimore: Johns Hopkins University Press, 2016.

Stinchcombe, William C. *The XYZ Affair*. Westport, CT: Greenwood Press, 1980.

71. ALIEN AND SEDITION ACTS

Brown, Katherine, B. "A Note on the Puritan Concept of Aristocracy." *Mississippi Valley Historical Review* 41 (1 June 1954): 105–112.

Carpenter, A. H. "Naturalization in England and the American Colonies." *American Historical Review* 9 (2 January 1904): 288–303.

Corry, John. "Keeping Speech Free in Troubled Times: Philosophy of Past Offers Guidance Today." *The Quill* (1 July–August 2002): 35.

Cooper, Thomas. *An Account of the Trial of Thomas Cooper*. Philadelphia: John Boiren, 1800.

Dye, Thomas R., and Harmon Zeigler. *The Irony of Democracy*. Millennial Edition. Fort Worth, TX: Summit Harcourt Brace College Publishers, 2000.

Elkins, Stanley, and Eric McKitrick. *The Age of Federalism*. New York: Oxford University Press, 1993.

Koch, Adriene, and Harry Amon. "The Virginia and Kentucky Resolutions: An Episode in Jefferson's and Madison's Defense of Civil Liberties." *William and Mary Quarterly* 5 (April 1948): 145–76.

Halperin, *The Alien and Sedition Acts of 1798*. Full ref. under 70.

72–73. REVOLUTION OF 1800 I & II

Alden, John R. *The American Revolution, 1775–1783*. New York: Harper, 1954.

Appleby, Joyce. *Capitalism and a New Social Order: The Republican Vision of the 1790s*. New York: New York University Press, 1984.

Bailyn, Bernard. *The Ideological Origins of the American Revolution*. Enlarged edition. Cambridge, MA: Harvard University Press, 1992.

Beard, Charles A. *An Economic Interpretation of the Constitution*, 1913. New York: Free Press, 1986.

Burns, James McGregor. *The Vineyard of Liberty*. Vol. 1 of *The American Experiment*. New York: Alfred A. Knopf, 1982.

Channing, Edward. *The Jeffersonian System, 1801–1811*, 1906. New York: Reprint Services, 1992.

Collinson, Simon. "President or King?" *History Today* 50 (11 November 2000), www.historytoday.com/simon-collinson/president-or-king.

Countryman, Edward. *The American Revolution*. New York: Hill and Wang, 1985.

Farrand, Max. *The Fathers of the Constitution*. New York: Elliots Books, 1921.

Fliegelman, Jay. *Prodigals and Pilgrims: The American Revolution against Patriarchal Authority, 1750–1800*. New York: Cambridge University Press, 1982.

Gipson, Lawrence H. *The Coming of the Revolution, 1763–1775*. New York: Harper, 1954.

Greene, Jack P. *The Reinterpretation of the American Revolution, 1763–1789*, 1968. Westport, CT: Greenwood Press, 1979.

Hofstadter, Richard. *The Idea of a Party System: The Rise of Legitimate Opposition in the United States, 1780–1840*. Berkeley: University of California Press, 1969.

Main, Jackson Turner. *The Social Structure of Revolutionary America*. Princeton, NJ: Princeton University Press, 1965.

McDonald, Forrest. *We the People: The Economic Origins of the Constitution*, 1958. New York: Transaction Books, 1992.

Middlekauff, Robert. *The Glorious Cause: The American Revolution, 1763–1789*. Vol. 3 of *The Oxford History of the United States*. Edited by, C. Vann Woodward. New York: Oxford University Press, 1982.

Miller, John C. *Triumph of Freedom, 1775–1783*, 1948. New York: Reprint Services, 1993.

———. *The Young Republic, 1789–1815*. New York: Free Press, 1970.

Morgan, Edmund S. *The Birth of the Republic, 1763–1789*, 3rd ed. Chicago: University of Chicago Press, 1992.

———. *The Challenge of the American Revolution*. New York: Norton, 1978.

Nash, Gary B. *Race, Class, and Politics*. Champaign, IL: University of Illinois Press, 1986.

———. *The Urban Crucible: Social Change, Political Consciousness, and the Origins of the American Revolution*, 1979. Cambridge, MA: Harvard University Press, 1990.

Nettels, Curtis P. *Emergence of a National Economy, 1775–1815*, 1962. New York: M. E. Sharpe, 1977.

Nevins, Allan. *The American States during and after the Revolution*, 1924. New York: Reprint Services, 1991.

Perkins, Bradford. *The Creation of a Republican Empire*. Vol. 1 of *The Cambridge History of American Foreign Relations*. New York: Cambridge, 1993.

———. *Prologue to War: England and the United States, 1805–1812*. Berkeley: University of California Press, 1961.

Rakove, Jack. *The Beginnings of National Politics: An Interpretive History of the Continental Congress*, 1979. Baltimore: Johns Hopkins University Press, 1982.

Reid, John Phillip. *Constitutional History of the American Revolution*, 4 vols. Madison, WI: University of Wisconsin Press 1987–1994.

Sharp, James Roger. *American Politics in the Early Republic: The New Nation in Crisis*. New Haven, CT: Yale University Press, 1993.

Stromberg, Joseph. "The Election of 1800." Mises Institute, http://www.mises .org/fullstory.asp?control=582.

Tucker, Robert W., and David C. Hendrickson. *Empire of Liberty: The Statecraft of Thomas Jefferson*. New York: Oxford University Press, 1990.

Wernick, Robert. "Mr. Justice Marshall Takes the Law in Hand." *Smithsonian* 29 (8 November 1998): 156–175.

Wood, Gordon S. *The Radicalism of the American Revolution*. New York: Alfred A. Knopf, 1992.

Wright, Esmond. *An Empire for Liberty: From Washington to Lincoln*. New York: Blackwell Publishing, 2018.

74. LOUISIANA PURCHASE

DeConde, Alexander. *This Affair of Louisiana*. New York: Scribner, 1976.

De Voto, Bernard. *The Louisiana Purchase*. Springfield, OH: Crowell-Collier, 1953.

Kastor, Peter J. *The Nation's Crucible: The Louisianan Purchase and the Creation of America*. New Haven, CT: Yale University Press, 2004.

Sprague, Marshall. *So Vast, So Beautiful a Land; Louisiana and the Purchase*. Boston: Little, Brown and Company, 1974.

75-77. HAMILTON AND BURR I, II, & III

Burr, Aaron. *Memoirs of Aaron Burr, with Miscellaneous Selections from his Correspondence*. Edited by Matthew L. Davis. New York: Harper and Brothers, 1836–1837.

Daniels, Jonathan. *Ordeal of Ambition: Jefferson, Hamilton, Burr*. Garden City, NY: Doubleday and Company, 1970.

Lomask, Milton. *Aaron Burr*. New York: Farrar, Straus and Giroux Publishing Company, 1982.

78. GUANO

Gootenberg, Paul. *Between Silver and Guano: Commercial Policy and the State in Post-Independence Peru*. Princeton, NJ: Princeton University Press, 1989.

Schwartz, Frederic D. "Does Guano Drive History?" *Invention and Technology* 19 (4, Spring 2004): 63, http://www.inventionandtech.com/content/does-guano -drive-history-0.

Skaggs, Jimmy M. *The Great Guano Rush: Entrepreneurs and American Overseas Expansion*. New York: St. Martin's Press, 1995.

79. LEWIS AND CLARK EXPEDITION

Ambrose, Stephen E. *Undaunted Courage: Meriwether Lewis, Thomas Jefferson, and the Opening of the American West*. New York: Simon and Schuster, 1996.

Appleman, Roy Edgar. *Louis and Clark: Historic Places Associated with their Transcontinental Exploration (1804–1806)*. Washington, DC: United States Government Printing Office, 1975.

Bakeless, John Edwin. *Louis and Clark: Partners in Discovery*. New York: W. Morrow Publishing Company, 1945.

Clark, Ella Elizabeth. *Sacagawea of the Louis and Clark Expedition*. Berkeley: University of California Press, 1979.

Louis, Meriwether. *The Journals of the Louis and Clark*. Edited by Bernard DeVoto. Boston: Houghton Mifflin Publishing, 1953.

80. ROBERT FULTON'S FOLLY

Dickinson, H. W. *Robert Fulton: Engineer and Artist*. New York: John Lane, 1912.

Flammang, James M. *Robert Fulton: Inventor and Steamboat Builder*. Berkeley Heights, NJ: Enslow Publishers, 1999.

"Fulton, Robert." *Encyclopedia Britannica*, 2003.

Morgan, John Smith. *Robert Fulton*. New York: Mason/Charter, 1977.

Philip, Cynthia Owen. *Robert Fulton: A Biography*. New York: Franklin Watts, 1985.

"Robert Fulton." Lemelson-MIT, http://lemelson.mit.edu/resources/robert-fulton.

81. NEW JERSEY AND THE WOMEN'S VOTE

Dowd, Gregory Evans. "Declarations of Dependence: War and Inequality in Revolutionary New Jersey, 1776–1815," in *A New Jersey Anthology*. Edited by Maxine N. Lurie. Newark, NJ: New Jersey Historical Society, 1994.

Fleming, Thomas J. *New Jersey: A Bicentennial History*. New York: W. W. Norton and Company, 1976.

82. END OF SLAVE TRADE

Madison, James. "Notes of the Debates of the Constitutional Convention in Philadelphia, 1787." Yale Law School, http://avalon.law.yale.edu/subject_menus/debcont.asp.

Rawley, James A. *The Transatlantic Slave Trade*. New York: Norton, 1981.

Weld, Theodore Dwight. *Slavery and the Internal Slave Trade in the United States*. New York: Arno Press, 1969.

White, John M. A. *Slavery in the American South*. New York: Harper and Row Publishers, 1971.

83-84. TIPPECANOE AND TECUMSEH TOO I & II

Drake, Benjamin. *The Life of Tecumseh and of His Brother the Prophet: With a*

Historical Sketch of the Shawnee Indians, 1858. Cincinnati: Anderson, Gates and Wright. Kraus Reprint, 1969.

Edmunds, R. David. *The Shawnee Prophet*. Lincoln, NE: University of Nebraska Press, 1983.

———. *Tecumseh and the Quest for Indian Leadership*. Boston: Little, Brown and Company, 1984.

Tucker, Glenn. *Tecumseh: Vision of Glory*. Indianapolis: Bobbs-Merrill, 1959.

85–86. WAR OF 1812 I & II

Hickey, Donald R. *The War of 1812, A Short History*. Champaign, IL: University of Illinois Press, 2012.

Hitsman, J. Mackay. *The Incredible War of 1812*. Toronto: University of Toronto Press, 1965, 27.

Remini, Robert V. *The Battle of New Orleans: Andrew Jackson and America's First Military Victory*. London: Penguin Books, 1999.

Zuehlke, Mark. *For Honour's Sake: The War of 1812 and the Brokering of an Uneasy Peace*. New York: Random House, 2007.

87. MISSOURI COMPROMISE

Devine, Robert A., et al. *America Past and Present*. New York: Longman, 1998.

McPherson, James M. *Battle Cry of Freedom: The Civil War Era*. New York: Oxford University Press, 1988.

"Missouri Compromise." Encyclopedia Britannica, http://www.britannica.com.

88. MONROE DOCTRINE

Clark, J. Reuben. *Memorandum on the Monroe Doctrine*. Washington, DC: Government Printing Office, 1930.

Perkins, Dexter. *The Monroe Doctrine, 1823–1826*. Cambridge, MA: Harvard University Press, 1965.

———. *The Monroe Doctrine, 1826–1867*. Baltimore: Johns Hopkins Press, 1933.

Thomas, David Y. *One Hundred Years of the Monroe Doctrine*. New York: The Macmillan Company, 1927.

89. THE STRANGE DEATH OF JEFFERSON AND ADAMS

Adams, John. *The Adams Papers, Series I: Diary and Autobiography*. Edited by L. H. Butterfield. Cambridge, MA: Harvard University Press, 1961.

Allison, John M. *Adams and Jefferson: The Story of a Friendship*. Norman, OK: University of Oklahoma Press, 1966.

Brodie, Fawn M. *Thomas Jefferson: An Intimate History*. New York: W. W. Norton and Company, 1974.

Jefferson, Thomas. *The Papers of Thomas Jefferson*. Edited by Julian P. Boyd. Princeton, NJ: Princeton University Press, 1950.

90. AMERICA'S FIRST RAILROAD

Williams, John Hoyt. *A Great and Shining Road.* New York: Times Books, 1988.

91. HAYNE-WEBSTER DEBATE

Baxter, Maurice. *One and Inseparable: Daniel Webster and the Union.* Cambridge, MA: Harvard University Press, 1984.

Ellis, Richard E. *The Union at Risk: Jacksonian Democracy, States Rights and the Nullification Crisis.* New York: Oxford University Press, 1987.

Jervey, Theodore Dehon. *Robert Y. Hayne and His Times.* New York: Macmillan Company, 1909.

Remini, Robert Vincent. *Daniel Webster: The Man and His Time.* New York: W. W. Norton, 1997.

Wheeler, Everett Pepperrell. *Daniel Webster, The Expounder of the Constitution.* New York: G. P. Putnam's Sons, 1905.

92-93. NAT TURNER SLAVE REBELLION I & II

Aptheker, Herbert. *American Negro Slave Revolt.* New York: International Publishers, 1963.

Ballagh, James C. *History of Slavery in Virginia.* Baltimore: Johns Hopkins Press, 1902.

Foner, Eric. *Nat Turner.* Englewood Cliffs, NJ: Prentice-Hall, 1971.

Greenberg, Kenneth S. *The Confessions of Nat Turner.* New York: St. Martin's Press, 1996.

Harding, Vincent. "God's Avenging Scourge." *Christian History* 3 (1999): 28-29.

Johnson, Roy F. *The Nat Turner Slave Insurrection.* Murfreesboro, NC: Johnson Publishing Company, 1966.

Oates, Stephen B. *The Fires of Jubilee.* New York: Harper and Row Publishers, 1975.

94. CYRUS MCCORMICK

Casson, Herbert Newton. *Cyrus Hall McCormick, His Life and Work.* Chicago: A. C. McClurg and Company, 1909.

Gies, Joseph. "The Great Reaper War," *American Heritage of Invention and Technology* 5 (3, 1989): 20-28.

Hutchinson, William Thomas. *Cyrus Hall McCormick.* New York: Century Company, 1930.

McCormick, Cyrus. *The Century of the Reaper.* Boston: Houghton Mifflin and Company, 1931.

95. JACKSON AND THE SECOND US BANK

Crouthamel, James L. "Did the Second Bank of the United States Bribe the Press?" *Journalism Quarterly* 36 (I, 1959): 35-44.

Ermine, Robert V. *Andrew Jackson and the Bank War: A Study in the Growth of Presidential Power*. New York: W. W. Norton and Company, 1967.

Gatell, Frank Otto. "Sober Second Thoughts on Van Buren, the Albany Regency, and the Wall Street Conspiracy." *Journal of American History* 53 (I, 1966): 19–40.

Govan, Thomas Payne. *Nicholas Biddle: Nationalist and Public Banker, 1786–1844*. Chicago: University of Chicago Press, 1959.

Macesich, George. "Sources of Monetary Disturbances in the United States, 1834–1845." *Journal of Economic History* 20 (3, 1960): 407–434.

McGrane, Reginald C. *The Correspondence of Nicholas Biddle: Dealing with National Affairs—1807–1844*. Boston: Houghton Mifflin Company, 1919.

Meerman, Jacob P. "The Climax of the Bank War: Biddle's Contraction, 1833–34." *Journal of Political Economy* 71 (4, 1963): 378–388.

Perkins, Edwin J. "Lost Opportunities for Compromise in the Bank War: A Reassessment of Jackson's Veto Message." *Business History Review* 61 (4, 1987): 531–550.

Sharp, James Roger. *The Jacksonians versus the Banks: Politics in the States after the Panic of 1837*. New York: Columbia University Press, 1970.

Taylor, George Rogers. *Jackson vs. Biddle's Bank: The Struggle Over the Second Bank of the United States*. London: D. C. Heath and Company, 1972.

96. COMPROMISE OF 1833

Peterson, Merrill D. *Olive Branch and Sword—The Compromise of 1833*. Baton Rouge, LA: Louisiana State University Press, 1982.

Weisberger, Bernard A. "The Nullifiers." *American Heritage* 46 (4 October 1995): 20–21.

97. ALEXIS DE TOCQUEVILLE

Blackmore, Tim. "The Dark Knight of Democracy: Tocqueville and Miller Cast Some Light on the Subject," *Journal of American Culture* 14 (1, 1991): 37–56.

Boesche, Roger, ed. *Alexis de Tocqueville: Selected Letters on Politics and Society*. James Toupin and Roger Boesche, trans. Berkeley: University of California Press, 1985.

Boesche, Roger. *The Strange Liberalism of Alexis de Tocqueville*. Ithaca and London: Cornell University Press, 1987.

Jardin, Andre. *Tocqueville: A Biography*. New York: Farrar, Straus and Giroux, 1988.

Kershner, Frederick, Jr. ed. *Tocqueville's America: The Great Quotations*. Columbus, OH: Ohio University Press, 1983.

Manent, Pierre. *Tocqueville and the Nature of Democracy*. Lanham, MD: Rowman and Littlefield Publishers, 1996.

Mayer, J. P., ed. *Alexis de Tocqueville: Journey to America*. George Lawrence, trans. New York: Doubleday and Company, 1971.

McCarthy, Eugene J. *America Revisited: 150 Years After Tocqueville*. New York: Doubleday and Company. 1978.

Pope, Whitney. *Alexis de Tocqueville: His Social and Political Theory*. Thousand Oaks, CA: SAGE Publications, 1986.

Stokes, Curtis. "Tocqueville and the Problem of Racial Inequality." *Journal of Negro History* 75 (1-2, 1990): 1-15.

Wood, W. Kirk. "Alexis de Tocqueville and the Myth of Democracy in America," *Southern Studies* 5 (3-4, 1994): 1-17.

98. SARAH ALDEN BRADFORD RIPLEY

Carlson, P. A. "Sarah Alden Ripley—Emerson's Other Aunt," *American Transcendental Quarterly*, Fall 1978.

Goodwin, Joan. W. *The Remarkable Mrs. Ripley: The Life of Sarah Alden Bradford Ripley*. Boston:

Northeastern University Press, 1999.

Perry, Bliss, ed. *The Heart of Emerson's Journal*. Mineola, NY: Dover Publishers, 1926.

Ripley, Sarah Alden Bradford. Letters. Schlesinger Library, Radcliffe Institute; Houghton Library, Harvard University; Concord Public Library, Concord, Massachusetts.

"Samuel and Sarah Ripley." Dictionary of Unitarian and Universalist Biography, http://uudb.org/articles/ripleyfamily.html.

99. TRAIL OF TEARS

Anderson, William L., ed. *Cherokee Removal: Before and After*. Athens, GA: University of Georgia Press, 1991.

Ehle, John. *Trail of Tears: The Rise and Fall of the Cherokee Nation*. New York: Doubleday and Company, 1988.

Filler, Lewis. *The Removal of the Cherokee Nation: Manifest Destiny or National Dishonor?* Boston: Heath Publishers, 1962.

Grinde, Donald. "Cherokee Removal an American Politics," *New England Social Studies Bulletin* 44 (2, 1987): 28-45, 53.

Satz, Ronald M. "The Cherokee Trail of Tears, a Sesquicentennial Perspective," *Georgia Historical Quarterly* 73 (3, 1989): 431-466.

100. AMISTAD

Cable, Mary. *Black Odyssey: The Case of the Slave Ship* Amistad. New York: Penguin Books, 1977.

Jackson, Donald Dale. "Mutiny on the *Amistad*," *Smithsonian* 28 (9 December 1997): 114-123.

Jones, Howard. *Mutiny on the* Amistad: *The Saga of a Slave Revolt and Its Impact on American Abolition, Law and Diplomacy*. New York: Oxford University Press, 1987.

101. JOHN C. CALHOUN

Bartlett, Irving H. *John C. Calhoun*. New York: W. W. Norton and Company, 1993.
"Calhoun, John C." Encyclopedia Britannica, http://www.britannica.com.
Niven, John. *John C. Calhoun and the Price of the Union*. Baton Rouge, LA:
    Louisiana State University Press, 1988.
Peterson, Merril D. *The Great Triumvirate*. New York: Oxford University Press, 1987.

102. THE BOWERY

Butsch, Richard. "Bowery Boys and Matinee Ladies: The Re-Gendering of
    Nineteenth Century American Theater Audiences." *American Quarterly* 46,
    (3, 1994): 374405.
Fields, Armond, and L. Marc Fields. *From the Bowery to Broadway: Lew Fields and
    the Roots of American Popular Theater*. New York: Oxford University Press, 1993.
Giamo, Benedict. *On the Bowery: Confronting Homelessness in American Society*. Iowa
    City: University of Iowa Press, 1989.
Gorn, Elliott J. "'Good-Bye Boys, I Die a True American': Homicide, Nativism,
    and Working-Class Culture in Antebellum New York City." *The Journal of
    American History* 74 (2 September 1987): 388–410.
Hodin, Mark. "Class, Consumption, and Ethnic Performance in Vaudeville."
    Prospects 22 (1997): 193–210.
Schisgall, Oscar. *The Bowery Savings Bank of New York: A Social and Financial History*.
    New York: American Management Associations, Publications Group, 1984.

103. SAM HOUSTON

Fehrenbach, T. R. *Lone Star: A History of Texas and the Texans*. New York: Collier
    Books, 1980.
Friend, Llerena B. *Sam Houston: The Great Designer*. Austin, TX: University of
    Texas Press, 1954.
Hitsman, J. Mackay. "The Texas War of 1835–1836." *History Today* 10 (2, 1960):
    116–123.
Houston, Samuel. *The Writings of Sam Houston: 1813–1863*. Eugene C. Barker and
    Amelia Williams, eds. Austin, TX: University of Texas Press, 1938–1943.
Marquis, James. *The Raven: A Biography of Sam Houston*. Indianapolis: Bobbs-
    Merrill, 1929.
Williams, John Hoyt. *Sam Houston: A Biography of the Father of Texas*. New York:
    Simon and Schuster, 1988.

104. TEXAS INVADES NEW MEXICO

Hogan, William Ransom. *The Texas Republic*. Norman, OK: University of
    Oklahoma Press, 1946.
Nance, Joseph Milton. *After San Jacinto: The Texas-Mexican Frontier, 1836–1841*.
    Austin, TX: University of Texas Press, 1963.

105. CHARLES DICKENS AND AMERICA

Abel, Ernest. "The Most Hated Man in America," *American History Illustrated* (22 August 1988): 10–15, 48.

Moss, Sidney. *Charles Dickens' Quarrel With America*. Troy, NY: Whiston Publishing, 1984.

Myerson, Joel, ed. *Studies in the American Renaissance*. Charlottesville, VA: University Press of Virginia, 1983.

Slater, Michael, ed. *Dickens on America and the Americans*. Austin, TX: University of Texas Press, 1978.

106. SOMER'S MUTINY

Barrows, Edward M. *The Great Commodore*. New York: Bobbs-Morrill Company, 1935.

Morison, Samuel Eliot. *Old Bruin: Commodore Matthew C. Perry, 1794–1858*. Boston: Little, Brown and Company, 1975.

107. SENATOR BENTON'S CONSPIRACY

Abbott, Carl. *Colorado: A History of the Centennial State*. Bolder, CO: Colorado State University Press, 1976.

Sprague, Marshall. *Colorado: A Bicentennial History*. New York: Norton Publishing Company, 1976.

108. FIFTY-FOUR FORTY OR FIGHT

Merk, Frederick. *The Oregon Question: Essays in Anglo-American Diplomacy*. Cambridge, MA: Belknap Press, 1967.

Polk, James Knox. *Polk: The Diary of a President, 1845–1849*. London: Longmans, Green Company, 1952.

Reeves, Jesse S. *American Diplomacy under Tyler and Polk*. Baltimore: Johns Hopkins Press, 1907.

109. EDGAR ALLAN POE

Mabbott, Thomas Ollive. *The Collected Works of Edgar Allan Poe*. Cambridge, MA: Belknap Press, 1969, 1978.

Poe, Edgar Allan. *The Edgar Allan Poe Audio Collection*. Narrated by Vincent Price and Basil Rathbone. New York: Caedmon Records, TC 1028, 2000.

Quinn, Arthur H. *Edgar Allan Poe: A Critical Biography*. New York: Appleton-Century-Crofts, 1941.

110. JAMES KNOX POLK AND "HAIL TO THE CHIEF"

Bergeron, Paul H. *The Presidency of James Knox Polk*. Lawrence, KS: University Press of Kansas, 1990.

"Hail to the Chief: The Origins and Legacies of an American Ceremonial Tune."
American Music 15 (Summer 1997): 123–136.

Holland, Barbara. *Hail to the Chiefs: How to Tell Your Polks from Your Tylers.* New
York: Ballantine Books, 1997.

Kane, Joseph Nathan. *Facts about the Presidents: A Compilation of Biographical and
Historical Information.* New York: H. W. Wilson Company, 1993.

Lindop, Edmund. *Presidents by Accident.* New York: Franklin Watts, 1991.

Scott, Walter. *The Lady of the Lake: A Poem in Six Cantos.* New York: T. Y. Crowell
and Company, 1883.

111. MIRACLE OF ANESTHESIA

Fenster, J. M. "How Nobody Invented Anesthesia," *American Heritage of Invention
and Technology* 12 (1, Summer 1996), http://www.inventionandtech.com
/content/how-nobody-invented-anesthesia-1.

Pernick, Martin S. *A Calculus of Suffering: Pain, Professionalism, and Anesthesia in
Nineteenth-Century America.* New York: Columbia University Press, 1985.

112. LINCOLN'S QUEST FOR CONGRESS

Findley, Paul. *Abraham Lincoln: The Crucible of Congress.* New York: Crown
Publishers, 1979.

Lincoln, Abraham. *The Collected Works of Abraham Lincoln.* Roy Basler, ed. New
Brunswick, NJ: Rutgers University Press, 1953, 1988.

Riddle, Donald W. *Congressman Abraham Lincoln.* Urbana, IL: University of Illinois
Press, 1957.

Thomas, Benjamin P. *Abraham Lincoln.* New York: Alfred A. Knopf, 1952.

113. DONNER PARTY TRAGEDY

Stewart, George R. *Ordeal by Hunger: The Story of the Donner Party.* Boston:
Houghton, Mifflin and Company, 1960.

114. MORMONS ARRIVE IN UTAH

Arrington, Leonard J. *The Mormon Experience: A History of the Latter-day Saints.*
New York: Alfred A. Knopf, 1979.

Lyman, Edward Leo. *Political Deliverance: The Mormon Quest for Utah Statehood.*
Urbana, IL: University of Illinois Press, 1986.

115. SENECA FALLS CONVENTION

Buhle, Mari Jo and Paul. *The Concise History of Woman Suffrage: Selections of the
History of Woman Suffrage by Elizabeth Cady Stanton, Susan B. Anthony, Matilda
Joslyn Gage and the National American Suffrage Association.* Urbana, IL: University
of Illinois Press, 1978.

Burnet, Constance Buel. *Five for Freedom: Lucretia Mott, Elizabeth Cady Stanton, Lucy Stone, Susan B. Anthony, Carrie Chapman Catt.* New York: Greenwood Press, 1968.

Stanton, Elizabeth Cady. *The Seneca Falls Convention, 1848.* Tucson, AZ: Kore Press, 2004.

116. *CALIFORNIA* DOCKS IN SAN FRANCISCO

Caughey, John Walton. *The California Gold Rush.* Berkeley: University of California Press, 1975.

Hulbert, Archer Butler. *49ers: The Chronicle of the California Trail.* Boston: Little, Brown and Company, 1931.

Morison, James. *By Sea to California, 1849–50: The Journal of Dr. James Morison.* Memphis, TN: Memphis State University Press, 1979.

Pomfret, John Edwin. *California Gold Rush Voyages, 1848–49: Three Original Narratives.* Westport, CT: Greenwood Press, 1974.

117. SECOND GREAT AWAKENING

Ahlstrom, Sydney E. *A Religious History of the American People.* New Haven, CT: Yale University Press, 1972.

Bedell, George C., Leo Sandon Jr., and Charles T. Wellborn. *Religion in America.* New York: Macmillan Publishing Company, 1982.

Cayton, Mary Kupiec. "Who Are the Evangelicals? Conservative and Liberal Identity in the Unitarian Controversy in Boston, 1804–1833." *Journal of Social History* 31 (1997): 85–108.

Clebsch, William A. *From Sacred to Profane America: The Role of Religion in American History.* New York: Harper and Row Publishers, 1968.

Finke, Roger, and Rodney Stark. *The Churching of America, 1776–1990.* New Brunswick, NJ: Rutgers University Press, 1992.

Gaustad, Edwin Scott. *A Religious History of America.* New York: Harper and Row Publishers, 1966.

Heimert, Alan. *Religion and the American Mind: From the Great Awakening to the Revolution.* Cambridge, MA: Harvard University Press, 1966.

Scott, Donald. "Evangelicalism, Revivalism, and the Second Great Awakening," National Humanities Center, http://nationalhumanitiescenter.org/tserve/nineteen/nkeyinfo/nevanrev.htm.

118. ABRAHAM LINCOLN'S ADVICE TO YOUNG LAWYERS

Lincoln, *The Collected Works of Abraham Lincoln.* Full ref. under 112.

119. HERMAN MELVILLE

Melville, Herman. *Moby-Dick: An Authoritative Text.* New York: W. W. Norton and Company, 1967.

Parker, Hershel. *Reading Billy Budd.* Evanston, IL: Northwestern University Press, 1990.

Wernick, Robert. "In Melville's Life, Fame Proved Fickle," *Smithsonian* 26 (4 July 1995) 100–112.

120. ELISHA GRAVES OTIS AND THE ELEVATOR

Goodwin, Jason. *Otis: Giving Rise to the Modern City.* New York: Ivan R. Dee, 2001.

Gross, David. "Upward Mobility," *Attache Magazine* (October 2001): 17–18.

121. WINDMILLS

Flavin, Christopher. *Windpower: A Turning Point.* Washington, DC: Worldwatch Institute, 1981.

Leuthner, Stuart. "The Windmills That Won the West," *American Heritage of Invention and Technology* 19 (2, Fall 2003): 56–59.

Thomason, Betty. "Windmills Helped Settle the West." American Windmills, https://www.windmills.net/?page_id=197.

Volta, Torrey. *Windcatchers: American Windmills of Yesterday and Tomorrow.* Brattleboro, VT: S. Greene Press, 1976.

122–123. KNOW-NOTHING PARTY I & II

Baker, Jean H. *Ambivalent Americans: The Know-Nothing Party in Maryland.* Baltimore: Johns Hopkins University Press, 1977.

Mulkern, John R. *The Know-Nothing Party in Massachusetts: The Rise and Fall of a People's Movement.* Boston: Northeastern University Press, 1990.

Wernick, Robert, "The Rise and Fall of a Fervid Third Party." *Smithsonian* (November 1, 1996): 150–158.

124. HARRIET TUBMAN

Buckmaster, Henrietta. *Let My People Go: The Story of the Underground Railroad and Growth of the Abolition Movement.* Boston: Beacon Press, 1959.

———. *Women Who Shaped History.* New York: Crowell-Collier Press, 1966.

Davidson, Nancy A. *Notable Black American Women.* Detroit and London: Gale Research, 1992.

Debman, Betty. "Great African-Americans." *Richmond Times Dispatch* (February 1, 2000): F1.

Eusebius, Sister Mary. "A Modern Moses: Harriet Tubman." *Journal of Negro Education* 19 (1): 16–27.

Heidish, Marcy. *A Woman Called Moses.* Boston: Houghton Mifflin Company, 1976.

Hines, Darlene Clark. *Black Women in America.* Brooklyn: Carlson Publishing, 1993.

Mallory, Maria. (1997). "Bound for Freedom: Retracing the Footsteps of Runaway Slaves." *U.S. News and World Report* 122 (4): 78.

Porter, Dorothy B. (1944). "An American Heroine." *Journal of Negro Education* 13 (1): 91–93.

"Roots of Resistance: The Story of the Underground Railroad," *American Experience*, directed by Orlando Bagwell (New York and Los Angeles: Public Broadcasting, 1990), video.

Wheat, Ellen Harkins. *Jacob Lawrence: The Frederick Douglass and Harriet Tubman Series of 1938–40*. Seattle and London: University of Washington Press, 1991.

125. BLEEDING KANSAS

Fehrenbacher, Don Edward. *The South and Three Sectional Crises*. Baton Rouge, LA: Louisiana State University Press, 1980.

Nichols, Alice. *Bleeding Kansas*. New York: Oxford University Press, 1954.

126. JOHN BROWN

Barrett, Tracy. *The Story of John Brown*. Brookfield, CT: Millbrook Press, 1993.

"Brown, John." Encyclopedia Britannica, https://www.britannica.com/biography/John-Brown-American-abolitionist.

Chowder, Ken. "The Father of American Terrorism." *American Heritage* (February/March 2000): 81–91.

McPherson, *Battle Cry of Freedom*. Full ref. under 87.

Vaughan, Donald. *The Everything Civil War Book*. Holbrook, MA: Adams Media Corporation, 2000.

127. DRED SCOTT DECISION

Fehrenbacher, Don Edward. *The Dred Scott Case: Its Significance in American Law and Politics*. New York: Oxford University Press, 1978.

——. *The South and Three Sectional Crises*. Baton Rouge, LA: Louisiana State University Press, 1981.

Nevins, Allan. *The Emergence of Lincoln*. New York: Scribner Publishing Company, 1950.

128. LINCOLN–DOUGLAS DEBATES

Angle, Paul M. Created Equal? *The Complete Lincoln Douglas Debates of 1858*. Chicago: University of Chicago Press, 1958.

Catton, Bruce. *The American Heritage Picture History of the Civil War*. New York: American Heritage Publishing Company, 1960, 1988.

Fehrenbacher, Don Edward. *Prelude to Greatness: Lincoln in the 1850's*. Palo Alto, CA: Stanford University Press, 1962.

Johannsen, Robert W., ed. *The Lincoln-Douglas Debates of 1858*. New York: Oxford University Press, 1965.

McPherson, *Battle Cry of Freedom*. Full ref. under 87.

129. HARRIET BEECHER STOWE

Wilson, Forrest. *Crusader in Crinoline*. Philadelphia: Lippincott Publishing Company, 1941.

130. TRANSATLANTIC CABLE

Barty-King, Hugh. *Girdle Round the Earth: The Story of Cable and Wireless*. London: Heinemann, 1979.

Chiles, J. R. "A Cable Under the Sea," *American Heritage of Invention & Technology* (Fall 1987): 34–41.

Cookson, Gillian, and Colin A. Hempstead. "The Transatlantic Telegraph Cable: Eighth Wonder of the World," *History Today* 50 (3 March 2000): 44–51.

——. *A Victorian Scientist and Engineer: Fleeming Jenkin and the Birth of Electrical Engineering*. London: Ashgate, 2000.

Hedrick, Daniel. *The Invisible Weapon: Telecommunications and International Politics, 1851–1945*. London: Oxford University Press, 1991.

Lienhard, John H. "A Transatlantic Cable," University of Houston, http://www.uh.edu/engines/epi59.htm.

131. CHARLES NALLE AND THE FUGITIVE SLAVE LAW

Bennett, *Before the Mayflower*. Full ref. under 14.

Foner, *History of Black Americans*. Full ref. under 14.

Franklin, *From Slavery to Freedom*. Full ref. under 14.

Roeder, *Jackie Robinson*. Full ref. under 14.

Toppin, *The Black American*. Full ref. under 14.

132. PONY EXPRESS

Blackstone, Sarah J. *Buckskins, Bullets, and Business: A History of Buffalo Bill's Wild West*. Westport, CT: Greenwood Press, 1986.

Russell, Don. *The Lives and Legends of Buffalo Bill*. Norman, OK: University of Oklahoma Press, 1960.

Sayers, Isabelle S. *Annie Oakley and Buffalo Bill's Wild West*. Mineola, NY: Dover Publications, 1981.

133. FREDERICK DOUGLASS AND THE BATTLE FOR FREEDOM

Conniff, Richard. "Frederick Douglass Always Knew He Was Meant to Be Free," *Smithsonian* 25 (11 February 1995): 115–127.

Robinson, Armstead. "A New Birth of Freedom: Frederick Douglass' Influence on Abraham Lincoln," unpublished essay, 1995.

Toppin, *The Black American*. Full ref. under 14.

134-135. SHOWDOWN IN CHARLESTON I & II

Brown, William Garrott. *The Lower South in American History*. New York: Macmillan, 1902.

Catton, Bruce. *The Coming Fury*. Vol. 1 of *The Centennial History of the Civil War*. New York: Doubleday Publishing Company, 1961.

Halstead, Murat. *Caucuses of 1860: A History of the National Conventions*. Columbus, OH: Follet, Foster, 1861.

Nichols, Roy Franklin. *The Disruption of American Democracy*. New York: Macmillan Company, 1948.

136-137. CIVIL WAR I & II

Catton, *The Coming Fury*. Full ref. under 135.

Flanigan, Jake. "For the Last Time, the American Civil War Was Not about States' Rights." Quartz.com, https://qz.com/378533/for-the-last-time-the -american-civil-war-was-not-about-states-rights/.

Loewen, James W. *Lies My History Teacher Told Me: Everything Your American History Textbook Got Wrong*. New York: New Press, 2008.

McPherson, *Battle Cry of Freedom*. Full ref. under 87.

Meyer, Jared, and Randall Meyer. "What Many Americans Get Wrong about States' Rights," The Federalist, http://thefederalist.com/2015/07/20/what -many-americans-get-wrong-about-states-rights/.

138. LINCOLN'S PRESIDENTIAL WIT

Conwell, Russell Herman. *Why Lincoln Laughed*. New York: Harper Publishing Company, 1922.

Gardner, Gerald. *All the President's Wits: The Power of Presidential Humor*. New York: William Morrow and Company, 1986.

Lincoln, Abraham. *Abraham Lincoln: His Speeches and Writings*. Roy P. Basler, ed. New York: World Publishing Company, 1946.

139-141. PHASES OF THE CIVIL WAR I, II, & III

Catton, *Picture History of the Civil War*. Full ref. under 128.

Hattaway, Herman, and Archer Jones. *How the North Won: A Military History of the Civil War*. Urbana, IL: University of Illinois Press, 1983.

Keegan, John. *The Face of Battle*. New York: Viking Press, 1977.

Mahon, John K. "Civil War Infantry Assault Tactics," *Military Affairs* 25 (1961): 57–68.

McPherson, *Battle Cry of Freedom*. Full ref. under 87.

McWhiney, Grady, and Perry D. Jamieson. *Attack and Die: Civil War Military Tactics and the Southern Heritage*. Tuscaloosa, AL: University of Alabama, 1982.

142. FORT SUMTER

Constable, George, ed. *The Time-Life History of the Civil War*. New York: Time-Life Books, 1990.

"Fort Sumter National Monument." Encyclopedia Britannica, http://www.britannica.com.

Latner, Richard. "Crisis at Fort Sumter," http://www.tulane.edu.

McPherson, *Battle Cry of Freedom*. Full ref. under 87.

143. STRUGGLE FOR MISSOURI

Catton, *The Coming Fury*. Full ref. under 135.

Fellman, Michael. *Inside War: The Guerilla Conflict in Missouri during the American Civil War*. New York: Oxford University Press, 1989.

Phillips, Christopher. *Damned Yankee: The Life of General Nathaniel Lyon*. Columbia, MO: University of Missouri Press, 1990.

144. DUPONT'S SALTPETER MISSION

Carr, William. *The du Ponts of Delaware*. Cornwall, N.Y.: The Cornwall Press, Inc., 1964.

Colby, Gerard. *Du Pont Dynasty*. Secaucus, NJ: Lyle Stuart Press, 1984.

Mosley, Leonard. *Blood Relations: The Rise and Fall of the du Ponts of Delaware*. New York: Atheneum, 1980.

Wall, Joseph Frazier. *Alfred I. Du Pont*. New York: Oxford University Press, 1990.

145. WEST VIRGINIA SECEDES FROM VIRGINIA

McPherson, *Battle Cry of Freedom*. Full ref. under 87.

Rice, Otis K. *West Virginia: A History*. Lexington, KY: University Press of Kentucky, 1985.

Richards, Michael P. "Lincoln and the Political Question: The Creation of the State of West Virginia." *Presidential Studies Quarterly* 27 (3, Summer 1997): 549–564.

"West Virginia." Encyclopedia Britannica, http://www.britannica.com.

"West Virginia Statehood," West Virginia Department of Arts, Culture and History, http://www.wvculture.org/history/archives/statehoo.html.

146. TRENT AFFAIR

Chalfant, Edward. "A War So Near: Imagined Steamers in the Trent Affair." *Journal of Confederate History* 6 (1990): 139–59.

Donald, David Herbert. *Lincoln*. New York: Simon and Schuster, 1995.

Goldsmith, Alistair. "Confederates on the Clyde." *History Today* 18 (8, 1998): 45–50.

Leibiger, Stuart. "Lincoln's 'White Elephants': The Trent Affair." *Lincoln Herald* 84 (2, 1982): 84–92.

147. STEPHEN RAMSEUR SEES THE DEATH OF THE WOODEN NAVY

Davis, William C. *Duel Between the First Ironclads*. Baton Rouge, LA: Louisiana State University Press, 1981.

Gallagher, Gary W. "The Fight between the Two Iron Monsters: The Monitor versus the Virginia as Described by Major Stephen Dodson Ramseur, C.S.A." *Civil War History* 30 (1984, 3): 268–271.

———. *Stephen Dodson Ramseur: Lee's Gallant General*. Chapel Hill, NC: University of North Carolina Press, 1985.

Miller, Edward. "The First Fight: Bound for Hampton Roads." *Civil War Times Illustrated* 20 (4, 1981): 22–31.

Peterkin, Ernest. "Building a Behemoth." *Civil War Times Illustrated* 20 (4, 1981): 12–21.

148. NEBRASKA AND THE HOMESTEAD ACT

Olson, James C. *History of Nebraska*. Lincoln, NE: University of Nebraska Press, 1966.

149–150. LINCOLN AND HIS ENEMIES I & II

Catton, Bruce. *Never Call Retreat: The Centennial History of the Civil War*. New York: Doubleday Publishing Company, 1965.

Goodwin, Doris Kerns. *Team of Rivals: The Political Genius of Abraham Lincoln*. New York: Simon and Schuster, 2006.

Harper, Robert S. *Lincoln and the Press*. New York: McGraw-Hill, 1951.

Oates, Stephen B. *With Malice toward None: The Life of Abraham Lincoln*. New York: Harper and Row Publishers, 1977.

151. MORRILL ACT

Johnson, Eldon L. "Misconceptions about the Early Land-Grant Colleges," *Journal of Higher Education* 52 (4, 1981): 333–351.

Preer, Jean. "Just and Equitable Division: Jim Crow and the 1890 Land-Grant College Act." *Prologue* 22 (4, 1990): 323–337.

152. LANE AND QUANTRILL

Breihan, Carl W. *Quantrill and His Civil War Guerrillas*. New York: Promontory Press, 1974.

Brownlee, Richard S. *Gray Ghosts of the Confederacy: Guerrilla Warfare in the West, 1861–1865*. Baton Rouge, LA: Louisiana State University Press, 1958.

Goodrich, Theodore. *Bloody Dawn: The Story of the Lawrence Massacre*. Kent, OH: Kent State University Press, 1991.

"Black Soldiers in the U.S. Military during the Civil War." National Archives and Records Administration, https://www.archives.gov/education/lessons/blacks -civil-war.

Burchard, Peter. *One Gallant Rush: Robert Gould Shaw and His Brave Black Regiment.* New York: St. Martin's Press, 1965.

Duncan, Russell. *Blue-Eyed Child of Fortune.* Athens, GA: University of Georgia Press, 1992.

Emilio, Luis F. *A Brave Black Regiment: History of the Fifty-Fourth Regiment of Massachusetts Volunteer Infantry 1863–1865.* Salem, NH: Ayer Company Publishing, 1990.

Fincher, Jack. "The Hard Fight Was Getting into the Fight at All." *Smithsonian* 21 (7, 1990): 42–51.

Glatthar, Joseph T. *Forged in Battle: The Civil War Alliance of Black Soldiers and White Officers.* New York: Penguin Books, 1990.

Hargrove, Hondon B. *Black Union Soldiers in the Civil War.* Jefferson, NC: McFarland and Company, 1988.

"History of the Colored Troops in the Civil War." American Civil War, http:// www.americancivilwar.com/colored/histofcoloredtroops.html.

Quarles, Benjamin. *The Negro in the Civil War.* New York: Da Capo Press, 1953.

Urwin, Gregory J. W. "I Want You to Prove Yourselves Men." *Civil War Times Illustrated* 28 (9, 1989): 42–51.

Westwood, Howard. C. *Black Troops, White Commanders and Freedmen during the Civil War.* Carbondale, IL: Southern Illinois University Press, 1992.

Wilson, Keith. "Thomas Webster and the 'Free Military School for Applicants for Commands of Colored Troops.'" *Civil War History* 29 (2, 1983): 101–122.

Berlin, Ira, Joseph P. Reidy, and Leslie S. Rowland. *Freedom's Soldiers: The Black Military Experience in the Civil War.* Cambridge: Cambridge University Press, 1998.

Blight, David W. "The Meaning of the Fight: Frederick Douglass and the Memory of the Fifty-Fourth Massachusetts." *The Massachusetts Review* 36 (1, Spring 1995): 141–153.

Cornish, Dudley Taylor. *The Sable Arm: Negro Troops in the Union Army, 1861–1865.* New York: W. W. Norton and Company, 1966.

Duncan, *Blue-Eyed Child of Fortune.* Full ref. under 153.

Emilio, *A Brave Black Regiment.* Full ref. under 153.

Fincher, "The Hard Fight." Full ref. under 153.

Flint, Allen. "Black Response to Colonel Shaw." *Phylon* 45 (3, 1984): 210–219.

Gooding, Corporal James Henry. *On the Altar of Freedom: A Black Soldier's Civil War Letters from the Front.* Edited by Virginia Matzke Adams. Amherst, MA: University of Massachusetts Press, 1991.

Grant, Susan-Mary. "Pride and Prejudice in the American Civil War." *History Today* 48 (9 September 1998): 41–49.

Hansen, Chadwick. "The 54th Massachusetts Volunteer Black Infantry as a Subject for American Artists." *Massachusetts Review* 16 (4, 1975): 745–759.

Mauldin, Curtis A. "Unassuming Valor: Sergeant William FL Carney and the Awarding of the Medal of Honor." *Proceedings and Papers of the Georgia Association of Historians* 12 (1991): 46–80.

McPherson, James M. "The 'Glory' Story." *New Republic* 202 (2–3 January 15, 1990): 22–27, https://newrepublic.com/article/91210/tnr-film-classics-glory-january-15-1990.

——. *The Negro's Civil War: How American Negroes Felt and Acted during the War for the Union*. New York: Pantheon Books, 1965.

——. *The Struggle for Equality: Abolitionists and the Negro in the Civil War and Reconstruction*. Princeton, NJ: Princeton University Press, 1964.

Quarles, Benjamin. *The Negro in the Civil War*. New York: Da Capo Press, 1989.

Scharnhorst, Gary. "From Soldier to Saint: Robert Gould Shaw and the Rhetoric of Racial Justice." *Civil War History* 34 (4, 1988): 308–322.

Stark, William C. "Forgotten Heroes: Black Recipients of the United States Congressional Medal of Honor in the American Civil War, 1863–1865, Part I." *Lincoln Herald* 88 (4, 1985): 122–130.

Westwood, *Black Troops*. Full ref. under 153.

Wise, Stephen R. *Gate of Hell: Campaign for Charleston Harbor, 1863*. Columbia, SC: University of South Carolina Press, 1994.

Yacovone, Donald, ed. *A Voice of Thunder: The Civil War Letters of George E. Stephens*. Chicago: University of Illinois Press, 1997.

Zwick, Edward, dir. *Glory*. 1989; Burbank, CA: RCA/Columbia Pictures Home Video, 1990. Videocassette.

155–156. CIVIL WAR WOMEN SPIES I & II

Galbraith, William, and Loretta Galbraith, eds. *A Lost Heroine of the Confederacy*. Jackson, MS: University Press of Mississippi, 1990.

Jones, Katharine M., ed. *Heroines of Dixie*. New York: Ballantine Books, 1955.

Kane, Harnett T. *Spies for the Blue and Gray*. New York: Hanover House, 1954.

Magness, Perre. "Women 'Fought' Quietly for South: Civil War Role Created Spies from Belles."

Markle, Donald E. *Spies and Spymasters of the Civil War*. New York: Hippocrene Books, 1994.

Commercial Appeal (12 March 1992): E2.

Massey, Mary Elizabeth. *Women in the Civil War*. Lincoln, NE: University of Nebraska Press, 1994.

Ryan, David D. *A Yankee Spy in Richmond*. Mechanicsville, PA: Stackpole Books, 1996.

Smith, Whitney. "Diaries Tell Vivid Story of Southern Heroine." *Commercial Appeal* 21 (July 1991): G4.

Vaughan, *The Everything Civil War Book*. Full ref. under 126.

157. STONEWALL JACKSON

Constable, *The Time-Life History of the Civil War*. Full ref. under 142.

"Jackson, Thomas Jonathan." Encyclopedia Britannica, http://www.britannica.com.

McPherson, *Battle Cry of Freedom*. Full ref. under 87.

Vaughan, *The Everything Civil War Book*. Full ref. under 126.

158. PICKETT'S CHARGE

Carmichael, Peter S., ed. *Audacity Personified: The Generalship of Robert E. Lee*. Baton Rouge, LA: Louisiana State University Press, 2004.

Hattaway, Herman, and Archer Jones. *How the North Won: A Military History of the Civil War*. Urbana, IL: University of Illinois Press, 1983.

McPherson, *Battle Cry of Freedom*. Full ref. under 87.

Pfanz, Harry W. *Gettysburg: Culp's Hill and Cemetery Hill*. Chapel Hill, NC: University of North Carolina Press, 1993.

Tucker, Glenn. *High Tide at Gettysburg*. Dayton, OH: Morningside House, 1983.

Wert, Jeffry. *Gettysburg: Day Three*. New York: Simon and Schuster, 1958.

159-160. GETTYSBURG ADDRESS I & II

Braden, Waldo. *Abraham Lincoln: Public Speaker*. Baton Rouge, LA: Louisiana State University Press, 1988.

Donald, *Lincoln*. Full ref. under 146.

"The Gettysburg Address." Library of Congress, http://www.loc.gov/exhibits/gadd/.

Hanchett, William. "Gettysburg Address." *Encyclopedia Americana*, 1996.

Holzer, Harold. "A Few Appropriate Remarks." *American History Illustrated* (23, 1988): 36-46.

Kunhardt, Philip B. "Lincoln at Gettysburg." *Life* (October 6, 1983): 97-112.

161. CITY POINT EXPLOSION

Rayburn, Ella S. "Sabotage at City Point." *Civil War Times Illustrated* 22 (2, 1983): 28-33.

Trudeau, Noah Andre. *The Last Citadel: Petersburg, Virginia, June 1864-1865*. Boston: Little, Brown and Company, 1991.

162. MR. LINCOLN'S CHRISTMAS GIFT

Bryan, Thomas Conn. *Confederate Georgia*. Athens, GA: University of Georgia, 1953.

Davis, Burke. *Sherman's March*. New York: Random House Publishers, 1980.

Glatthaar, Joseph T. *The March to the Sea and Beyond: Sherman's Troops in the Savannah and Carolinas Campaigns*. New York: New York University Press, 1985.

163. THE DOCTORS MAYO

Clapesattle, Helen. *The Doctors Mayo*. Minneapolis: University of Minnesota Press, 1941.

164. RAPHAEL SEMMES

McCorvey, Thomas C. *Alabama Historical Sketches*. Charlottesville, VA: University of Virginia Press, 1960.

165. JOHN SINGLETON MOSBY

Gibboney, Douglas. "Bested at Berryville," *Civil War Times Illustrated* 24 (8, 1985): 36-39.

"John Singleton Mosby," Civil War Home, http://www.civilwarhome.com/mosbybio.htm.

Siepel, Kevin H. "The Gray Ghost in Mufti: The Postwar Career of John S. Mosby," *Virginia Cavalcade* 36 (2, 1986): 74-87.

Schuchman, W. Red Sky. "The Gray Ghost," *Mankind* 3 (7, 1972): 56-64.

Wert, Jeffry D. *Mosby's Rangers*. New York: Simon and Schuster, 1990.

166. MATHEW BRADY

Donald, *Lincoln*. Full ref. under 146.

Kelbaugh, Ross J. *Introduction to Civil War Photography*. Gettysburg, PA: Thomas Publications, 1991.

Panzer, Mary. *Mathew Brady and the Image of History*. Washington, DC: Smithsonian Institution Press, 1997.

Zeller, Bob. *The Civil War in Depth: History in 3-D*. San Francisco: Chronicle Books, 1997.

167-168. LINCOLN'S VISION I & II

Braden, Abraham Lincoln: Public Speaker. Full ref. under 160.

Donald, *Lincoln*. Full ref. under 146.

"Gettysburg Address." Library of Congress, http://www.loc.gov/exhibits/gadd/.

Hanchett, "Gettysburg Address." Full ref. under 160.

Holzer, "A Few Appropriate Remarks." Full ref. under 159-160.

Kunhardt, "Lincoln at Gettysburg." Full ref. under 160.

White, Ronald C., Jr. *Lincoln's Greatest Speech: The Second Inaugural*. New York: Simon and Schuster, 2002.

169. MAN PURSUED BY WAR

Catton, *Never Call Retreat*. Full ref. under 150.

Cauble, Frank P. *Biography of Wilmer McLean*. Lynchburg, VA: H. E. Howard, 1987.

170. THE HAUNTED MAJOR RATHBONE

Bishop, Jim. *The Day Lincoln Was Shot*. New York: Harper Publishing Company, 1955.

Cisenachiml, Otto. *In the Shadow of Lincoln's Death*. New York: W. Funk Publishers, 1940.

"Last Witness to Abraham Lincoln Assassination," *I've Got a Secret*, 1956, YouTube, https://www.youtube.com/watch?v=1RPoymt3Jx4. Video.

Smith, Gene. "The Haunted Major," *American Heritage* 45 (1 February/March 1994): 110–111.

Weichmann, Louis J. *The True History of the Assassination of Abraham Lincoln and of the Conspiracy of 1865*. New York: Alfred A. Knopf, 1975.

171. COLLINS'S OVERLAND TELEGRAPH

Collins, Perry M. *Siberian Journey: Down the Amur to the Pacific, 1856–1857*. Madison, WI: University of Wisconsin Press, 1962.

Thompson, Robert Luther. *Wiring A Continent: The History of the Telegraph Industry of the United States*. Princeton, NJ: Princeton University Press, 1947.

172. GREAT EASTERN

Stewart, Doug. "The Curse of the Great Eastern." *Smithsonian* 25 (8 November 1994): 62–77.

173. BOZEMAN TRAIL

Drew, Marilyn J. "A Brief History of the Bozeman Trail." Wyoming State Historical Society, https://www.wyohistory.org/encyclopedia/brief-history -bozeman-trail.

Johnson, Dorothy M. *The Bloody Bozeman: The Perilous Trail to Montana's Gold*. New York: McGraw-Hill, 1971.

McCaig, Donald. "The Bozeman Trail." *Smithsonian* 31 (7 October 2000): 88–101.

174. LAURA INGALLS WILDER

Cech, John, ed. *American Writers for Children 1900–1960*. Vol. 2. Detroit: Bruccoli Clark, 1983.

Davidson, Cathy N., and Linda Martin-Wagner, eds. *The Oxford Companion to Women's Writing in the United States*. New York: Oxford University Press, 1995.

Hipple, Ted, ed. *Writers for Young Adults*. Vol. 3. New York: Scribner, 1997.

Magill, Frank N., ed. "Wilder, Laura Ingalls." *Cyclopedia of World Authors*. 3rd ed. Vol. 5. Englewood Cliffs, NJ: Salem Press, 1997.

Miller, John E. *Becoming Laura Ingalls Wilder*. Columbia, MO: University of Missouri Press, 1998.

——. *Laura Ingalls Wilder's Little Town: Where History and Literature Meet.* Lawrence, KS: University of Kansas, 1994.

Spaeth, Janet. *Laura Ingalls Wilder.* Boston: Twayne Publishers, 1987.

Vedder, Polly A. "Laura Elizabeth Ingalls Wilder: 1867–1957." *Contemporary Authors Online.* Farmington Hills, MI: Gale Group, 1999.

175. ANDREW JOHNSON'S IMPEACHMENT

Benedict, Michael Les. *The Impeachment of Andrew Johnson.* New York: W. W. Norton and Company, 1973.

Kennedy, John F. *Profiles in Courage.* New York: Harper and Row Publishers, 1964.

Riddleberger, Patrick W. *1866: The Critical Year Revisited.* Carbondale, IL: Southern Illinois University, 1979.

176–177. BIG FOUR OF THE CENTRAL PACIFIC I & II

Brown, D. Alexander. *Hear that Lonesome Whistle Blow: Railroads in the West.* New York: Holt, Rienhart and Winston, 1977.

Silver, John F. *Iron Road to the West: American Railroads in the 1850s.* New York: Columbia University Press, 1978.

Williams, John Hoyt. *A Great and Shining Road: The Epic Story of the Transcontinental Railroad.* New York: Times Books, 1988.

178. BELLE HUNTINGTON

Evans, Cerinda. *Collis Potter Huntington.* Newport News, VA: Mariners' Museum, 1954.

Rouse, Parke, Jr. "Belle Huntington, Her Men and Her Muse." *Virginia Magazine of History and Biography* 88 (4 October 1980): 387–400.

179. SAMUEL TILDEN AND TAMMANY HALL

Flick, Alexander Clarence. *Samuel Jones Tilden: A Study in Political Sagacity.* Port Washington, NY: Kennikat Press, 1963.

Mushkat, Jerome. *Tammany: The Evolution of a Political Machine, 1789–1865.* Syracuse, NY: Syracuse University Press, 1971.

Werner, Morris Robert. *Tammany Hall.* Garden City, NY: Doubleday, Doran and Company, 1928.

180. NEW YORK'S FIRST SUBWAY

Allen, Oliver E. "New York's Secret Subway." *American Heritage of Invention and Technology* 12 (3, Winter 1997): 45–48.

181. GREAT CHICAGO FIRE OF 1871

Liddy, Colbert Elias. *Chicago in the Great Conflagration*. New York: Viking Press, 1971.

Miller, Ross. "The Great Fire and the Myth of Chicago," *Chicago History* (1990, 1-2): 4-31.

Pauly, John J. "The Great Chicago Fire as a National Event." *American Quarterly* 36 (5, 1984): 668-683.

Sawislak, Karen. "Smoldering City." *Chicago History* 17 (3-4, 1988-9): 70-101.

182. THE KLAN CLAIMS A VICTIM

Bennett, *Before the Mayflower*. Full ref. under 14.

Foner, *History of Black Americans*. Full ref. under 14.

Franklin, *From Slavery to Freedom*. Full ref. under 14.

Toppin, *The Black American*. Full ref. under 14.

183. JOSEPH GLIDDEN AND BARBED WIRE

Ellwood House Museum, http://www.ellwoodhouse.org/#home-section.

McCallum, Henry D. *The Wire That Fenced the West*. Norman, OK: University of Oklahoma, 1965.

Monaghan, Jay, ed. *The Book of the American West*. New York: Bonanza Books, 1963.

Morgan, Ted. *The Shovel of Stars: The Making of the American West*. New York: Simon and Schuster, 1995.

O'Connor, Clyde A., and Martha A. Sandweiss, eds. *The Oxford History of the American West*. New York: Oxford University Press, 1994.

Ray, Emily, and Wynell Schamel. "Glidden's Patent Application for Barbed Wire." *Social Education* 61 (1 January 1997): 53-56.

184. TRIAL OF HENRY WARD BEECHER

Clark, Clifford E., Jr. *Henry Ward Beecher: Spokesman for a Middle-Class America*. Chicago: University of Illinois Press, 1982.

McLoughlin, William G. *The Meaning of Henry Ward Beecher: An Essay on the Shifting Values of Mid-Victorian America, 1840–1870*. New York: Alfred A. Knopf, 1970.

185. GEORGE WESTINGHOUSE

Leupp, Francis Ellington. *George Westinghouse: His Life and Achievements*. Boston: Little, Brown and Company, 1918.

Millard, A. J. *Edison and the Business of Innovation*. Baltimore: Johns Hopkins University Press, 1990.

Wohleber, Curt. "'St. George' Westinghouse." *American Heritage of Invention and Technology* 12 (3, Winter 1997): 28-42.

186. BUFFALO SOLDIERS

Stiles, T. J. "Buffalo Soldiers." *Smithsonian* 29 (9 December 1998): 82–94.

187. DEMISE OF GEORGE ARMSTRONG CUSTER

Ambrose, Stephen E. *Crazy Horse and Custer: The Parallel Lives of Two American Warriors.* New York: Meridian Publishing, 1986.

Connell, Evan S. *Son of the Morning Star.* San Francisco: North Point Press, 1984.

Graham, William Alexander. *The Custer Myth: A Source Book of Custeriana.* New York: Bonanza Books, 1953.

Rosenberg, Bruce A. *Custer and the Epic of Defeat.* University Park, PA: Pennsylvania State University Press, 1974.

Utley, Robert Marshall. *Cavalier in Buckskin: George Armstrong Custer and the Western Military Frontier.* Norman, OK: University of Oklahoma Press, 1988.

188. ELECTION CRISIS OF 1876

Davison, Kenneth E. *The Presidency of Rutherford B. Hayes.* Westport, CT: Greenwood Press, 1972.

Eckenrode, H. J. *Rutherford B. Hayes: Statesman of Reunion.* New York: Dodd, Mead and Company, 1930.

Flick, Alexander Clarence. *Samuel Jones Tilden: A Study in Political Sagacity.* Port Washington, NY: Kennikat Press, 1963.

Hoogenboom, Ari Arthur. *The Presidency of Rutherford B. Hayes.* Lawrence, KS: University Press of Kansas, 1988.

189. EDISON'S PHONOGRAPH

Baldwin, Neil. *Edison: Inventing the Century.* New York: Hyperion, 1995.

Josephson, Matthew. *Edison: A Biography.* London: Eyre and Spottiswoode, 1961.

Millard, Edison and the Business of Innovation. Full ref. under 185.

Spencer, Len. "The First Recorded Promotional Message on the Edison Phonograph, Edison Studios, West Orange, New Jersey, 1906." *Great Speeches of the Twentieth Century, Volume Two: The Changing World.* Santa Monica, CA: Rhino Records, 1991. 33 1/3 rpm LP.

190. NEZ PERCE WAR

Beal, Merrill D. *I Will Fight No More Forever: Chief Joseph and the Nez Perce War.* Seattle: University of Washington Press, 1963.

Howard, Oliver O. *Nez Perce Joseph.* Boston: Lee and Shepherd Publishing Company, 1881.

McWhorter, Lucullus Virgil. *Yellow Wolf: His Own Story.* Caldwell, ID: Caxton Printers, 1940.

191. WILLIAM CULLEN BRYANT

Bryant, William Cullen. "Thanatopsis." In *Harvard Classics: English Poetry from Tennyson to Whitman*. Vol. 42. New York: P. F. Collier and Son Company, 1910.

Lynes, Russell. "Countryman-Poet Let Some Fresh Air into Old New York." *Smithsonian* 4 (12 March 1974): 80–87.

192. CARRY NATION

Day, Robert. "Carry from Kansas Became a Nation All unto Herself," *Smithsonian* 20 (1, 1989): 147–164.

Madison, Arnold. *Carry Nation*. Nashville, TN: T. Nelson, 1977.

Willard, Francis Elizabeth. *Woman and Temperance: Or, The Work and Workers of the Woman's Christian Temperance Union*. New York: Arno Press, 1972.

193. PHINEAS TAYLOR BARNUM AND JUMBOMANIA

Saxon, A. H. *P. T. Barnum: The Legend and the Man*. New York: Columbia University Press, 1989.

194. ANATOMY OF A PRESIDENTIAL SCANDAL

Nevins, Allan. *Grover Cleveland: A Study in Courage*. New York: Dodd, Meade, and Company, 1932.

Welch, Richard E. *The Presidencies of Grover Cleveland*. Lawrence, KS: University Press of Kansas, 1988.

195. EDISON VS. WESTINGHOUSE

Leupp, *George Westinghouse*. Full ref. under 185.

Millard, *Edison and the Business of Innovation*. Full ref. under 185.

Wohleber, "'St. George' Westinghouse." Full ref. under 185.

196. HAYMARKET INCIDENT

Avrich, Paul. *The Haymarket Tragedy*. Princeton, NJ: Princeton University Press, 1984.

David, Henry. *The History of the Haymarket Affair: A Study in the American Social-Revolutionary and Labor Movements*. New York: Russell and Russell Publishing Company, 1958.

Roediger, Dave, and Franklin Rosemont, Eds. *Haymarket Scrapbook*. Chicago: C. H. Kerr Publishing Company, 1986.

Schindler, Burton. "The Haymarket Bomb." *American History Illustrated* 21 (4, 1986): 20–27.

197. JOHNSTOWN FLOOD

Jackson, Donald Dale. "For Gods Sake, Get Out, The Dam's Broke." *Smithsonian* 20 (2 May 1989): 50–61.

Kinney, Doris G. "After the Flood," *Life* 12 (May 1989): 144–148.

McCullough, David G. *The Johnstown Flood*. New York: Simon and Schuster, 1968.

198. MASSACRE AT WOUNDED KNEE

Brown, Dee. *Bury My Heart at Wounded Knee: An Indian History of the American West*. New York: H. Holt, 2001.

Ostler, Jeffrey. "Conquest and the State: Why the U.S. Employed Massive Military Force to Suppress the Lakota Ghost Dance." *Pacific Historical Review* 65 (May 1996): 217–249.

Taylor, Walt. "Wounded Knee (1890)—Unquenchable Spirit (1990)." *Canadian Dimension* (January-February 1991): 13–16.

Utley, Robert M. *The Last Days of the Sioux Nation*. New Haven, CT: Yale University Press, 1963.

199. FLYING WEDGE

Hill, Dean. *Football through the Years*. New York: Gridiron Publishing Company, 1940.

McCallum, John Dennis. *Ivy League Football since 1872*. New York: Stein and Day Publishing, 1977.

Porter. David L., ed. *Biographical Dictionary of American Sports*. New York: Greenwood Press, 1987.

McQuilken, Scott A., and Ronald A. Smith, "The Rise and Fall of the Flying Wedge: Football's Most Controversial Play." *Journal of Sport History* 20 (1, 1993): 57–64.

200. JOHN PIERPONT MORGAN BAILS OUT US GOVERNMENT

Allen, Frederick Lewis. *The Great Pierpont Morgan*. New York: Harper, 1949.

Carosso, Vincent P. *The Morgans: Private International Bankers, 1854–1913*. Cambridge, MA: Harvard University Press, 1987.

Sinclair, Andrew. *Corsair: The Life of J. Pierpont Morgan*. Boston: Little, Brown and Company, 1981.

Wheeler, George. *Pierpont Morgan and Friends: The Anatomy of a Myth*. Englewood Cliffs, NJ: Prentice-Hall, 1973.

Winkler, John K. *Morgan the Magnificent: The Life J. Pierpont Morgan (1837–1913)*. Garden City, NY: Garden City Publishing Company, 1930.

201. WILLIAM JENNINGS BRYAN AND THE CROSS OF GOLD

Bryan, William Jennings. "Scopes Monkey Trial and the Advocates," 1921. YouTube, https://www.youtube.com/watch?v=UV2wRCcWJa8&list =PLU1cLSAI7OzXnDrUgRpEJyWtQIzYaa4N2&index=6. Audio. William Jennings Bryan reprises his "cross of gold" speech.

Weisberger, Bernard A. "Election in Silver and Gold." *American Heritage* (October 1996): 16–17.

202. GEORGE WASHINGTON CARVER

Benitez, Mirna. *George Washington Carver: Plant Doctor*. Milwaukee: Raintree Publishing, 1989.

Fishbein, Toby. "The Legacy of George Washington Carver." Iowa State University, https://digitalcollections.lib.iastate.edu/george-washington-carver/biography.

Holt, Rackham. *George Washington Carver: An American Biography*. Garden City, NY: Doubleday, 1943.

McMurry, Linda O. *George Washington Carver: Scientist and Symbol*. New York: Oxford University Press, 1981.

Micucci, Charles. *The Life and Times of the Peanut*. Boston: Houghton Mifflin, 1997.

203. SOUSA'S GREATEST MARCH

Bierley, Paul E. *John Philip Sousa: American Phenomenon*. New York: Century-Appelton Crofts, 1973.

"Sousa's Greatest," *American Heritage* (May/June 1997): 106.

"The Stars and Stripes Forever," US Marine Band, 2009. YouTube, https://www.youtube.com/watch?v=a-7XWhyvIpE&t=137s. Video.

204. HOMER PLESSY AND SEPARATE BUT EQUAL

Abraham, Henry Julian. *Freedom and the Court: Civil Rights and Liberties in the United States*. New York: Oxford University Press, 1982.

Medley, Keith Weldon. "The Sad Story of How 'Separate but Equal' Was Born." *Smithsonian* 24 (11 February 1994): 105–117.

205. REVOLUTION IN PARADISE

Wyndette, Oive. *Islands of Destiny: A History of Hawaii*. Rutland, VT: C. E. Tuttle Company, 1968.

206. GALVESTON HURRICANE

Fox, Stephen. "For a While, It Was Fun." *Smithsonian* (September 1999): 128–142.

207. SUSAN BROWNELL ANTHONY

Anticaglia, Elizabeth. *Twelve American Women*. Chicago: Nelson-Hall Company, 1980.

Barry, Kathleen. *Susan B. Anthony: A Biography of a Singular Feminist*. New York: New York University Press, 1988.

Riegel, Robert Edgar. *American Feminists*. Lawrence, KS: University of Kansas Press, 1963.

208. MODEL T

Flink, James J. "Unplanned Obsolescence." *American Heritage of Invention and Technology* 12 (1, Summer 1996): 58–62.

209–210. SAGA OF LEO FRANK I & II

Dinnerstein, Leonard. "The Fate of Leo Frank." *American Heritage* (October 1996): 99–109.

———. *The Leo Frank Case.* Athens, GA: The University of Georgia, 1987.

Lindemann, Albert S. *The Jew Accused: Three Anti-Semitic Affairs (Dreyfus, Beilis, Frank), 1894–1915.* New York: Cambridge University Press, 1991.

211. HENRY FORD AND THE $5 WORKDAY

Conot, Robert. *American Odyssey.* Detroit: Wayne State University Press, 1986.

Ford, Henry, and Samuel Crowther. *My Life and Work.* Garden City, NY: Doubleday Publishing Company, 1922.

Nevins, Alan, and Frank E. Hill. *Ford: The Times, the Man, the Company.* New York: Scribner, 1954.

212. EDUCATION UNDER JIM CROW

Curry, J. L. M. *A Brief Sketch of George Peabody, and a History of the Peabody Education Fund through Thirty Years.* Cambridge, MA: University Press, 1898.

Embree, Edwin, and Julia Waxman. *Investment in People: The Story of the Julius Rosenwald Fund.* New York: Harper and Brothers, 1949.

Harlan, Louis R. *Booker T. Washington: The Wizard of Tuskegee, 1901–1915.* New York: Oxford University Press, 1983.

Westin, Barry. "The Effect of Philanthropy upon Public Education in the Jim Crow South: North Carolina and the Rosenwald Fund, 1917–1933." Unpublished essay, 1999.

Wiebe, Robert H. *The Search for Order.* New York: Hill and Wang, 1967.

213. FLU EPIDEMIC OF 1918

Associated Press, The. "Genetic Analysis Links 1918 Pandemic Flu to American Pigs." *Richmond Times-Dispatch*, March 21, 1997: A9.

Collier, Richard. *The Plague of the Spanish Lady: The Influenza Pandemic of 1918–1919.* London: Macmillan Publishing Company, 1974.

Crosby, Alfred W. *Epidemic and Peace, 1918.* Westport, CT: Greewood Press, 1976.

Phillips, Howard. "South Africa's Worst Demographic Disaster: The Spanish Influenza Epidemic of 1918." *South African Historical Journal* 20 (1988): 57–73.

214. WILSON AND THE LEAGUE OF NATIONS

Bailey, Thomas A. *Wilson and the Peacemakers.* New York: Macmillan, 1947.

Garraty, John A. *Henry Cabot Lodge: A Biography*. New York: Alfred A. Knopf, 1968.

Widenor, William C. *Henry Cabot Lodge and the Search for an American Foreign Policy*. Berkeley: University of California Press, 1980.

215. THE PALMER RAIDS

Gentry, Curt. *J. Edgar Hoover: The Man and the Secrets*. New York: Norton Publishing Company, 1991.

Powers, Richard Gid. *Secrecy and Power: The Life of J. Edgar Hoover*. New York: Free Press, 1987.

Theoharis, Athan G. *The Boss: J. Edgar Hoover and the Great American Inquisition*. Philadelphia: Temple University Press, 1966.

216. BLACK SOX SCANDAL

Asinof, Eliot. *Eight Men Out*. New York: H. Holt, 1987.

Danzig, Allison, and Joe Reichler. *Baseball: An Illustrated History*. Englewood Cliffs, NJ: Prentice-Hall, 1959.

Gropman, Donald. *Say It Ain't So, Joe!* New York: Citadel Press, 2001.

Luhrs, Victor. *The Great Baseball Mystery*. South Brunswick, NJ: A. S. Barnes, 1966.

Thompson, Lewis, and Charles Boswell. "Say it Ain't So, Joe." *American Heritage* 11 (4 June 1960): 24–27, 88–93.

217. BOOKER T. WASHINGTON VS. W. E. B. DU BOIS

Harlan, Louis R. *Booker T. Washington: The Making of Black Leader*. New York: Oxford University Press, 2011.

Hawkins, Hugh. *Booker T. Washington and His Critics: Black Leadership in Crisis*. Lexington, MA: D. C. Heath Publishing Company, 1974.

Reed, Adolph L., Jr. "W. E. B. Du Bois: A Perspective on the Bases of His Political Thought," *Political Theory* 13 (3, 1985): 431–455.

218. TEAPOT DOME SCANDAL

Bates, J. Leonard. *The Origins of Teapot Dome*. Urbana, IL: University of Illinois Press, 1963.

McCartney, Laton. *The Teapot Dome Scandal: How Big Oil Bought the Harding White House and Tried to Steal the Country*. New York: Random House, 2008.

Noggle, Burl. *Teapot Dome: Oil and Politics in the 1920s*. Baton Rouge, LA: Louisiana State University Press, 1962.

Werner, M. R., and John Starr. *Teapot Dome*. New York: Viking Press, 1959.

219. SACCO AND VANZETTI

Avrich, Paul. *Sacco and Vanzetti–The Anarchist Background*. Princeton, NJ: Princeton University Press, 1991.

Kaiser, David, and William Young. *Postmortem.* Amherst, MA: University of Massachusetts Press, 1985.

Russell, Francis. *Sacco and Vanzetti: The Case Resolved.* New York: Harper and Row Publishers, 1986.

220. "RHAPSODY IN BLUE"

Gershwin, George. "I Got Rhythm," *Crazy for You,* 1992. YouTube, https://www .youtube.com/watch?v=AnrqYKWuvB0&list=PLPtFzRgqEWTv4Hmj6G1ObOss _pxnZw8AD&index=13. Audio. *Crazy for You* was the 1990 revival of *Girl Crazy* from 1930.

———. "Rhapsody in Blue." New York Philharmonic. Leonard Bernstein. Recorded in 1976, YouTube, https://www.youtube.com/watch?v=cH2PH0auTUU. Video.

Peyser, Joan. *The Memory of All That: The Life of George Gershwin.* New York: Simon and Schuster, 1993.

Rosenberg, Deena. *Fascinating Rhythm: The Collaboration of George and Ira Gershwin.* New York: Dutton Publishing Company, 1991.

Schwartz, Charles. *Gershwin: His Life and Music.* Indianapolis: Bobbs-Merrill, 1973.

221. SCOPES'S MONKEY TRIAL

De Camp, L. Sprague. *The Great Monkey Trial.* Garden City, NY: Doubleday Publishers, 1969.

Ginger, Ray. *Six Days or Forever? Tennessee v. John Thomas Scopes.* London: Oxford University Press, 1974.

Glad, Paul W. *The Trumpet Soundeth: William Jennings Bryan and His Democracy, 1896–1912.* Lincoln, NE: University of Nebraska Press, 1960.

Kramer, Stanley, dir. *Inherit the Wind.* 1960; Universal City, CA: United Artists. YouTube, https://www.youtube.com/watch?v=vtNdYsoool8. Video. The clip shows the dramatic climax of *Inherit the Wind,* the film derived from the Pulitzer Prize–winning play of the same name. It is an effective, though in part fictional, examination of the issues surrounding the Scopes trial, featuring Spencer Tracy and Fredric March as the two legal antagonists: Brady (Bryan) and Drummond (Darrow).

Scopes, John Thomas. *Center of the Storm: Memoirs of John Thomas Scopes.* New York: Holt, Rinehart and Winston, 1967.

Tierney, Kevin. *Darrow: A Biography.* New York: Crowell, 1979.

222. EUGENICS

Brown, Michael, et al., eds. *Nationalism and Ethnic Conflict.* Cambridge, MA: MIT Press, 1997.

Bureau of Vital Statistics. *Eugenics in Relation to the New Family and the Law on*

Racial Integrity. Richmond, VA: Davis Bottom, Superintendent of Public Printing, 1924.

Goddard, Henry Herbert. *The Kallikak Family.* New York: Macmillan Company, 1927.

Haller, Mark H. *Eugenics.* New Brunswick, NJ: Rutgers University Press, 1963.

Ingle, Dwight J. *Who Should Have Children?* Indianapolis and New York: Bobbs-Merrill, 1973.

Packard, Vance. *The People Shapers.* Boston and Toronto: Little, Brown and Company, 1977.

Popenoe, Paul, and Roswell Hill Johnson. *Applied Eugenics.* New York: Macmillan Company, 1926.

Ramsey, Paul. *Fabricated Man.* New Haven and London: Yale University Press, 1970.

Rountree, *Pocahontas's People.* Full ref. under 10.

223. COURT-MARTIAL OF BILLY MITCHELL

Hurley, Alfred F. *Billy Mitchell: Crusader for Air Power.* Bloomington, IN: Indiana University Press, 1975.

Schwarz, Frederic D. "The Time Machine: The Court-Martial of Billy Mitchell." *American Heritage* (October 2000): 95–98.

Waller, Douglas C. *A Question of Loyalty: General Billy Mitchell and the Court-Martial That Gripped the Nation.* New York: HarperCollins Publishers, 2004.

224. FOOD AND DRUG ADMINISTRATION

Carson, Gerald H. "Who Put the Borax in Dr. Wiley's Butter?" *American Heritage* (October 1960): 59–62, 95.

Food and Drug Administration, http://www.fda.gov/.

Marti-Ibanez, Felix, and Henry Welch, eds. *The Impact of the Food and Drug Administration on Our Society.* New York: MD Publications, 1956.

Ricardo-Campbell, Rita, *Food Safety Regulation.* Washington, DC: American Enterprise Institute for Public Policy Research, 1974.

225. MAKING PICTURES TALK

Crafton, Donald. *The Talkies: American Cinema's Transition to Sound, 1926–1931.* New York: Charles Scribner's Sons, 1997.

Eyman, Scott. *The Speed of Sound: Hollywood and the Talkie Revolution 1926–1930.* New York: Simon and Schuster, 1997.

Wohleber, Curt. "How the Movies Learned to Talk." *American Heritage of Invention and Technology* 10 (3, Winter 1995): 36–46.

226-228. CAUSES OF THE GREAT DEPRESSION I, II, & III

"Causes of the Great Depression." History on the Net, https://www .historyonthenet.com/causes-of-the-great-depression/.

Devine, Robert A., et al. *America Past and Present*. New York: Longman, 1998.

"Great Depression." Encyclopedia Britannica, http://www.britannica.com.

Prescott, Edward C. "Some Observations on the Great Depression." Abstract.
Federal Reserve Bank of Minneapolis Quarterly Review 23 (Winter 1999): 25–32.

229. AL CAPONE AND THE ST. VALENTINE'S DAY MASSACRE

Kobler, John. *Capone: The Life and World of Al Capone*. New York: Putnam
Publishing, 1971.

Mitchell, John G. "What the Public Wanted, It Seemed, Was a Vice and Bootleg
Business Netting Sixty Million Dollars a Year—and Many Gangland Funerals."
American Heritage (February 1979): 84–93.

230. BABE RUTH

Burleigh, Robert, and Mike Wimmer. *Home Run*. San Diego: Harcourt Brace and
Company, 1998.

Creamer, Robert. *Babe: The Legend Comes to Life*. New York: Simon and Schuster,
1992.

———. "Rutholotry, or Why Everyone Loves the Babe." *Smithsonian* 25 (11 February
1995): 68–78.

Ruth, Babe. *Babe Ruth's Own Book of Baseball*. Lincoln, NE: University of Nebraska
Press, 1992.

231. HYBRID SEED CORN

Bauman, L. F., and P. L. Crane. *National Corn Handbook*. West Lafayette, IN:
Purdue University.

Fitzgerald, Deborah. "Farmers Deskilled: Hybrid Corn and Farmers' Work,"
Technology and Culture 34 (2, 1992): 324–343.

Lamar, Howard R., ed. "Corn Production." In *The New Encyclopedia of the
American West*. New Haven, CT: Yale University Press, 1998.

Phillips, Charles, and Alan Axelrod. "Corn Growing." In *The New Encyclopedia
of the American West*. Howard R. Lamar, ed. New Haven, CT: Yale University
Press, 1998.

Socolofsky, Homer E. "The World Food Crisis and Progress in Wheat Breeding."
Agricultural History 43(4, 1969): 423–437.

232. CIVILIAN CONSERVATION CORPS

Brinkley, Douglas. *Rightful Heritage: Franklin D. Roosevelt and the Land of America*.
New York: HarperCollins, 2016.

Jackson, Donald Dale. "To the CCC: Thanks for the Memories and the
Monuments." *Smithsonian* 25 (9 December 1994): 66–81.

Maher, Neil M. *Nature's New Deal: The Civilian Conservation Corps and the Roots of the American Environmental Movement.* New York: Oxford University Press, 2008.

Salmon, John A. *The Civilian Conservation Corps, 1933–1942: A New Deal Case Study.* Durham, NC: Duke University Press, 1967.

233. TENNESSEE VALLEY AUTHORITY

Hargrove, Erwin C., and Paul K. Conkin, eds. *TVA: Fifty Years of Grass-Roots Bureaucracy.* Urbana, IL: University of Illinois Press, 1983.

Lilienthal, David E. *TVA: Democracy on the March.* New York: Harper and Brothers, 1953.

Morgan, Arthur E. *The Making of the TVA.* Buffalo, NY: Prometheus Books, 1974.

Shapiro, Edward. "The Southern Agrarians and the Tennessee Valley Authority." *American Quarterly* 22 (4, Winter 1970): 791–806.

234. FLYING BLIND

Davenport, William Wyatt. *Gyro! The Life and Times of Lawrence Sperry.* New York: Scribner Publishing Company, 1978.

Heppenheimer, T. A. "Flying Blind." *American Heritage of Invention and Technology* 4 (10, Spring 1995): 54–63.

Lindbergh, Charles Augustus. *The Spirit of St. Louis.* New York: Charles H. Scribner and Sons, 1953.

Reynolds, Quentin James. The Amazing Mr. Doolittle: A Biography of Lieutenant General James H. Doolittle. New York: Arno Press, 1972.

235. ALBERT EINSTEIN

Crelinsten, Jeffrey. "Einstein, Relativity, and the Press: The Myth of Incomprehensibility." *The Physics Teacher* (February 1980): 115–122.

Einstein, Albert, and Stephen Hawking. *A Stubbornly Persistent Illusion: The Essential Scientific Writings of Albert Einstein.* Philadelphia: Running Press, 2007.

Missner, Marshall. "Why Einstein Became Famous in America." *Social Studies of Science* 15 (1985): 267–291.

Rosenfeld, Albert. "A Three Million Year Trip in Fifty-Five Years." *Life* (May 24, 1963): 35–37.

Schilpp, Paul Arthur. *Albert Einstein: Philosopher-Scientist.* New York: Harper, 1959.

Westin, R. Barry. "American Response to the Concept of Time in Relativity Theory with Particular Attention to the Twins Paradox." Unpublished essay, August 3, 1988.

236. SOCIAL SECURITY

Beard, Charles A., and George H. E. Smith. *The Old Deal and the New.* New York: The Macmillan Company, 1940.

Biles, Roger. A New Deal for the American People. DeKalb, IL: Northern Illinois University Press, 1991.

Brock, William R. *Welfare, Democracy, and the New Deal.* Cambridge, MA: Cambridge University Press, 1988.

Cohen, Lizabeth. *Making a New Deal.* Cambridge, MA: Cambridge University Press, 1990.

Davis, Kenneth S. *FDR and The New Deal 1933–1937: A History.* New York: Random House, 1986.

Ekirch, Arthur A., Jr. *Ideologies and Utopias: The Impact of the New Deal on American Thought.* Chicago: Quadrangle Books, 1969.

Farnham, Rebecca, and Irene Link. *Effects of The Works Program on Rural Relief.* New York: Da Capo Press, 1971.

Flynn, John T. *The Roosevelt Myth.* New York: Garden City Publishing Company, 1948.

Freidel, Frank, ed. *The New Deal and the American People.* Englewood Cliffs, NJ: Prentice Hall, 1964.

Leuchtenburg, William E. *Franklin D. Roosevelt and the New Deal.* New York: Harper and Row Publishers, 1963.

Rauch, Basil. *The History of the New Deal.* New York: Capricorn Books, 1963.

Schlesinger, Arthur M., Jr. *The Coming of the New Deal.* Boston: Houghton Mifflin Company, 1958.

Sitkoff, Harvard, ed. *Fifty Years Later: The New Deal Evaluated.* New York: Alfred A. Knopf, 1985.

United States Social Security Administration, http://www.ssa.gov.

237. DILLINGER AND HOOVER

Demaris, Ovid. *The Director.* New York: Harper and Row Publishers, 1975.

Ellis, Mark, "J. Edgar Hoover and the 'Red Summer' of 1919." *The Journal of American Studies* 28, (April 1994): 39–59.

Floyd, Craig W., and Kelley Lang Helms, eds. *To Serve and Protect.* Paducah, KY: Turner Publishing Company, 1995.

Girardin, G. Russell, and William J. Helmere. *Dillinger: The Untold Story.* Indianapolis: Indiana University Press, 1994.

Klungness, Elizabeth. "The Lookout." *American Heritage* 48 (April 1997): 35–37.

Miller, Jim. "A Flawed Law-and-Order Hero: New Light on a Crimefighter's Life—and Obsessions." *Newsweek* (March 16, 1987): 74.

Nash, J. Robert. *The Dillinger Dossier.* Highland Park, IL: December Press, 1970.

Sorel, Nancy Caldwell. "First Encounters: J. Edgar Hoover and Emma Goldman." *Atlantic Monthly* 271 (January 1993): 105.

Summers, Anthony. *Official and Confidential: The Secret Life of J. Edgar Hoover.* New York: G. P. Putnam's Sons, 1993.

Thomas, Evan. "Mr. God Goes to Washington." *Newsweek* (September 23, 1991): 56.

238. FDR AND THE COURT-PACKING PLAN

"F.D.R.'s Scheme (Expanding Size of U.S. Supreme Court)." *Time* 124 (October 8, 1984): 34.

Kyvig, David. "The Road Not Taken." *Political Science Quarterly* 103 (3, Fall, 1989): 463–481.

Schlesinger, Arthur M., Jr. "Roosevelt and the Courts," *Society* 24 (November/December 1986): 53–57.

239. CRASH OF THE *HINDENBURG*

Dick, Harold G. *The Golden Age of the Great Passenger Airships, Graf Zeppelin and Hindenburg.* Washington, DC: Smithsonian Institution Press, 1985.

"Hindenburg Crash—How It Really Sounded," 1937. YouTube, https://www.youtube.com/watch?v=pUVDmXvXcbk. Video.

"Hindenburg Disaster: Real Zeppelin Explosion Footage," 1937. YouTube, https://www.youtube.com/watch?v=CgWHbpMVQ1U. Video.

Hoehling, Adolph A. *Who Destroyed the Hindenburg?* Boston: Little, Brown and Company, 1962.

Meyer, Henry Cord. *Airshipmen, Businessmen, and Politics, 1890–1940.* Washington, DC: Smithsonian Institution Press, 1991.

Mooney, Michael Macdonald. *The Hindenburg.* New York: Dodd, Mead Publishing, 1972.

Vaeth, Joseph. *Graf Zeppelin: The Adventures of an Aerial Globetrotter.* New York: Harper Publishing Company, 1959.

240. PEGGY MARSH WRITES HER BOOK

Edwards, Anne. *Road to Tara: The Life of Margaret Mitchell.* New Haven, CT: Ticknor and Fields Publishing, 1983.

Fleming, Victor, dir. *Gone with the Wind.* 1939; Beverly Hills, CA: Metro-Goldwyn-Mayer. YouTube, https://www.youtube.com/watch?v=6Gj5aLQIEQo. Video. The clip shows the end scene.

Hanson, Elizabeth I. *Margaret Mitchell.* Boston: Twayne Publishers, 1991.

Mitchell, Margaret. *Margaret Mitchell: Reporter.* Edited by Patrick Allen. Columbia, SC: University of South Carolina Press, 2010.

Pyron, Darden Asbury. *Southern Daughter: The Life of Margaret Mitchell.* New York: Oxford University Press, 1991.

241. PANIC BROADCAST

Cantril, Hadley. *The Invasion from Mars.* Princeton, NJ: Princeton University Press, 1940.

Koch, Howard. *The Panic Broadcast*. New York: Avon Books, 1970.

"War of the Worlds," *American Experience*, directed by Cathleen O'Connell (Boston: Public Broadcasting, 2013), YouTube, https://www.youtube.com /watch?v=qqjY24Q5KYY. Video.

Wells, H. G. *A Critical Edition of the War of the Worlds*. Edited by David Y. Hughes and Harold Geduld. Bloomington, IN: Indiana University Press, 1993.

Wells, Orson, dir. "The War of the Worlds," *Mercury Theater*, 1938, YouTube, https://www.youtube.com/watch?v=Xs0K4ApWl4g. Audio.

242. LOUIS-SCHMELING FIGHT

"The Fight," *American Experience*, directed by Barak Goodman (Boston: Public Broadcasting, 2004). YouTube, https://www.youtube.com/watch?v =6MfOPoQ8rug. Video.

"Joe Louis vs. Max Schmeling—First Round Knockout," 1938. YouTube, https:// www.youtube.com/watch?v=2LNzWHuygpw. Radio broadcast and video.

"Joe Louis vs. Max Schmeling II," 1938. YouTube, https://www.youtube.com /watch?v=6BLGdFQPh8c. Video.

Mead, Chris. *Champion: Black Hero in White America*. New York: Scribner, 1985.

243. JOHN STEINBECK AND *THE GRAPES OF WRATH*

"John Steinbeck—Voice of the Dust Bowl Refugees," BBC World Service. https:// www.bbc.co.uk/programmes/p03m11z0. Audio.

Levant, Howard. *The Novels of John Steinbeck*. Columbia, MO: University of Missouri Press, 1974.

Owens, Louis. *The Grapes of Wrath: Trouble in the Promised Land*. Boston: Twayne Publishers, 1989.

Shillinglaw, Susan. "John Steinbeck." *American National Biography* 8 (1999): 624-626.

Turkel, Studs. "Hard Times Remembered." *American Heritage* (August 1973): 43-45.

244. LOU GEHRIG

Graham, Frank. *Lou Gehrig: A Quiet Hero*. New York: G. P. Putnam's Sons, 1942.

Hageman, William. *New York Yankees: Seasons of Glory*. Middle Village, NY: Jonathan David Publishers, 1999.

"Lou Gehrig and Babe Ruth Address the Crowd on Lou Gehrig Appreciation Day at Yankee Stadium," 1939. YouTube, https://www.youtube.com/watch?v =Bak7WAHW_iQ. Video. The audio is rough and variable, so take care with the volume!

Meany, Thomas. *The Magnificent Yankees*. New York: Grosset and Dunlap, 1952.

245. THE WIT OF FRANKLIN DELANO ROOSEVELT

"FDR Mocks Republican Promises," YouTube, https://www.youtube.com/watch
?v=Pb-7Dpp-LPk. Video.

"FDR Talks about the Republican Attacks on His Dog Fala," YouTube, https://
www.youtube.com/watch?v=6esaEdUv1ZM. Video.

Leuchtenberg, William Edward. *The FDR Years: On Roosevelt and His Legacy*. New
York: Columbia University Press, 1995.

Morgan, Ted. FDR: *A Biography*. New York: Simon and Schuster, 1985.

Tugwell, Rexford G. *The Democratic President: A Biography of Franklin D. Roosevelt*.
Garden City, NY: Doubleday and Company, 1957.

246. THE PROBLEM WITH CHARLES LINDBERGH

Dunn, Susan. *1940: FDR, Willkie, Lindbergh, Hitler—The Election Amid the Storm*.
New Haven, CT: Yale University Press, 2013.

Gill, Brendan. *Lindbergh Alone*. St. Paul, MN: Minnesota Historical Society Press,
2002.

Lindbergh, Charles Augustus. *The Spirit of St. Louis*. New York: Scribner, 1953
and 1977.

Ross, Walter Stanford. *The Last Hero: Charles Augustus Lindbergh*. New York:
Harper and Row Publishers, 1967.

247. SERGEANT ELLIOTT'S DISCOVERY

Baker, Leonard. *Roosevelt and Pearl Harbor*. New York: Macmillan, 1970.

Elliott, George E., Jr. "There's Nothing Wrong with Our Radar!" Edited by David
J. Castello. Pearl-Harbor.com, http://pearl-harbor.com/georgeelliott/.

Esposito, Vincent J. *A Concise History of World War II*. New York: Praeger, 1964

Overy, Richard. *The Oxford Illustrated History of World War II*. New York: Oxford
University Press, 2015. Online resource.

Prange, Gordon Williams, and Katherine V. Dillon. *Pearl Harbor: The Verdict of
History*. New York: McGraw-Hill, 1986.

Sulzberger, Cyrus Leo, and David G. McCullough. *The American Heritage Picture
History of World War II*. New York: American Heritage Publishing Company and
Simon and Schuster, 1966.

248. DOOLITTLE RAID

Doolittle, James H. *I Could Never Be so Lucky Again: An Autobiography*. New York:
Bantam Books, 1991.

"Doolittle Raid over Tokyo—WWII Newsreel," YouTube, https://www.youtube
.com/watch?v=-yXzYxUC93A.

Potter, E. B. *Bull Halsey*. Annapolis, MD: Naval Institute Press, 1985.

Sweetman, Jack. "Great Sea Battles of World War II: The Halsey-Doolittle Raid." *Naval History* 9 (3 May/June 1995).

249. BATTLE OF MIDWAY

"The Battle of Midway," National WWII Museum, https://www.nationalww2museum .org/war/articles/battle-midway.

Desselle, John R. "A Cruise through 'The Battle of Midway.'" The Sextent, http://usnhistory.navylive.dodlive.mil/2016/06/03/a-cruise-through-the -battle-of-midway-2/.

Matloff, Maurice, ed. *American Military History*. Washington, DC: Office of the Chief of Military History, United States Army, 1969.

Morrison, Samuel Eliot. *Coral Sea, Midway and Submarine Actions, May 1942– August 1942*. Vol. 4 of *History of the United States Naval Operations in WWII*. Boston: Little, Brown and Company, 1949.

Sweetman, Jack. "Midway." *Naval History* 9 (3 May/June 1995): 34–35.

250. JAPANESE AMERICAN CONCENTRATION CAMPS

"A Family Gathering," *American Experience*, directed by Lise Yasui and Ann Tegnell (Alexandria, VA: Public Broadcasting, 1989), video.

Bosworth, Allan R. *America's Concentration Camps*. New York: W. W. Norton and Company, 1967.

Daniels, Roger. *Concentration Camps: North American Japanese in the United States and Canada during World War II*. Miami, FL: Robert E. Krieger Publishing Company, 1981.

Omori, Emiko. *Rabbit in the Moon*. San Francisco: Wabi-Sabi Productions, 1999.

Tateishi, John. *And Justice for All*. Seattle: University of Washington Press, 1984.

Ten Broek, Jacobus, E. H. Barnhart, and F. W. Matson. *Prejudice, War and the Constitution*. Berkeley: University of California Press, 1968.

Weglyn, Michi. *Years of Infamy: The Untold Story of America's Concentration Camps*. New York: Morrow, 1976.

251. PT BOATS

Domagalski, John J. *Under a Blood Red Sun: The Remarkable Story of PT Boats in the Philippines and the Rescue of General MacArthur*. Electronic Book. Havertown, PA: Casmate, 2016.

Donavan, Robert J. *PT109: John F. Kennedy in World War II*. New York: McGraw-Hill, 1961.

Keresey, Dick. "Farthest Forward." *American Heritage* (July–August 1998): 60–73.

Konstam, Angus. *PT Boat Squadrons: U.S. Navy Torpedo Boats*. Hersham, UK: Ian Allan Publishing, 2005.

252. ARMED SERVICES RADIO

Briggs, Asa. *The World at War. Vol. 3 of The History of Broadcasting.* Oxford, UK: Oxford University Press, 1970.

Christman, Trent. *Brass Button Broadcasters.* New York: Turner Publishing, 1997.

Morley, Patrick. "Allies on the Airwaves." *History Today* 49 (1 January 1999): 28–33.

Reynolds, David. *Rich Relations.* New York: HarperCollins, 1995.

253. ROSIE THE RIVETER

Four Vagabonds, "Rosie the Riveter," 1943. YouTube, https://www.youtube.com /watch?v=AE2z_N1fM5E. Video.

Hartmann, Susan M. *The Home Front and Beyond: American Women in the 1940s.* Boston: Twayne Publishers, 1982.

Streitmatter, Rodger. *Mightier Than the Sword: How the News Media Have Shaped American History.* Boulder, CO: Westview Press, 1997.

Wise, Nancy Baker. *A Mouthful of Rivets: Women at Work in World War II.* San Francisco: Jossey-Bass Publishing Company, 1994.

254. GI BILL OF RIGHTS

Altschuler, Glenn C., and Stuart M. Blumin. *The GI Bill: The New Deal for Veterans.* New York: Oxford University Press, 2009.

Bennett, Michael J. *When Dreams Come True: The GI Bill and the Making of Modern America.* Washington, DC: Potomac Books, 1996.

Kiester, Edwin, Jr. "Uncle Sam Wants You . . . to Go to College." *Smithsonian* 25 (8 November 1994): 128–142.

255. D-DAY

Ambrose, Stephen E. *D-Day, June 6, 1944: The Climactic Battle of World War II.* New York: Simon and Schuster, 1994.

Penrose, Jane. *The D-Day Companion: Leading Historians Explore History's Greatest Amphibious Assault.* Oxford: Osprey, 2004.

Ryan, Cornelius. *The Longest Day: June 6, 1944.* New York: Simon and Schuster, 1994.

256. JACKIE ROBINSON STAYS PUT

Bennett, *Before the Mayflower.* Full ref. under 14.

"Classic Jackie Robinson Footage," 2012. YouTube, https://www.youtube.com /watch?v=bt17YLJWaJQ. Video.

Foner, *History of Black Americans.* Full ref. under 14.

Franklin, *From Slavery to Freedom.* Full ref. under 14.

Roeder, *Jackie Robinson.* Full ref. under 14.

Toppin, *The Black American.* Full ref. under 14.

257. USS *INDIANAPOLIS*

Buell, Thomas. *Master of Sea Power: A Biography of Fleet Admiral Ernest J. King.* Boston: Little, Brown and Company, 1979.

Kurzman, Dan. *Fatal Voyage: The Sinking of the USS* Indianapolis. New York: Atheneum Publishing Company, 1990.

Potter, E.B. *Nimitz*. Annapolis, MD: Naval Institute Press, 1976.

Rogow, Arnold A. *James Forrestal*. New York: Macmillan, 1963.

"Missing the USS *Indianapolis*," *Sea Tales* (1997). YouTube, https://www.youtube .com/watch?v=QeHJTp35o8s&t=1537s. Video.

258. ATOMIC DAWN

Christman, Al. "The Atom Bomb: Making It Happen." *American Heritage of Invention and Technology* 11 (1, Summer 1995): 22-35.

Cooper, Dan. "The Atom Bomb: Making It Possible."*American Heritage of Invention and Technology* 11 (1, Summer 1995): 10-21.

Genion, William, ed. *The Affects of the Atomic Bombs on Hiroshima and Nagasaki by the United States Strategic Bombing Survey.* Sante Fe, NM: Genion Publishing, 1973.

Groves, Leslie R. *Now It Can Be Told*. New York: Harper and Row Publishers, 1962.

"Hiroshima Atomic Bomb." *A Day That Shook the World*, 1945. YouTube, https:// www.youtube.com/watch?v=t19kvUiHvAE.

Maddox, Robert James. "The Biggest Decision: Why We Had to Drop the Atomic Bomb." *American Heritage* 46 (3 May/June 1995): 70-77.

Stehling, Kurt R. "World Shaking Week in December: When the Work in Quiet Lab in Berlin and a Walk in the Snow in Sweden Opened Up the Pandora's Box of Fission." *Smithsonian* 4 (9 December 1973): 88-89.

Wyden, Peter. *Day One: Before Hiroshima and After.* New York: Simon and Schuster Publishing Company, 1984.

259. CREATION OF THE UNITED NATIONS

Evan, Herbert V. *The United Nations*. Cambridge, MA: Harvard University Press, 1948.

Johnsen, Julia E. *United Nations or World Government.* New York: H. W. Wilson Company, 1947.

Luard, Evan. *The Years of Western Domination, 1945-1955.* Vol. 1 of *A History of the United Nations.* New York: St. Martin's Press, 1982.

Mingst, Karen A., and Margaret P. *The United Nations in the Post-Cold War Era.* Boulder, CO: Westview Press, 1995.

"United Nations: History," Infoplease, http://www.infoplease.com/ce6/history /A0861704.html.

260. CHURCHILL'S IRON-CURTAIN SPEECH

Barker, Elisabeth. *Churchill and Eden at War*. New York: St. Martin's Press, 1978.

"Churchill's Missouri Speech," Movietone News, 1946. YouTube, https://www
.youtube.com/watch?v=X2FM3_h33Tg. Video.

Churchill, Winston Spencer. *Winston S. Churchill: His Complete Speeches,
1897–1963*. Edited by Robert Rhodes James. New York: Chelsea House
Publishers, 1974.

Harbutt, Fraser J. *The Iron Curtain: Churchill, America, and the Origins of the Cold
War*. New York: Oxford University Press, 1986.

261. COLE PORTER'S BREAKTHROUGH

Furia, Philip. *The Poets of Tin Pan Alley: A History of America's Great Lyricists*. New
York: Oxford University Press, 1990.

Maxwell, Elsa. *R.S.V.P.: Elsa Maxwell's Own Story*. Boston: Little, Brown and
Company, 1954.

Porter, Cole. "So in Love," *Kiss Me Kate*, 1953, YouTube, https://www.youtube
.com/watch?v=WeiOFZy1dx4. Video.

———."Wundabar," *Kiss Me Kate*, 1953, YouTube, https://www.youtube.com
/watch?v=cK5wCmfvAPA. Video.

Schwartz, Charles. *Cole Porter: A Biography*. New York: Da Capo Press, 1979.

262. HARRY TRUMAN'S 1948 DILEMMA

McCoy, Donald R. *The Presidency of Harry S. Truman*. Lawrence, KS: University
Press of Kansas, 1984.

McCullough, David. *Truman*. New York: Simon and Schuster, 1992.

Schilts, Randy. *Conduct Unbecoming*. New York: St. Martin's Press, 1993.

263. BERLIN AIRLIFT

Collier, Richard. *Bridge Across the Sky*. New York: McGraw-Hill, 1978.

Harrington, Daniel F. "United States, United Nations and the Berlin Blockade."
Historian: A Journal of History 52 (2 February 1990): 262–285.

McLellan, David S. *Dean Acheson: The State Department Years*. New York: Dodd,
Mead and Company, 1976.

Pennacchio, Charles F. "The East German Communists and the Origins of the
Berlin Blockade Crisis." *East European Quarterly* 3 (1995): 293–311.

Spitzer, Neil. "Dividing a City." *Wilson Quarterly* 3 (1988): 100–113.

264. ED SULLIVAN

Barthelme, Donald, "And Now Let's Hear It for the Ed Sullivan Show!" In *Guilty
Pleasures*. New York: Farrar, Straus and Giroux, 1974.

Bowles, Jerry. *A Thousand Sundays: The Story of the Ed Sullivan Show.* New York: Putnam, 1980.

Leonard, John. "The Ed Sullivan Age." *American Heritage* (May/June 1997): 42–61.

Maguire, James. *Impresario: The Life and Times of Ed Sullivan.* New York: Billboard Books, 2006.

265. TRUMAN AND MACARTHUR

Appleman, Roy Edgar. *Ridgway Duels for Korea.* College Station, TX: Texas A&M University Press, 1990.

Devine, Robert A., et al. *America Past and Present.* New York: Longman, 1998.

Fehrenbach, T. R. *This Kind of War: The Classic Korean War History.* Dulles, VA: Brassey's, 2000.

Halberstam, David. "The Coldest Winter: America and the Korean War." *Smithsonian* 38 (8 November 2007): 56–64.

Manchester, William Raymond. *American Caesar: Douglas MacArthur, 1880–1964.* Boston: Little, Brown and Company, 1978.

McCullough, David. *Truman.* New York: Simon and Schuster, 1992.

Stokesbury, James. L. *A Short History of the Korean War.* New York: Morrow, 1988.

266. BROWN V. BOARD OF EDUCATION

Dorgan, Howard, and Calvin M. Logue, eds. *A New Diversity in Contemporary Southern Rhetoric.* Baton Rouge, LA: Louisiana State University Press, 1987.

Eaton, Susan E., and Gary Orfield. *Dismantling Desegregation.* New York: The New Press, 1996.

Schultz, Fred. *Sources: Notable Selections in Education.* Guilford, CT: The Dushkin Publishing Group, 1995.

Wilson, Paul E. *A Time to Lose: Representing Kansas in* Brown v. Board of Education. Lawrence, KS: University of Kansas Press, 1995.

267. JOSEPH MCCARTHY

"Army-McCarthy Hearings," 2009. YouTube, https://www.youtube.com/watch?v=fqQD4dzVkwk. Video. Joseph Welsh, US army counsel, excoriates Senator Joseph McCarthy, beginning his decline.

Brown, Steven R., and John D. Ellithorp. "Emotional Experiences in Political Groups: The Case of the McCarthy Phenomenon." *American Political Science Review* 64 (2 June 1970): 349–366.

Buckley, William Frank, Jr., and L. Brent Bozell. *McCarthy and His Enemies.* Chicago: Regnery House, 1954.

Cook, Fred J. *The Nightmare Decade: The Life and Times of Joseph McCarthy.* New York: Random House, 1971.

Doherty, Thomas. "Point of Order." *History Today* 48 (8, 1998): 33–37.

"Edward R. Murrow's Final Reply to Senator Joseph McCarthy's *See It Now* Appearance," April 13, 1954," 2015. YouTube, https://www.youtube.com /watch?v=8wMiPkaofjw. Video.

Rovere, Richard Halworth. *Senator Joe McCarthy*. New York: Harcourt and Brace, 1959.

Wiebe, G. D. "The Army-McCarthy Hearings and the Public Conscience." *Public Opinion Quarterly* 22 (4, Winter 1958–1959): 490–502.

268. BATTLE FOR COLOR TELEVISION

Abramson, Albert. *The History of Television, 1942 to 2000*. New York: McFarland and Company, 2003.

Burns, R. W. *Television: An International History of the Formative Years*. New York: IET, 1998.

Fisher, David E., and Marshall Jon Fisher, "The Color War." *American Heritage of Invention and Technology* 12 (3, Winter 1997): 8–18.

Lebar, Stanley. "The Color War Goes to the Moon." *American Heritage of Invention and Technology* 13 (2, Summer 1997): 52–54.

269. POLIO

Black, Kathryn. *In the Shadow of Polio: A Personal and Social History*. New York: Perseus, 1997.

Klein, Aaron E. *Trial by Fury: The Polio Vaccine Controversy*. New York: Doubleday, 1972.

McGrew, Roderick E. *Encyclopedia of Medical History*. New York: McGraw-Hill Company, 1985.

Smith, Jane. *Patenting the Sun: Polio and the Salk Vaccine*. New York: Morrow and Company, 1990.

270. MIKE KING FINDS HIS CALLING

Bishop, Jim. *The Days of Martin Luther King, Jr.* New York: Putnam Publishing Company, 1971.

Davis, Lenwood G. *I Have a Dream: The Life and Times of Martin Luther King, Jr.* Westport, CT: Negro Universities Press, 1973.

King, Coretta Scott. *My Life with Martin Luther King, Jr.* New York: Holt, Rinehart and Winston, 1969.

King, Martin Luther, Jr. "Martin Luther King Speech, Holt Street Baptist Church," 1955. YouTube, https://www.youtube.com/watch?v=GGtp7kCi _LA. Audio.

Lewis, David L. *King: A Biography*. Urbana, IL: University of Illinois Press, 1978.

Oates, Stephen B. *Let the Trumpet Sound: The Life of Martin Luther King, Jr.* New York: Harper and Row, 1982.

271. MALCOLM MCLEAN

Cudahy, Brian J. *Box Boats: How Container Ships Changed the World*. New York: Fordham University Press, 2006.

Levinson, Marc. *The Box: How the Shipping Container Made the World Smaller and the World Economy Bigger*. Princeton, NJ: Princeton University Press, 2006.

Patton, Phil. "Agents of Change." *American Heritage* 45 (8 December 1994): 88-109.

272. INTEGRATION COMES TO LITTLE ROCK

Brownelle, Herbert. "Eisenhower's Civil Rights Program: A Personal Assessment." *Presidential Studies Quarterly* 21 (2, 1991): 235-242.

Freyer, Tony Allan. *The Little Rock Crisis: A Constitutional Interpretation*. Westport, CT: Greenwood Press, 1984.

Hauckby, Elizabeth. *Crisis at Central High: Little Rock, 1957-58*. Baton Rouge, LA: Louisiana State University Press, 1980.

Spitzberg, Irving J. *Racial Politics in Little Rock: 1954-64*. NewYork: Garland Publishing Company, 1987.

273-274. MASSIVE RESISTANCE I & II

Bartley, Numan V. *The Rise of Massive Resistance: Race and Politics in the South during the 1950's*. Baton Rouge, LA: Louisiana State University Press, 1969.

Cornell Law School. "U.S. Constitution: 14th Amendment," http://www.law .cornell.edu/constitution/constitution.amendmentxiv.html.

Ely, James W., Jr. *The Crisis of Conservative Virginia: The Byrd Organization and the Politics of Massive Resistance*. Knoxville, TN: University of Tennessee Press, 1976.

Hamilton, John Alfred. "Prince Edward's Massive Resistance." *Nieman Reports* 53 (1999): 141-147.

Lassiter, Matthew D., and Andrew B. Lewis. *The Moderates' Dilemma: Massive Resistance to School Desegregation in Virginia*. Charlottesville, VA: University Press of Virginia, 1998.

MacLean, Nancy. *Democracy in Chains: The Deep History of the Radical Right's Stealth Plan for America*. New York: Viking, Penguin Random House, 2017.

Martin, Waldo E., Jr. *Brown v. Board of Education*. Berkeley: University of California, 1998.

Mayer, Michael S. "*Brown v. Board of Education*: A Civil Rights Milestone and Its Troubled Legacy." *Journal of Southern History* 68 (2002): 740-743.

Morrow, Lance. "Prince Edward and the Past." *Time* 134 (November 20, 1989): 58-59.

Norton, Mary Beth, et al. *A People and a Nation*. Boston: Houghton Mifflin Company, 1994.

Smith, J. Douglas. *Managing White Supremacy: Race, Politics, and Citizenship in Jim Crow Virginia*. Chapel Hill, NC: University of North Carolina Press, 2002.

Wilhoit, Francis M. *The Politics of Massive Resistance*. New York: George Braziller, 1973.

Wolters, Raymond. *The Burden of Brown: Thirty Years of School Desegregation*. Knoxville, TN: University of Tennessee Press, 1984.

275. FIRST PRESIDENTIAL TELEVISION DEBATE

Nixon, Richard Milhous. *The Memoirs of Richard Nixon*. New York: Grosset and Dunlap, 1978.

Schlesinger, Arthur M., Jr. *A Thousand Days: John F. Kennedy in the White House*. Boston: Houghton Mifflin, 1965.

Schroeder, Alan. *Presidential Debates: Fifty Years of High-Risk TV*. New York: Columbia University Press, 2008.

White, Theodore S. *The Making of the President, 1960*. New York: Atheneum, 1961.

276. PRESIDENTIAL WIT

Bradley, Benjamin. *Conversations with Kennedy*. New York: Norton Publishing Company, 1962.

Conwell, Why Lincoln Laughed. Full ref. under 138.

Gardner, Gerald. *All the President's Wits: The Power of Presidential Humor*. New York: William Morrow and Company, 1986.

Lincoln, *Speeches and Writings*. Full ref. under 138.

Manchester, William. *Portrait of a President*. Boston: Little, Brown and Company, 1962.

Sorensen, Theodore C. *Kennedy*. New York: Harper and Row, 1965.

277. LUNCHEON RACISM

Carson, Clayborne. "American Civil Rights Movement." Encyclopedia Britannica, https://www.britannica.com/event/American-civil-rights-movement.

Cozzens, Lisa. "Sit-Ins." Watson.org, http://watson.org/~lisa/blackhistory /civilrights-55-65/sit-ins.html.

Ling, Peter. "Racism for Lunch." *History Today* 50 (2 February 2000): 36–38.

"Sit-Ins." *News & Record*, https://www.greensboro.com/sit-ins/. Photos and text.

Williams, Juan. *Eyes on the Prize*. New York: Viking, 1987.

Yeingst, William, and Lonnie Bunch. "Sitting for Justice." National Museum of American History, http://amhistory.si.edu/docs/Yeingst_Bunch_Sitting_for _Justice_1996.pdf.

278. CUBAN MISSILE CRISIS

Dinerstein, Herbert Samuel. *The Making of a Missile Crisis: October 1962*. Baltimore: Johns Hopkins Press, 1976.

Dooley, Brian. "The Cuban Missile Crisis—Thirty Years On," *History Today* 42 (October 1992): 6–8.

Fursenko, Aleksandr Vasilevich. *One Hell of a Gamble: Khrushchev, Castro, and Kennedy: 1958–1964*. New York: W. W. Norton, 1997.

Garthoff, Raymond F. *Reflections on the Cuban Missile Crisis*. Washington, DC: Brookings Institution, 1987.

Kennedy, Robert F. *Thirteen Days: A Memoir of the Cuban Missile Crisis*. New York: W. W. Norton, 1969.

Lebow, Richard Ned. "Domestic Politics and the Cuban Missile Crisis: The Traditional and Revisionist Interpretations Reevaluated." *Diplomatic History* 14 (4, Fall 1990): 471–492.

Medland, William J. "The Cuban Missile Crisis: Evolving Historical Perspectives." *The History Teacher* 23 (4 August 1990): 433–447.

Scott, Len, and Steve Smith. "Lessons of October: Historians, Political Scientists, Policy Makers and the Cuban Missile Crisis." *International Affairs* 70 (4, 1994): 659–684.

279. DDT AND THE MODERN ENVIRONMENTAL MOVEMENT

Alston, Lee J. "Farm Foreclosures in the United States During the Interwar Period." *Journal of Economic History* 43 (4, 1983): 885–903.

Blair, Cornelia, et al., eds. *The Environment: A Revolution in Attitudes*. Detroit, Gale Group, 2001.

Carson, Rachel. *Silent Spring*. New York: Houghton Mifflin Company, 1962.

Gore, Al. "Introduction." In *Silent Spring*, Rachel Carson. New York: Houghton Mifflin Company, 1994.

Hoag, Dana L. *Agricultural Crisis in America*. Santa Barbara, CA: ABC-CLIO, 1999.

Lewis, Richard J. *Hazardous Chemicals Desk Reference*. New York: Van Nostrand Reinhold, 1993.

McNeill, J. R. *Something New Under the Sun: An Environmental History of the Twentieth-Century World*. New York: W. W. Norton and Company, 2000.

Rasmussen, Wayne D. "The Impact of Technological Change on American Agriculture, 1862–1962." *Journal of Economic History* 22 (4, 1962): 578–591.

Rausser, Gordon C. "Predatory versus Productive Government: The Case of U.S. Agricultural Policies." *Journal of Economic Perspectives* 6 (3, 1992): 133–157.

Reece, C. H. "The Role of the Chemical Industry in Improving the Effectiveness of Agriculture." *Philosophical Transactions of the Royal Society of London. Series B, Biological Sciences* 310 (1144, 1985): 201–211.

Rodale, Ardath. "Organic Farming." In *Encyclopedia of Rural America: The Land and People*. Gary A. Goreham, ed. Santa Barbara, CA: ABC-CLIO, 1997.

Ruttan, Vernon W. "Changing Role of Public and Private Sectors in Agricultural Research." *Science* 216 (4541, 1982): 23–29.

280. US SUPREME COURT VS. SCHOOL PRAYER

Bickel, Alexander M. *Politics and the Warren Court*. New York: Da Capo Press, 1973.

Rice, Arnold S. *The Warren Court, 1953–1969*. Millwood, NY: Associated Faculty Press, 1987.

Spaeth, Harold J. *Studies in US Supreme Court Behavior*. New York: Garland Publishers, 1990.

281. FREEDOM SUMMER

Balser, Deborah. "The Impact of Environmental Factors on Factionalism and Schism on Movement Organizations." *Social Forces* 76 (1, 1997): 199–201.

Belfrage, Sally. *Freedom Summer*. New York: Viking Press, 1965.

Bond, Julian. "SNCC: What We Did." *Monthly Review* 52 (15, 2000): 14–25.

Cozzens, Lisa. "Mississippi and Freedom Summer." Watson.org, www.watson.org /lisa/blackhistory/civil rights-55-66/mississippi-html.

Greenberg, Cheryl Lynn. *A Circle of Trust: Remembering SNCC*. New Brunswick, NJ: Rutgers University Press, 1998.

Miller, Mike. "Mentors." *Social Policy* 30 (12, 1999): 38–41.

"Mississippi Burning Movie Clip." *Mississippi Burning*, directed by Alan Parker (Metro Goldwyn Mayer, 1988), YouTube, https://www.youtube.com/watch ?v=W5QmfT1Zpbc.

Randall, Herbert, and Bobs M. Tusa. *Faces of Freedom Summer*. Tuscaloosa, AL: University of Alabama Press, 2001.

Sugden, Jane. "A Veteran of Mississippi." *People Weekly* 32 (12, 1989): 61–63.

"Three CORE Members Murdered in Mississippi." Congress of Racial Equality, http://core-online.org/History/freedom_summer.htm.

"The True Story of Mississippi Burning." *The FBI Files*, directed by Jeffrey Fine (Discovery Channel, 1999). YouTube, https://www.youtube.com/watch ?v=N1gedv0tDpk. Video.

Zengerle, Jason. "Raleigh Dispatch: Laughter and Forgetting." *New Republic* (May 1, 2000): 14–17.

282. SELMA, ALABAMA

Bishop, Jim. *The Days of Martin Luther King, Jr.* New York: Putnam Publishing Company, 1971.

Garrow, David. J. "The Voting Rights Act in Historical Perspective." *Georgia Historical Quarterly* 74 (3, 1990): 377–398.

King, Coretta Scott. *My Life with Martin Luther King, Jr.* Full ref. under 270.

Oates, *Let the Trumpet Sound*. Full ref. under 270.

Oates, Stephen B. "The Week the World Watched Selma." *American Heritage* 33 (4, 1982): 48–63.

283. REAGAN VS. BROWN

Dallek, Matthew. "Liberalism Overthrown." *American Heritage* 47 (October 1996): 39-60.

Rarick, Ethan. *California Rising: The Life and Times of Pat Brown.* Berkeley: University of California Press, 2005.

Reagan, Ronald, Kiron K. Skinner, Annelise Graebner Anderson, and Martin Anderson. *Reagan's Path to Victory: The Shaping of Ronald Reagan's Vision: Selected Writings.* New York: Free Press, 2004.

Will, George F. "The Legacy of the Sixties." *American Heritage* 47 (October 1996): 54-60.

284. APOLLO I TRAGEDY

Giblin, Robin. "Fire in the Cockpit." *American Heritage of Invention and Technology* 13 (4, Spring 1998): 46-55.

Murray, Charles, and Catherine Cox. *Apollo: The Race to the Moon.* New York: Simon and Schuster, 1989.

285. ASSASSINATION AND NIXON'S SOUTHERN STRATEGY

Aistrup, Joseph. *The Southern Strategy Revisited: Republican Top-Down Advancement in the South.* Lexington, KY: University Press of Kentucky, 1996.

Allen, Mike. "RNC Chief to Say It Was 'Wrong' to Exploit Racial Conflict for Votes." *Washington Post,* July 14, 2005, http://www.washingtonpost.com /wp-dyn/content/article/2005/07/13/AR2005071302342_pf.html.

Kurlansky, Mark. *1968: The Year That Rocked the World.* New York: Ballantine Books, 2004.

Phillips, Kevin. *The Emerging Republican Majority.* New Rochelle, NY: Arlington House, 1969.

Risen, Clay. "The Myth of 'the Southern Strategy.'" *New York Times Magazine,* December 10, 2006, http://www.nytimes.com/2006/12/10/magazine /10Section2b.t-4.html.

Stanley, Harold. "Southern Partisan Changes: Dealignment, Realignment, or Both?" *Journal of Politics* 50 (1 February 1988): 64-88.

286. STONEWALL UPRISING

Carter, David. *Stonewall: The Riots That Sparked the Gay Revolution.* New York: St. Martin's Press, 2004.

Edsall, Nicholas. *Toward Stonewall: Homosexuality and Society in the Modern Western World.* Charlottesville, VA: University of Virginia Press, 2003.

Fejes, Fred. *Gay Rights and Moral Panic: The Origins of America's Debate on Homosexuality.* New York: Palgrave MacMillan, 2008.

Ridinger, Robert B. Marks. *The Gay and Lesbian Movement: References and Resources.* New York: G. K. Hall, 1996.

Shepherd, Simon, and Mick Wallis. *Coming on Strong: Gay Politics and Culture.* Boston: Unwin Hyman, 1989.

Shilts, Randy. *Conduct Unbecoming.* New York: St. Martin's Press, 1993.

287. APOLLO 11

Brooks, Courtney G., James M. Grimwood, and Lloyd S. Swenson Jr. *Chariots for Apollo: A History of Manned Lunar Spacecraft.* Washington, DC: Scientific and Technical Information Branch, NASA, 1979.

Chaiken, Andrew. *A Man on the Moon: The Voyages of the Apollo Astronauts.* New York: Viking, 1994.

Compton, William. *Where No Man Has Gone Before: A History of Apollo Lunar Exploration Missions.* Washington, DC: US Government Printing Office, 1989.

Hansen, James R. *First Man: The Life of Neil A. Armstrong.* New York: Simon and Schuster, 2005.

Murray, Charles, and Catherine Bly Cox. *Apollo: The Race to the Moon.* New York: Simon and Schuster, 1989.

Swanson, Glen E. *Before This Decade Is Out: Personal Reflections on the Apollo Program.* Washington, DC: National Aeronautic and Space Administration, 1999.

288. MIRANDA DECISION

Baker, Liva. *Miranda: Crime, Law, and Politics.* New York: Atheneum Publishing Company, 1983.

Levy, Leonard W. *Origins of the Fifth Amendment.* New York: Macmillan, 1969.

Milner, Neal A. *The Court and Local Law Enforcement: The Impact of Miranda.* Beverly Hills, CA: Sage Publications, 1971.

Patton, Phil. "Agents of Change." *American Heritage* 45 (8 December 1994): 42–56.

Soltero, Carlos R. "Miranda v. Arizona (1966) and the Rights of the Criminally Accused." In *Latinos and American Law: Landmark Supreme Court Cases.* Austin, TX: University of Texas Press, 2006.

Stuart, Gary L. *Miranda: The Story of America's Right to Remain Silent.* Tucson, AZ: University of Arizona Press, 2004.

289. WATERGATE AND THE RESIGNATION OF RICHARD NIXON

White, Theodore Harold. *Breach of Faith: The Fall of Richard Nixon.* New York: Atheneum Publishers, 1975.

Woodward, Bob, and Carl Bernstein. *The Final Days.* New York: Simon and Schuster, 2005.

Schudson, Michael. *Watergate in American Memory: How We Remember, Forget, and Reconstruct the Past.* New York: Basic Books, 1992.

290. US LEAVES SAIGON

Addington, Larry H. *America's War in Vietnam: A Short Narrative History.* Bloomington, IN: Indiana University Press, 2000.

Burns, Ken, Lynn Novick, and Geoffrey C. Ward, dirs. *The Vietnam War.* 2017; Arlington, VA: PBS Distribution, 2017. DVD.

Karnow, Stanley. *Vietnam: A History.* New York: Viking, 1991.

"Vietnam: A Television History," *American Experience,* directed by Judith Vecchione, Austin Hoyt, Martin Smith, and Bruce Palling (Boston: Public Broadcasting, 1983), 2004. DVD.

291. IRAN HOSTAGE CRISIS

Bakhash, Shaul. *The Reign of the Ayatollahs: Iran and the Islamic Revolution.* New York: Basic Books, 1984.

Bowden, Mark. *Guests of the Ayatollah: The Iran Hostage Crisis: The First Battle in America's War with Militant Islam.* New York: Grove Press, 2006.

Ebtekar, Massoumeh, and Fred Reed. *Takeover in Tehran: The Inside Story of the 1979 U.S. Embassy Capture.* Burnaby, BC: Talonbooks, 2000.

Sick, Gary. *October Surprise: America's Hostages in Iran and the Election of Ronald Reagan.* New York: Random House, 1991.

292. "THERE YOU GO AGAIN"

Morris, Kenneth Earl. *Jimmy Carter: American Moralist.* Athens, GA: University of Georgia Press, 1996.

Pemberton, William E. *Exit with Honor: The Life and Presidency of Ronald Reagan.* Armonk, NY: M. E. Sharpe, 1997.

Reagan, et al., *Reagan's Path to Victory.* Full ref. under 283.

White, Theodore H. *America in Search of Itself: The Making of the President, 1956–1980.* New York: Harper and Row, 1982.

Wooten, James T. *Dasher: The Roots and the Rising of Jimmy Carter.* New York: Summit Books, 1978.

293. WILLIE HORTON AND THE POLITICS OF RACE

Barilleaux, Ryan J., and Mark J. Rozell. *Power and Prudence: The Presidency of George H. W. Bush.* College Station, TX: Texas A&M University Press, 2004.

Brady, John Joseph. *Bad Boy: The Life and Politics of Lee Atwater.* Reading, MA: Addison-Wesley Publishing Company, 1997.

Lamis, Alexander P. *The Two-Party South.* New York: Oxford University Press, 1990.

Germond, Jack W., and Jules Witcover. *Whose Broad Stripes and Bright Stars: The Trivial Pursuit of the Presidency, 1988.* New York: Warner Books, 1989.

Wicker, Tom. *George Herbert Walker Bush.* New York: Lipper/Viking, 2004.

294. REPUBLICAN REVOLUTION

Janda, Kenneth, Jeffrey M. Berry, and Jerry Goldman. *The Challenge of Democracy: Government in America.* Boston: Houghton Mifflin, 2008.

——. *Interpreting the Republican Revolution, 1994–1995: A Supplement to Accompany The Challenge of Democracy: Government in America.* Boston: Houghton Mifflin, 1996.

McSweeney, Dean, and John E. Owens. *The Republican Takeover of Congress.* Hampshire, England: Macmillan, 1998.

Shafer, Byron E. *Present Discontents: American Politics in the Very Late Twentieth Century.* Chatham, NJ: Chatham House Publishers, 1997.

295. SEX, LIES, AND IMPEACHMENT

Baker, Peter. *The Breach: Inside the Impeachment and Trial of William Jefferson Clinton.* New York: Scribner, 2000.

Blumenthal, Sidney. *The Clinton Wars.* New York: Farrar, Straus and Giroux, 2003.

Clinton, Hillary Rodham. *Living History.* New York: Simon and Schuster, 2003.

296. BUSH V. GORE

Brinkley, Douglas. *36 Days: The Complete Chronicle of the 2000 Presidential Election Crisis.* New York: Times Books, 2001.

Bugliosi, Vincent. *The Betrayal of America: How the Supreme Court Undermined the Constitution and Chose Our President.* New York: Thunder's Mouth Press, 2001.

Dershowitz, Alan M. *Supreme Injustice: How the High Court Hijacked Election 2000.* New York: Oxford University Press, 2001.

Dover, E. D. *Missed Opportunity: Gore, Incumbency, and Television in Election 2000.* Westport, CT: Praeger, 2002.

Posner, Richard A. *Breaking the Deadlock: The 2000 Election, the Constitution, and the Courts.* Princeton, NJ: Princeton University Press, 2001.

Toobin, Jeffrey. *Too Close To Call: The Thirty-Six-Day Battle to Decide the 2000 Election.* New York: Random House, 2001.

297. 9/11 AND ASYMMETRIC WARFARE

Arreguin-Toft, Ivan. *How the Weak Win Wars: A Theory of Asymmetric Conflict.* New York: Cambridge University Press, 2005.

Friedman, George. *America's Secret War: Inside the Hidden Worldwide Struggle between the United States and Its Enemies.* London: Little, Brown and Company, 2004.

Merom, Gil. *How Democracies Lose Small Wars*. New York: Cambridge University Press, 2003.

Schroefl, Joseph. *Political Asymmetries in the Era of Globalization*. New York: Peter Lang, 2007.

298. SMARTPHONES

Bonczek, Rose Burnett, Roger Manix, David Storck, Valerie Clayman Pye, and Michael Flanagan. *Turn That Thing Off: Collaboration and Technology in 21st-Century Actor Training*. New York: Routledge, 2018.

Merchant, Brian. *The One Device: The Secret History of the iPhone*. New York: Little, Brown and Company, 2017.

Tinnell, John. *Actionable Media: Digital Communication beyond the Desktop*. New York: Oxford University Press, 2018.

299. ELECTION OF THE FIRST AFRICAN AMERICAN PRESIDENT

Clayton, Dewey. *The Presidential Campaign of Barack Obama: A Critical Analysis of a Racially Transcendent Strategy*. New York: Routledge, 2010.

Jolivétte, Andrew. *Obama and the Biracial Factor: The Battle of a New American Majority*. Chicago: Policy Press, 2012.

Thomas, Evan. *A Long Time Coming: The Inspiring Combative 2008 Campaign and the Election of Barack Obama*. New York: Public Affairs, 2009.

Todd, Chuck, Sheldon R. Gawiser, Ana Maria Arumi, and G. Evans Witt. *How Barack Obama Won: A State-by-State Guide to the Historic 2008 Presidential Election*. New York: Vintage Books, 2009.

300. ADVENT OF GENDER-NEUTRAL MARRIAGE

Cretney, Stephen Michael. *Same Sex Relationships: From "Odious Crime" to "Gay Marriage."* New York: Oxford University, 2006.

Phy-Olsen, Allene. *Same-Sex Marriage*. Westport, CT: Greenwood Press, 2006.

Richardson-Self, Louise. *Justifying Same-Sex Marriage: A Philosophical Investigation*. New York: Rowman and Littlefield International, 2015.

Rimmerman, Craig A., and Clyde Wilcox. *The Politics of Same-Sex Marriage*. Chicago: University of Chicago Press, 2007.

ABOUT THE AUTHOR

Dan Roberts is Executive Producer and Host of the award-winning radio series *A Moment in Time*. Created to excite and enlighten the public about the past and its relevance to the present and impact on the future, *A Moment in Time* is a captivating historical narrative that is currently broadcast worldwide.

After receiving a BA in history from Presbyterian College in 1969, Roberts served as an officer in the US Army, including a tour in Vietnam where he was awarded the Bronze Star in 1971. Roberts began training as a Presbyterian minister and completed his professional education at Princeton Theological Seminary in 1974. In August, 1986, he served as guest chaplain of the United States Senate.

In 1990, Roberts obtained a master's degree from the University of Richmond and, in 1997, a PhD in early modern British history and American colonial history from the University of Virginia. He is currently a Professor of Liberal Arts and History at the University of Richmond and serves as Chair of the Department of Liberal Arts at the School of Professional and Continuing Studies. He has been a guest contributor and columnist for *Education Week*, *USA Today*, *Scripps-Howard* papers, and *Richmond Times-Dispatch*. He is often heard as a history commentator on CNN, CNN Headline News, and Fox News.

Dan is a popular jazz pianist and an avid reader. He travels each year to a part of the world for research in his continuous quest to bring history to life. He also spends a great deal of time on the road as a popular speaker for corporations, organizations, and national audiences.

Roberts has three children: Heather Elizabeth Roberts Gill, Kathleen Roberts, and Daniel McDonald Roberts, III. He also has two lovely granddaughters: Ava McKenzie Hunt and Gerika Gill.

ABOUT FAMILIUS

VISIT OUR WEBSITE: WWW.FAMILIUS.COM

Familius is a global trade publishing company that publishes books and other content to help families be happy. We believe that the family is the fundamental unit of society and that happy families are the foundation of a happy life. We recognize that every family looks different, and we passionately believe in helping all families find greater joy. To that end, we publish books for children and adults that invite families to live the Familius Nine Habits of Happy Family Life: *love together, play together, learn together, work together, talk together, heal together, read together, eat together,* and *laugh together.* Founded in 2012, Familius is located in Sanger, California.

JOIN OUR FAMILY

There are lots of ways to connect with us! Subscribe to our newsletters at www.familius.com to receive uplifting daily inspiration, essays from our Pater Familius, a free ebook every month, and the first word on special discounts and Familius news.

GET BULK DISCOUNTS

If you feel a few friends and family might benefit from what you've read, let us know and we'll be happy to provide you with quantity discounts. Simply email us at orders@familius.com.

CONNECT

Facebook: www.facebook.com/paterfamilius
Twitter: @familiustalk, @paterfamilius1
Pinterest: www.pinterest.com/familius
Instagram: @familiustalk

*The most important work you ever do will
be within the walls of your own home.*